Far Eastern Magic

Illustrated Introduction to the Mystical
Symbols and Scripts of Indian and Chinese
Cosmic Philosophy

M B JACKSON

GREEN MAGIC

Green Magic
53 Brooks Road
Street
Somerset
BA16 0PP
England
www.greenmagicpublishing.com

Designed and typeset by Carrigboy, Wells, UK
www.carrigboy.co.uk

ISBN 978 1 915580 37 5

GREEN MAGIC

Contents

Far Eastern Magic

The term 'Far Eastern Magic' refers to a wide range of esoteric and hidden spiritual practices rooted in the cultures of the Far East, often characterized by elements of mysticism, magic and traditions of Hindu, Buddhist and Daoist cosmologies and metaphysics.

Hindus consider the universe to be divine and cyclical with constant creation and destruction through Shabda Brahman, or universal creation through sound. In Buddhist cosmology, the physical universe is seen as a series of stacked planes or realms corresponding to mental states or dhyanas, stages of meditative absorption.

Daoist cosmology views the universe as a unified system where heaven, earth and man are interconnected and harmonious, in balance with the primordial energy of chi, the dualistic principles of yin and yang, the interactive cycle of the five elements and the symbolism of the four auspicious beasts, the totem guardian animals of the four cardinal compass points and cosmic order.

While having distinct origins, Indian and Chinese cosmologies share fundamental concepts like an ultimate ineffable reality and a cyclical view of the universe. Concerning ultimate reality, both traditions believe in a primordial, all-encompassing principle that is the source of all existence. In Hinduism, this is Brahman, the unchanging, infinite and divine source of the cosmos. In Daoism, it is the Dao (the Way), the ineffable and natural order that governs the universe.

Both cosmologies describe time as cyclical, involving continuous periods of creation and destruction. In Hinduism, this is associated with the Trimurti or Trinity of Gods – Brahma, Vishnu and Shiva. In Daoism, the universe arises from the undifferentiated void called Yu and moves through cycles of change and ultimately returns to Dao. In both religions, the creator gods, Brahma and Pangu, emerged from a cosmic egg.

In Hinduism, the universal soul or Brahman is present within the individual human soul or Atam and the human body reflects the structure of the cosmos. Daoism sees the human body as a miniature version of the universe with internal landscapes and energies mirroring those of nature.

Both believe in a vital life force, an essential energy that animates all of creation. In India it is known as Prahna, in China it is called Qi or Chi. Both also believe there is a deep, inherent connection between the human being or microcosm and the universe or macrocosm.

Their concepts of elements in the organization of the material world differ in their philosophical systems. Hinduism typically organizes the world into five elements of earth, water, fire, air and ether. Daoism uses a different system of the five transitions, phases or elements of wood, fire, earth, metal and water.

THEOSOPHY

Far Eastern metaphysical concepts merged into Western occultism primarily through the Theosophical Society during the 19th-century occult revival. Rather than a single event, the fusion was a multi-staged process of cultural exchange that began in the 18th century and accelerated throughout the 19th into the 20th century.

In the 18th century, Western scholars of Orientalism translated ancient Sanskrit texts, making Indian religious and philosophical ideas about the universal knowledge of cultures available to the West for the first time. In 1769, a Jesuit monk sent a copy of the hexagrams of the I-Ching to Gottfried Leibnitz, who had recently invented binary notation.

Founded in 1875 by Russian occultist Madame Helena Blavatsky, the Theosophical Society was a primary vehicle for interpreting Indian concepts into Western occult thought. Theosophy posited a 'universal brotherhood' and an ancient 'secret doctrine' that blended Eastern and Western traditions. It introduced karma, reincarnation, chakras and the kundalini system.

Theosophical and occult ideas became influential during the 1960s counter-culture movement; practices like yoga and feng shui directly influenced the rise of the New Age phenomena between the 1970s and the 1990s.

The integration of Chinese metaphysics was less direct and systematic than Indian metaphysics, but still occurred primarily through Theosophy and other esotericism. In the early 20th century, occult novels like 'The Golem' by Gustav Mayrinks, began to incorporate Chinese imagery and themes. He used Theosophy as a framework to incorporate Buddhist concepts and the Daoist Taijitu or yin-yang symbol.

Western esotericism was receptive to Daoist notions of nature such as Dao – The Way, and Chi – vital life energy, which mirrored some existing Western concepts. Chinese concepts like the five phases and the dynamic interplay of yin and yang were incorporated with correlated cosmologies popular in the occult world. These ideas were used to analyze situations and human conditions.

In the 1960s, principles such as feng shui and I-Ching divination that drew upon these metaphysical principles gained popularity in the West, particularly within New Age circles.

In general, Indian metaphysics was largely adapted to create a universal, transcultural spiritual history. Chinese metaphysics was assimilated in a more fragmented way, often through the adaptation of specific Daoist, Buddhist and folklore concepts to fit existing Western occult models.

INDIAN MYSTICISM

Indian Mysticism

India is the original home of four of the world's major religions – Hinduism, Jainism, Buddhism and Sikhism – all of which have their roots in the ancient Vedic-Brahman religion. Vedism constituted the religious ideas and practices prevalent amongst some of the Indo-Aryan people who entered the Indus Valley from Iran around 1500 BCE. Veda was the name of their religion, and their priests were called Brahmins. Vedic Brahmins spoke the refined Indo-Aryan dialect called Sanskrit.

Originally received by Brahma from the Supreme Lord Krishna, the word Vedas means knowledge. Vedic Sanskrit has its own grammar, and it is only used in the Vedas – no new book can be composed in Vedic Sanskrit. The words have accents akin to musical notes, and a word's meaning can change drastically if the accent of its letters is changed.

Brahmanism is a later development from Vedism but remained true to the Vedic worldview, remolding the religious ideas and practices of non-Vedic Indian and Asian traditions.

Zoroastrianism, Judaism, Christianity and Islam arrived in India during the first millennium CE and have influenced Vedic development. Its modern name, Hinduism, which includes Shivaism, was introduced in British colonial days to distinguish it from Islam.

Jainism and Buddhism split from Vedism during the 6th century BCE. Jainism remains a minority religion, and Buddhism is no longer practiced in India. Sikhism is the most recent religion, founded by Guru Nanak (1469–1538) as an attempt to synthesize Hinduism and Islam into one formal belief system.

Around 200 BCE, Hinduism and Buddhism spread from mainland India to Southeast Asia and the Orient. Today, it is only practiced in India, Java and Bali, having been replaced by Buddhism, Christianity and Islam everywhere else.

Early Buddhism divided into two main schools – Hinayana or the Little Vehicle, and Mahayana or the Great Vehicle. The traditional school of Hinayana, also known as Theravada, is the closest to the original teachings of Buddha. Its sutras, written in Pali, the native Sanskrit dialect of Buddha, were carried southeast from India to Sri Lanka, Burma, Thailand, Cambodia, Laos, Malaya, Java and Indonesia.

Written in the Siddhamatrika script, the Sanskrit sutras of the mystical school of Mahayana or the Great Vehicle were carried north from India to Nepal, Tibet, Mongolia, China, Korea and Japan, creating the Vajrayana and Chen/Zen schools.

Pratik
Hinduism

Parasparopgraho Jivanam
Jainism

Dharma Wheel
Buddhist

Lotus flower
Buddhist

Tilaka (Trident)
Shivaism

Khanda
Sikhism

Mahayana emphasizes the bodhisattva's ideal, where enlightened beings postpone their own enlightenment to help others achieve enlightenment. The Vajrayana School or the Secret Vehicle was developed in Tibet and is also called Tantric Buddhism. It emphasizes esoteric practices and rituals like mantras, mandalas and mudras to achieve rapid spiritual awakening.

SHABDA BRAHMAN

According to ancient Hindu texts, the world was created through sound. Brahman, the Ultimate Reality, is composed of two forms of sound called Nada Brahman and Shabda Brahman. Both concepts highlight the sacred and transformative power of sound.

Nada Brahman is the pure, subtle, internal or 'unstuck' sound that exists beyond physical manifestation, accessible only through deep meditation and quiet contemplation. Shabda Brahman represents its expression into the world.

Shabda Brahman is the more external, manifest concept of sound – the external sound and word of the Vedas, the 'cosmic sound' that creates the universe and is present in all things.

Shabda, meaning 'sound', is said to be a manifestation of the primordial sound Om/Aum that emerged from Nada, reverberating through the universe like ripples in water, returning back to Shabda as his wives, the 50 bija-mantra that are the Matrikas, the Mother sounds of the Sanskrit language, the vowels and consonants that form the basis of the Sanskrit alphabet.

The individual sounds and letters of the Sanskrit alphabet are not just symbols but powerful bija-mantra or seed-mantra. The external manifestation of Shabda Brahman, such as spoken mantra, can lead to the realization of the inner, unstruck Nada Brahman through meditation and focus. This can be aided by the use of visualization practices that include detailed geometric imagery of deities and cosmic principles, as yantras or mandalas, to help transform the practitioner's mind.

The 50 bija-mantra are arranged in a specific order called the Matrika Chakra, a circular sequence that represents the cosmic manifestation of the universe. The Matrika Chakra is said to have originated from the cosmic sound of Lord Shiva's drum, which represents the primordial sound of creation or Om/Aum.

This circular arrangement of the letters of the Sanskrit alphabet is also known as the Varnamala of Bija, meaning 'circle of colours', reflecting the letter order according to their colour, or just Aksaramala, meaning 'circle of letters'.

अ आ इ ई उ ऊ

a   aa   i   ii   u   uu

Sanskrit Letters - Vowels /Svara

अं आं इं ईं उं ऊं

Am   Aam   Im   Iim   Um   Uum

Matrikas (Mothers)

हं हीं हीः

Hri   Hrim   Hrih

Bija   Bija-Mantra

Bija (seed syllables)

Mantra - Om Mani Pad Me Hum

Mantra Chakra

Chakra Bija

Dharma Mandala

Simple Yantra

Trimurti and Tridevi

To understand Hindu cosmology and its metaphysical structure, the relationship between the different gods of the Trimurti and its relationship to OM, its partnership with Shakti or female energy and the cult of Tantra, the science of the Divine Word is required.

Indian cosmology is portrayed by a large pantheon of gods and goddesses; these deities exist as married couples who represent the individual aspects of Brahman, the Supreme Consciousness, who brought about Creation as Shabda Brahaman or Transcendental Sound by reverberating as the Supreme Syllable, Om/Aum, from which all 51 sound vibrations of the Vedic Sanskrit language are derived.

Brahaman is the supreme consciousness, and from this sphere is born the living cosmos. The cosmos evolves through three stages: creation, preservation and destruction. In the Hindu pantheon, Brahma, Vishnu and Shiva represent these three aspects, respectively. Together in their capacity as universal life itself, they are called the Trimurti. This triple aspect of creation is also symbolized in the supreme bija-mantra OM, in which the three individual sounds A U M correspond to the three stages and gods of the Trimurti, respectively. Their wives, Sarasvati, Lakshmi and Parvati, are a trinity of goddesses known as the Tridevi.

BRAHMA AND SARASVATI

Not to be confused with Brahman, the Supreme Cosmic Spirit, Brahma is the first god of the Trimurti, the Deva or Creator of the universe, and all living things are said to have evolved from him. He is seen as a god of the intellect and of the mind, the source of all knowledge in the universe, credited as the inventor of all the arts of civilization: music, letters, mathematics and calendars. He inscribed the Vedic texts in Sanskrit on leaves of gold.

Brahma's female consort is Sarasvati, goddess of eloquence, inventor of the Sanskrit language, music and poetry. As the goddess Vak, she is the voice, the representation of the spoken word. The name Sarasvati comes from 'saras' meaning 'flow' and 'wati' meaning 'she who has...' – i.e., 'she who has flow'. So, Sarasvati is a symbol of knowledge; its flow (or growth) is like a river, and knowledge is supremely alluring, like a beautiful woman.

A tributary of the mighty Indus River was named after her, also an alternative name for the Indus Valley script and the meaning of the name of the Sharada script – Sharada being an alternative name for Sarasvati, and Sharadadesh being an archaic name for Kashmir.

Brahma
God of Cation - First god of the Trimurti

Sarasvatti
Goddess of eloquence, poetry, music - Consort of Brahma

VISHNU AND LAKSHMI

Vishnu, the second god of the Trimurti, is considered the preserver and protector of the universe. He is also known for his various avatars, including Krishna and Rama. He is believed to incarnate on earth in times of need to restore balance and protect dharma. Vishnu's wife is Lakshmi, the goddess of wealth, fortune, beauty, fertility, royal power and abundance – often pictured sitting on a lotus flower or leaf. She is the ideal of a Hindu wife, exemplifying loyalty and devotion to her husband.

SHIVA AND PARVATI

Shiva is the third god of the Trimurti, responsible for the destruction of the universe. However, in Hindu mythology, creation always follows destruction; therefore, Shiva is also associated with a reproductive force, restoring what was destroyed. Most Shivaites agree that in his highest form, Para Shiva, Shiva is both male and female at once, containing both the male Shiva and his female counterpart, the goddess, Shakti.

As this destroyer/reproductive force, Shiva is the Nataraja, the 'Lord of the Cosmic Dance'. He is the creator of dance, rhythm, and music. He is also said to have spoken, or beaten out on a drum, the first sixteen rhythmic syllables ever pronounced, which formed the basis of the Sanskrit language.

His wife, Parvati, is the goddess of power, energy, harmony, love, devotion and motherhood. She and Shiva are the parents of Ganesha, the elephant-headed god of writing and business. Philosophically, she is regarded as Shiva's Shakti, or feminine divine power or energy. Shakti is the source of power that energizes Shiva, who is incomplete without her.

KALI, CONSORT OF SHIVA

Shiva's female consort is the goddess Kali, a fearsome goddess of destruction. She is often seen standing on Shiva's body, suggesting that without the power of Kali or Shakti, Shiva as masculine energy is inert. Kali is the foremost of the Mahavidyas, ten ferocious tantric goddesses, Matrikas who fought the demon, Rutabija, on behalf of Shiva.

Kali wears a necklace made of severed human heads, which are variously enumerated. Containing 108, representing the number of countable beads on a Japamala, or rosary for repeating mantras. 50, 51 and 52 beads represent the sounds of Vedic Sanskrit in the form of the Varnamala of Bija with which Kali destroys, re-creates and preserves the universe. Hindus believe that Sanskrit is the dynamic language of the goddess – each letter represents a feminine energy (Shakti), a form of Kali. Therefore, she is seen as the mother of all language, of all bija, mantra and shashtra.

Kali - Consort of Shiva
Goddess of death, destruction and rebirth

Shabda – Sound

Over the millennia, Indic philosophers have devoted a large portion of their time to the study of the creation of the cosmos through sound vibration or Shabda. This is an Eastern concept, as opposed to the Western, whose creation is through light. Both these concepts of creation are mentioned right at the beginning of the Bible in the lines, 'In the beginning was the Word (sound) and the Word was with God' and 'God said, Let There Be Light' and behold there was light.

According to Hindu philosophy, Shabda is more ancient than gods and men. It precedes creation; it is eternal, indivisible, creative and imperceptible in its subtle form. Sound is what you hear with your ear. Wherever there is motion and vibration of any kind – that is sound. There is movement in all that exists. All movement (and objects) emits sound, whether you hear it or not. Atoms in objects spin and make a sound. The planets spin and make sound; they are the individual sounds of the musical scale, and when they are heard together, they make the sound humans call silence.

The primordial sound Om generates the cosmic energy that spreads like ripples through a pond and becomes the immediate progenitor of the universe. Om is Shabda Brahman, all sounds; the audible, unlettered Dhvani and the visual, lettered Varna are vibrations of Om. The primordial sound is the subtlest, and as it descends from Para Nada (silence), it assumes gross forms, eventually resulting in speech (vak, vox).

Shabda Brahman is the Father, and Nada Brahman is the Mother, the Matrika. She is the originator of the five subtle elements, the five gross elements, the five motor organs, the five sensory organs, the four karanas, the three gunas and the others.

DHVANI AND VARNA (AUDIBLE AND VISUAL SOUND)

Shabda is divided into two distinct forms: audible, unlettered sound, called Dhvani, and visual, lettered sound, called Varna. Dhavani or 'mere sounds' includes vocal or non-vocal sounds with or without meaning, emitted by men, animals and natural objects, like a roar, thunder, drumbeat, laughter, crying, or expressions of fright, anger, etc. Varna or visual, articulated speech can be put down in letters.

A simple explanation of the difference between Dhvani and Varna can be heard when walking along the street listening to traffic, buildings, birds, wind, dogs, sirens, alarms, rustling leaves and human conversation, all of which are Dhvani. Only those sounds heard in conversation between people are Varna.

Dhavani is the acoustic aspect of Shabda. It carries vibration, frequency and decibel. This includes the science of pronunciation and chanting (shishka), one of the six Vendangas and the energy associated with seed sounds, the basis of mantra. Once sound explodes from Sphorta, it is registered by the ear and is deified as Shabda Brahman.

For Dhvani to aquire its qualities, the gunas pervade the sound. When the latent mental sound acquires the guna called rajas, she is called dhvani or sound. Dhvani contains the seed sounds, svara or vowels and bija or seed syllables that make up mantra. The bija or bija-mantra sound 'Om' is Dhvani. From Om was derived all the dhavani, the audible, unlettered sounds, and all the Varna or visual, lettered sounds.

Varnas are visual, vocal, articulate, meaningful sounds. Once a sound has been made, it produces a colour or shade of colour (light). Varna is a Sanskrit word meaning colour, shade, group, and the sounds of Sanskrit can be ordered by their colour into groups. The term Varna covers all visual sounds, including svara and aksara (vowels and consonants).

The combination of Varnas to form words, their sequencing and ordering, is called vyakarana (grammar). The study of ordinary words is called nirukta. It is based on the physical effect or reaction to various natural phenomena and the sounds corresponding to those effects. Chandas is the study or meter, the arrangement of syllable groups with different lengths. These are three of the six vendangas.

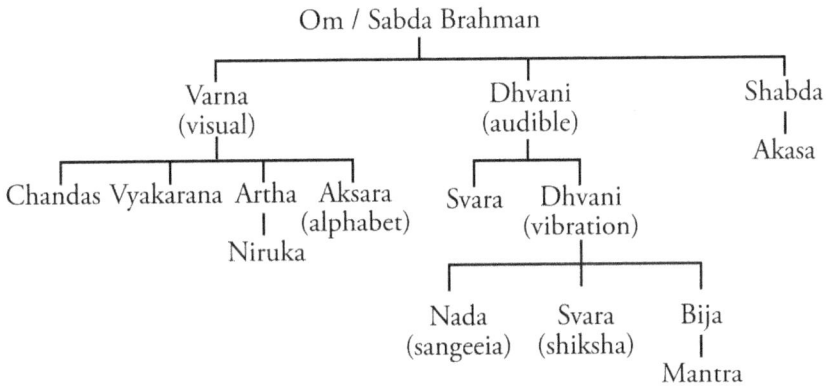

Om / Sabda Brahman

Varna (visual) — Dhvani (audible) — Shabda | Akasa

Chandas Vyakarana Artha Aksara (alphabet) | Niruka — Svara Dhvani (vibration)

Nada (sangeeia) — Svara (shiksha) — Bija | Mantra

Descent of sound from vibration to audible and visual sound

Vak – Speech

In Vedic sound theory, Vak, pronounced 'vach', meaning 'to speak', corresponds to the Latin term 'vox', meaning 'voice'. In Tantra, it is said that the universe was set in motion by the primordial throb or 'adya spanda', and that all objects in the universe are created by sound, as sound precedes the formation of objects.

The rhythms of cosmic vibration issue forth from four levels that correspond to the various levels in manifestation, giving each Sanskrit letter four states of sound. Vak, the power of speech that sprouts in Para, gives forth leaves in Pasyanti, buds forth in Madhyana, and blossoms in Vaikhari.

1/ Para-Vak – undifferentiated word. No movement, supreme speech, an indication of sound, it is a sprout.

2/ Pasyanti – is creative thought and action by Bindhu and abides in the mind. It is the word and the object seen in and by the mind. It is will. The sprout becomes leaves.

3/ Madhyana – in the middle between visual and spoken word. It is knowledge. The buds show up.

4/ Vaikhari – spoken letter or word. Articulation of letters, words and sentences. Expressed ideas. Chanting of mantras. It is action. It is a blossom.

Articulated speech or Vak can be visualized by Varnas, vocal, articulate, meaningful sounds. The Varnas or letter sounds are the body of the goddess - Matrika, Kali, Kundalini – while Vak is an alternative name for Sarasvati, the goddess of speech.

The Sanskrit alphabet starts with an 'A' and ends in 'ha' – no matter what language a person speaks, when they suddenly know the meaning of something, they will say 'Aha', the first and last sound of Sanskrit. This is the universal mind saying that it has comprehended something from beginning to end, from A to Z, from A to Ha. When the mind becomes amused, it just repeats the last sound of Sanskrit over and over again, ha ha ha ha ha. Therefore, the Sanskrit word for laughter is Ha, or Ha's for multiple laughter.

Om / Sabda Brahman

Varna
(articulate)

Dhvani
(unarticulate)

Sanskrit
(language)

Para Vak

Pasyanti

Madhayana

Vaikhari

Vak / Vox
(speech/voice)

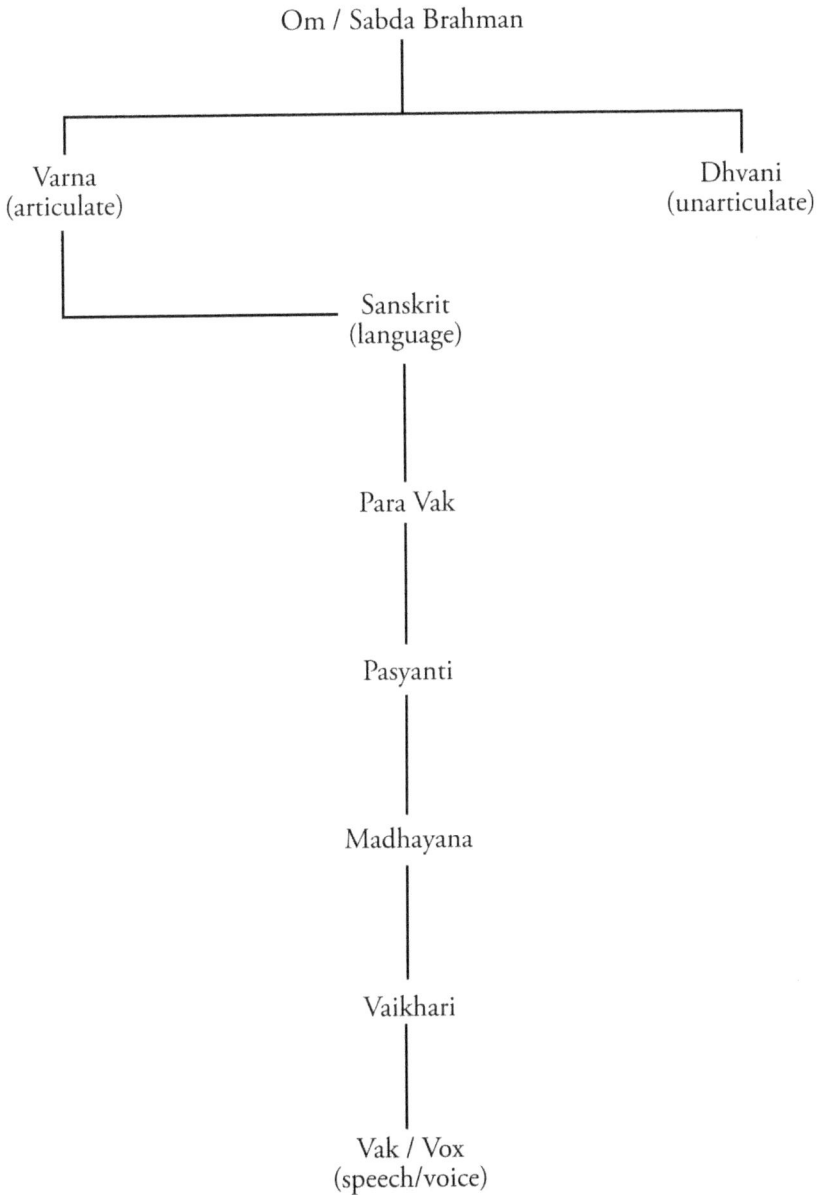

Descent of sound from subtle vibration to gross speech

Brahmi Abugida (Sanskrit)

Brahmi abugida is a Western academic term used to describe the Sanskrit alphabet called the Varnamala or Aksaramala in India. The term 'abugida' denotes its alpha-syllabic function. The system was first developed around 250 BCE, to write the Sanskrit dialect of Magdhi Prakrit, also called Pali. It was later extended to write Vedic Sanskrit.

All the letters are capital forms, written from left to right. In northern India, the horizontal bar called Shiro Rekha, from which each letter hangs, characterizes the script. In southern India, it is characterized by being rounded. These calligraphic distinctions are the result of employing different writing materials.

Following independence in the 1950s, the Devanagari script was chosen as the official Sanskrit script of India due to its strong religious and cultural associations, although Sanskrit can be written in any one of the many Brahmi-derived scripts.

The number of letters the Indian alphabet contains varies depending on which language it is being used to write. Vedic Sanskrit requires 50, 51 or 52 letters, with Classical Sanskrit requiring only 46. Prakrits or dialects like Hindi require 44, while Pali requires only 42. At its most elaborate, it is composed of 52 letters, employing 16 vowels, 11 of which are in frequent use – a, aa, u, uu, i, ii, ri, e, ai, o, au. Its 33 to 36 consonant-syllables are arranged in a logical scheme according to the order of speech organs involved – throat, palate, the teeth and lips – allowing them to be divided into two sets and eight groups called vargas, which are subdivided into categories called ganas.

It employs three forms of phoneme or letter. Independent vowels called svara, and modifying vowels called matra. Consonant-syllables called vyanjana and conjunct consonants called samyoka. The vowel-consonants 'am' and 'ah' are signified by ayogavahah, special diacritic marks.

There are four basic forms of punctuation: the dash or horizontal bar; the vertical bar; dot; and circle. Sentences are marked at the end by a perpendicular stroke called Viram, two such strokes are used at the end of a text. Word boundaries are not marked, as the horizontal top bars are usually linked to form an unbroken line. The line is only broken between words with a final vowel, diphthong, nasal (anusvara) or weak aspirant (visarga) and words with an initial consonant. Rather than writing a succession of individual words, Sanskrit orthography is sensitive to breath groups representing connected discourse.

Spelling has been eliminated in Sanskrit because every sound has been correctly analyzed and placed into its phonetic classification, and the consonants and the vowels, which have different functions, have been assigned definite modes of behaviour.

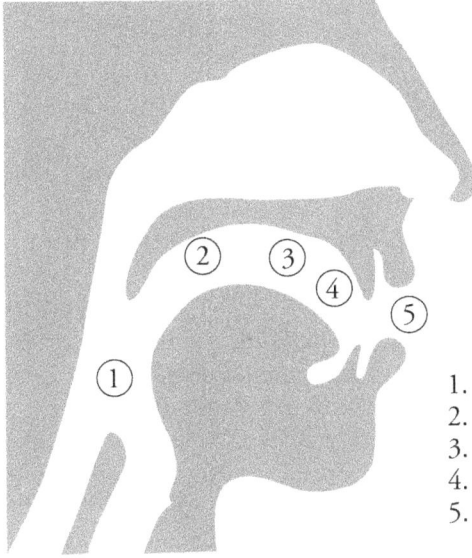

1. Gutturals
2. Palatals
3. Cerebrals
4. Dentals
5. Labials

Tongue placement positions for Sanskrit

group/catagory varga/gana	mute-consonants sparsa				nasals anunasika	semi-vowels antahstha	sibilants usman
	-V-A	-V+A	+V-A	+V+A	+V	+V	-V
gutterals kanthya	क ka	ख kha	ग ga	घ gha	ङ na		ह ha
palatals talavya	च ca	छ cha	ज ja	झ jha	ञ na	य ya	श sa
cerebrals (retroflex) murdhanya	ट tta	ठ ttha	ड dda	ढ ddha	ण na	र ra	ष sa
dentals dantya	त ta	थ tha	द da	ध dha	न na	ल la	स sa
labials osthya	प pa	फ pha	ब ba	भ bha	म ma	व va	

-V non-voiced;   -A non-aspirate;   +V voiced;   +A aspirate

Consonants (vyanjana)

Brahmi Lipi (Script)

India, its mysticism, its alphabet and its scripts all have their origins in the Indus Valley civilization that evolved along the banks of the Indus River that flows between Pakistan and northwest India, in north Sindh and south Punjab.

At its peak, between 2500 and 1900 BCE, the major cities of the Indus Valley ranked alongside those of Mesopotamia and Egypt. Prior to its discovery in 1921, no-one had even suspected the existence of such a civilization in India. This archaic civilization disappeared around 1900 BCE, 300 years before the arrival of Aryan-speaking people from Iran who became the Hindus of India.

The noun 'India' is derived from the local appellation for the people of the Indus Valley and beyond. In Sanskrit it is Sindhu, in Persian it is Hindu, in Greek it is Indus and in English it is India. India's ancient name for itself was Bharatavarsha, named after a legendary ancient emperor. Its modern name has been shortened to 'Bharat'.

INDUS VALLEY SCRIPT

The Indus Valley script is the usual name given to the pictographic system employed by the ancient people whose culture was established along the banks of the Indus River. More recently, the script has been called Mohen-jo-Darro script and Harappan script, after the people of the area. Even more recently, it has been termed the Sarasvati script, after the river and area where most of the artefacts have been found.

About 3500 Indus Valley inscriptions are known. They were found carved onto seal stones, pottery, copper tablets, bronze implements, and bone and ivory rods. The Indus Valley inscriptions are brief; the average has less than four signs to a line and five signs in a text. The longest inscription is only 20 signs, in three lines.

Scholars tend to agree that there are about 400 Indus signs in all (plus or minus 25). This means that there are too many signs to be an alphabet or syllabary. Leading to the conclusion that it must be a mixed script of pictograms and logograms, like the scripts of Babylon and Egypt.

The Indus script still defies decipherment because the language spoken in the ancient Indus Valley is not known. Although linguists now think that the Indus people spoke a mixed language of Austro-Asian and Dravidian. Due to this, it looks unlikely that the script will ever be deciphered, as many of its signs are so simplified and schematic that their pictorial meaning is difficult to perceive – condemning it to remain an unknown script, writing an unknown language.

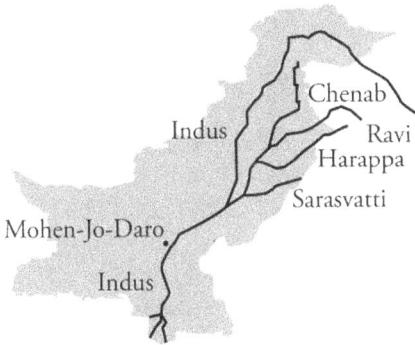

Indus Valley civilization (Pakistan)
2500 - 1900 BCE

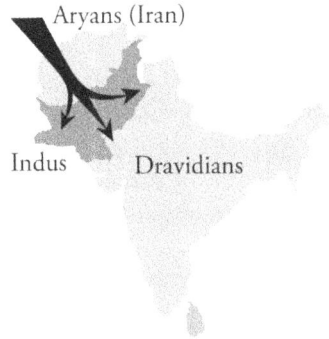

Aryan migration
1600 BCE

Indus pictograms

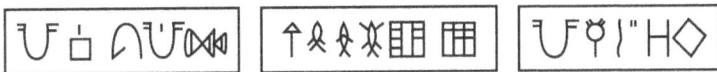

Seal inscriptions

a	i	u	e	o	ka	kha	ga	gha	ca	cha

ja	jha	tta	ttha	dda	ddha	ta	tha	da	dha	na

pa	pha	ba	bha	ma		ya	ra	la	va	sa	sa	sa	ha

Pre-Brahmic Indus/Tamil script

BRAHMI LIPI

Named Brahmi after the Vedic priests who invented it, Brahmi Lipi or Brahmi script is the original script from which all Indian scripts and their Southeast Asian variants are derived. It is the parent script of the world's largest script family, due to the spread of Hinduism and Buddhism.

Its ancient origins are disputed. Some scholars perceive that Brahmi Lipi is a native Indian invention, separate from the Western alphabet, theorizing that the Brahmi script evolved from the Harappan script of the Indus Valley, although anyone has yet to prove this. The earliest examples of Brahmi Lipi are found in Anuradhapura, Sri Lanka, with short inscriptions in copper and on broken pottery, dated between the 6th and the 4th centuries BCE, but these are scarce.

Brahmi Lipi was sparingly utilized, if at all, until the advent of Buddhism and, to a lesser extent, Jainism. Buddha insisted that his teachings be given to all people in their own language. King Asoka's conversion to Buddhism created the edicts, which are written in Magdhi Prakrit, a common form of Sanskrit and the native tongue of Buddha, also known as Pali. It is now called Mauryan Brahmi, after Maurya, Ashoka's kingdom.

Over the millennia, Brahmi Lipi has undergone certain transformations. From the proto-Brahmi scripts of Bhattiprolu and Tamil, to its standardization and institution as Asokan Brahmi, into a dynastic Mauryan variant which can be divided into two stages: Uttari (ancient) and Daksimi (modern). By the 6th century CE, the modern form had evolved into northern and southern variants, which would be the inspiration for the modern scripts of the Indian subcontinent.

At the time of its creation, Brahmi Lipi was called Leth or Lett; the name Brahmi is said to have come from a Jain legend. According to South Indian myth, a Jain monk called Vrushabhadeva explained the script to his daughters, Brahmi and Soundhary. Therefore, as a mark of this, the written script is called Brahmi,and the numerals are called Soundhary.

According to Tamil tradition, the Brahmi letter shapes were formed on a schema or grid, a geometric representation of the cosmos. The letter forms based on the position of the speech organs during pronunciation, complying with phonetic rationales, were transcribed into geometric forms using the schema.

Western scholars support the notion that their pictographic source is based on Indus Valley script with influences from the Western alphabet.

Schema   A   I   U   E   O

ka   kha   ga   gha   na   ca   cha   ja   jha   na

tta   ttha   dda   ddha   na   ta   tha   da   dha   na

pa   pha   ba   bha   ma   ya   ra   la   va   sa   ha

a   i   u   e   o

ka   kha   ga   gha   na   ca   cha   ja   jha   na   tta   ttha   dda   ddha   na

ta   tha   da   dha   na   pa   pha   ba   bha   ma   ya   ra   la   va   sa   ha

Geometric forms

a   i   u   e   o

ka   kha   ga   gha   na   ca   cha   ja   jha   na   tta   ttha   dda   ddha   na

ta   tha   da   dha   na   pa   pha   ba   bha   ma   ya   ra   la   va   sa   ha

Cursive forms

a   aa   i   ii   u   uu   e   oo   am

ka   kha   ga   gha   ca   cha   ja   na   tta   ttha   dda   ddha   na

ta   tha   da   dha   na   pa   pha   ba   ma   ya   ra   la   va   sa   sa   sa   ha

Mauryan Brahmi

Sacred Scripts (North)

Brahmi Lipi established itself as a religious script, used for recording the Buddhist sutras written in its local variant, making all Indian scripts sacred. Over the centuries, various northern and southern variants have acquired their own individual sacred status, used for writing religious texts, mantra, bija and seals within Hinduism, Jainism, Buddhism and Sikhism.

NORTHERN BRAHMI / GUPTA

The scripts of northern India slowly evolved through successive dynastic variants, from the Brahm Lipi of the Mauryan Empire, 4th–1st century BCE, through to the Late Brahmi script of the Gupta dynasty, 3rd–5th century CE. After the 6th century, the Late Gupta script became known as Siddhamatrika or Siddham script and evolved into Western and Eastern variants, which influenced the character of the regionalized medieval scripts that replaced the Late Gupta script across northern India by the 10th century.

SIDDHAMATRIKA

Siddhamatrika is the name given to a calligraphic refinement of the Late Gupta script, from which the later Sarada, Nagari and Bangla scripts are descended. It was employed to write Sanskrit texts between the 6th and 13th centuries CE. It was a formal style created by writing Gupta Brahmi with a square-nibbed bamboo pen to form the capital letters individually in Indian ink on manuscripts made of birch bark. The leaves or pages were gathered together, holes were drilled into them, and they were bound with string to create books. The Siddham script became synonymous with Mahayana Buddhism.

During the Gupta era, Buddhism was at its height in India, and Sanskrit texts were transported along the Silk Road, making their way to China, Tibet and Japan. Buddhist Tantrics considered it important to preserve the Sanskrit pronunciation of mantras. Since Chinese characters are not suitable for translating Sanskrit, the use of the Siddham script was retained and preserved in East Asia, and the writing of Siddham survived where Tantric Buddhism persisted. Therefore, more attention was paid to the letterforms of Siddham.

Outside of India, Tantric Buddhists abandoned the square-nibbed pen in favour of the brush, and Siddham assumed its place in Asian calligraphy. Particular importance was placed on the faithful reproduction of bija and mantra composed in Siddham. In contrast to Devanagari in India, Siddham in China and Japan was never used for anything but sacred writing.

अ आ ़ ़ ३ ३ ़ ़ १ ़ ़ ़ ३ ३ ़ ़
a aa i ii u uu ri rri li lli e ai o au am ah

क ख ग घ ़ च छ ज झ ़ ़ ़ ़ ़
ka kha ga gha na ca cha ja jha na tta ttha dda ddha na

त थ द ध न ब भ म य र ल व स स स ह ल्ल क्ष
ta tha da dha na ba bha ma ya ra la va sa sa sa ha lla ksha

Late Gupta - Western variant

अ आ ़ ़ ़ ़ ़ ़
a aa i ii u e ai o

क ख ग घ च छ ज ़ ़ ़ ़ ़ ़
ka kha ga gha ca cha ja na tta ttha dda ddha na

त थ द ध न प फ ब भ म य र स ़
ta tha da dha na pa pha ba bha ma ya ra sa la

Late Gupta - Eastern variant

अ आ ़ ़ ़ ़ ़ ़
a aa i i u u ri rii

़ ़ ़ ़ ़ ़ ़ ़
i i e ai o au am ah

़ ़ ़ ़ ़ ़ ़ ़ ़
ka kha ga gha na ca cha ja jha na

़ ़ ़ ़ ़ ़ ़ ़ ़
tta ttha dda ddha na ta tha da dha na

़ ़ ़ ़ ़ ़ ़ ़ ़
pa pha ba bha ma ya ra la va

़ ़ ़ ़ ़ ़
sa sa sa ha la ksa

Late Gupta / Siddhamatrika / Bonji

Following the annexation of trade and pilgrim routes by Islamic expansion in the 8th century, the practice of writing Siddham script was preserved and reached its zenith with the Japanese Shingon school of Buddhism, producing the largest number of Siddham master calligraphers. The most renowned was Kukai, aka Kobi Dashi, the monk who first introduced Siddhamatrika to Japan, bringing it back with him from China during the 9th century. Siddhamatrika is revered by Shingon Buddhists as 'Bonji', meaning 'Sanskrit script' or 'Buddhist characters', used to write out mantras and sutras in Sanskrit using a brush pen.

Today, none of the original Gupta texts in Siddhamatrika exist; only the Chinese and Japanese variants of this formal script are known. Since the 7th or 8th centuries, Siddhamatrika has been exclusively used for seed syllables, or bija and mantras. Nothing original has been composed in the script in India, China or Japan.

SARADA (SHARADA)

From the 8th century CE, the Siddham script evolved into northwest regional variants that produced two sacred forms. In Kashmir, Punjab and Sindh (Pakistan), it became parent to the Sarada script. In turn, Sarada became the parent of other northwestern scripts, including Landa, the parent of Gurmukhi, the sacred script of Sikhism. Sarada is also allied with Nagari, built on the same system, but the letterforms differ.

Originally used by the educated Hindu minority in Kashmir, it was the first regional script developed for writing Vedic texts in Sanskrit. This probably qualifies Sarada as India's only true religious script.

Today, Sarada is a nearly extinct regional script employed in the northwest states of Punjab, Jammu and Kashmir to write Sanskrit and Kashmiri. The Kashmiri script is essentially a more modern version of the Sarada script. Small groups of Brahmins (Jyotishis and Purohits) continue to use Sarada for writing and calculating astrological and ritual formulas.

GURMUKHI

Originally derived from the Sarada variant Landa, mixed with influences from the Nagari script style, the Gurmukhi script was invented in the 16th century by the second Sikh Guru, Angad Dev, to replace the Landa script for writing the Punjabi language. It has also been adapted to write Braj Bhasha, Sanskrit and Sindhi. With the penning of Guru Grantha Sahib's 1430 pages in Gurmukhi, it became the principal script of the Sikhs. The name comes from the old Punjabi word 'gurmukhi', which translates as "the script that issued from the mouth of the Guru."

Ashokan 3th c. bce	Kusnan 2th c. bce	Gupta 4th c. ce	Late Gupta 6-12th c. ce	Sharada 9th c. ce	Nagari 11th c. ce	Bangla 10th c. ce	Kashmiri 14th c. ce

Development of northern script styles for the independent vowel A

a aa i ii u uu e o

ka kha ga gha na ca cha ja jha na tta ttha dda ddha na

ta tha da dha na pa pha ba bha ma ya ra la va sa sa sa ha

Sarada 8th-10th century

a aa i ii u uu ri rii li lii e ai o au an am ah

ka kha ga gha na ca cha ja jha na tta ttha dda ddha na

tta ttha dda ddha na pa pha ba bha ma ya ra la lla va sa sa sa ha

Modern Sarada / Kashmiri

a a i i u ǔ e ai o au

ka kha ga gha na ca cha ja jha na

tta ttha dda ddha na ta tha da dha na

pa pha ba bha ma ya ra la va ra sa ha

gya nha mha rha lha rha sa za la tr

Gurmukhi

By the 8th century CE, the Siddham script had evolved into regional scripts used across central and northern India. The most influential and most widely used of all being the Nagari script style.

The term Nagari is derived from the Sanskrit word 'nagar', meaning 'urban', 'city' or 'metropolitan' script. It was the dominant script form in the Middle Ages, used to write Sanskrit between 1000 and 1200 CE, replacing the Siddham script. Between the 14th and 18th centuries, the script developed nearer to its present-day Devanagari form.

Traditionally written from left to right, using a script of capital letters, the Nagari script style is defined by hanging letters from a visible headline or 'matra'. This was made possible by the use of writing with a square-cut nibbed pen on tree bark that allowed for the use of straight lines. Nagari has the headline stroke at the top of individual letters but lacks the long connecting line that groups letters into words. The later extended horizontal line came to define the Devanagari script.

NANDINAGARI

Central and southwest India produced a regional Nagari variant called Nandinagari, used between the 8th and 19th centuries to write Sanskrit inscriptions and texts in southern Maharashtra, Karnataka and Andhra Pradesh. Archaic forms of Nandinagari are dated back as far as the 6th and 7th centuries, but its form was firmly established by the 10th century. It has never been used for printing and, as such, lacks refinement and standardization. The meaning of its name is obscure, but it may be related to its locality or the worship of Shiva.

DEVANAGARI

Devanagari has been the official script of India since 1944, employed to write Sanskrit and its dialects, including Hindi, the most spoken language in India and fourth in the world. Over the centuries, it has evolved two variants – a southern variant derived from Nandinagari, and a northern variant with influences from the Sarada script.

The name Devanagari is made up of two Sanskrit words: 'Deva', which means 'god, Brahmin, celestial', and 'nagari', meaning 'urban, metropolitan, city'. In English, this can be translated two ways: 'heavenly/sacred script of the city' or 'script of the city of the gods or priests'. It has been known by this name since the 11th century CE, due to its ubiquitous use for writing Sanskrit. At the beginning of the 21st century, it is commonly called by its nickname of 'Deva Lipi', or 'godly, holy, sacred script'.

झ	आ	इ	ई	उ	ऊ
a	aa	i	ii	u	uu

ri	li	e	ai	o	au

फ	रव	ग	प्प	ड	व	क	ड	न	ण
ka	kha	ga	gha	na	ca	cha	ja	jha	na

tta	thha	dda	dhha	na	ta	tha	da	dha	na

प	पर	क	न	म
pa	pha	ba	bha	ma

ya	ra	la	va	sa	sa	sa	ha

Nandinagari

अ	आ	इ	ई	उ	ऊ	ऋ	ॠ
a	aa	i	ii	u	uu	ri	rii

लृ	लॄ	ए	ऐ	ओ	औ	अं	अः
li	lii	e	ai	o	au	am	ah

क	ख	ग	घ	ङ	च	छ	ज	झ	ञ
ka	kha	ga	gha	na	ca	cha	ja	jha	na

ट	ठ	ड	ढ	ण	त	थ	द	ध	न
tta	ttha	dda	ddha	na	ta	tha	da	dha	na

प	फ	ब	भ	म	य	र	ल	व	श	ष	स	ह
pa	pha	ba	bha	ma	ya	ra	la	va	sa	sa	sa	ha

Southern Devanagari (standard / classic)

It wasn't until independence from Britain in 1947 that an Indian government established Devanagari as a national writing system, not only for writing standardized Sanskrit and Hindi but also adapted to write other Indian languages and dialects.

EASTERN NAGARI / BANGLA LIPI / BENGALI SCRIPT

During the first millennium CE, Kolkata (Calcutta), the capital city of Bengal, was a hub of Sanskrit literature written in the Siddham script. The sister script of the western Nagari, Bangla Lipi or Bengali script evolved out of the eastern variant of Siddham script around 1000 CE.

Originally Bangla was not associated with any particular language but was often used in the middle kingdoms of India and in the Pala Empire. Its proto form for writing Bengali and Assamese was called Gaudi. Later, it continued to be used specifically in the Bengal region and came to be called Bangla, meaning Bengali.

Bengali is the second most spoken language in India and the seventh most in the world. It is an eastern Sanskrit dialect known as Magadhi Prakrit, which evolved as a distinct regional language between 1000–1200 CE.

During the Islamic Mughal domination of a large part of India, 1526–1857, Bengalis used an adapted language called Dobhashi Bengali, written in Arabic-Persian script, for writing Islamic texts and the Bengali language. In 1880, the British Indian government changed the script of the Bengali language and replaced it with Bangala, the original script of Bengal before Muslim rule.

Standardized into its modern form by Iswar Chanda, under the reign of the East India Company, the current printed form first appeared in 1778, when Charles Wilkins developed printing in Bengali with a few archaic letters modernized in the 19th century. Today it is the official script of Bangladesh – although Muslim, they still speak Bengali.

Since 1971, Bengal has been divided in two. East Bengal gained independence from Hindu India to become the Republic of Bangladesh, a Muslim nation in which the Koran can be written in Arabic, Persian or Bengali Lipi, making it the only non-Arabic script used to write the Koran.

ऋ आ इ ई उ ऊ ऋ ॠ
a   aa   i   ii   u   uu   ri   rii

ऌ ॡ ए ऐ ओ औ अं अः
li   lii   e   ai   o   au   am   ah

क ख ग घ ङ च छ ज झ ञ
ka kha ga gha na ca cha ja jha na

ट ठ ड ढ ण त थ द ध न
tta ttha dda ddha na ta tha da dha na

प फ ब भ म य र ल व श ष स ह
pa pha ba bha ma ya ra la va sa sa sa ha

Northern Devanagari (modern - Late Sarada)

অ আ ই ঈ উ ঊ
a   aa   i   ii   u   uu

ঋ এ ঐ ও ঔ
ri   e   ai   o   au

ক খ গ ঘ ঙ চ ছ জ ঝ ঞ
ka kha ga gha na ca cha ja jha na

ট ঠ ড ঢ ণ ত থ দ ধ ন
tta ttha dda ddha na ta tha da dha na

প ফ ব ভ ম য র ল শ ষ স হ য় ড় ঢ়
pa pha ba bha ma ya ra la sa sa sa ha ya a ha

Bangla / Bengali

The Siddham script and its Nagari calligraphic variants used for writing Sanskrit texts spread from northwest India to Nepal and Tibet by the 10th century CE, creating new script styles for making new copies of Mahayana Buddhist sutras in Sanskrit.

All Nepalese and some Tibetan scripts are of the Kutila calligraphic style. The term 'kutil' means 'crooked' or 'bent', referring to the right-angled downstroke created by a sharp twist of the pen at the end of a letter's vertical downstroke. It first appeared as a calligraphic style in conjunction with the Siddham script and is found in both Devanagari and Bangla calligraphy.

RANJANA / KUTILA / NEPALI LIPI

The Nepalese script called Ranjana, meaning 'pleasant, delightful', is considered to be the world's second most beautiful and artistic script. Derived from Siddham, it has the angular or squarish appearance of Nagari script.

Composed of thick and thin lines, a thick-lined script can mark the paper for a longer duration, Ranjana is revered as a sacred script commonly used by Buddhist monks for writing the Sanskrit titles of books which have been translated from Sanskrit. It is also used for inscribing 'Om Mani Padme Hum' and other mantras and bija mantras on prayer wheels, shrines, temples and monasteries.

Ranjana is also used to form stacked syllables called Kutaksara (heaped syllables), used for condensing mantras and mystical monograms written vertically in columns, instead of horizontally in lines. Since they serve as a kind of shorthand for mantras, only the specialist or the initiate that may have helped in their development can decipher such complex figures.

The best-known example is the mantra of Kalachakra – the powerful ten in Tibetan. It contains in compressed form the seven bija and the three parts of the nasalization sign. Other forms of Kutasksara include the seven-letter monogram.

Originating in northeast India during the 10th century, Ranjana was used for writing Sanskrit texts and mantras during the Pala dynasty, under whose reign Indian Buddhism flourished for the last time.

The script spread to Magadha and then to Nepal and Tibet. Under the influence of Tibetan monks, it was used for Buddhist inscriptions in China and Japan as early as the 13th century. The main function of Ranjana in Nepal and Tibet is its preferred use for ornamental inscriptions of mantras and bijas written in gold with a red outline.

a	aa	i	ii	u	uu	ri	rii

e	o	ai	au	am	ah

ka	kha	ga	gha	na	ca	cha	ja	jha	ne

ta	tha	da	dha	na	ta	tha	da	dha	na

pa	pha	ba	bha	ma	ya	ra	la	va	sa	sa	sa	ha

Ranjana

ka		ca		tta		ta
kha		cha		ttha		tha
ga		ja		dda		da
gha		jha		ddha		dha
na		na		na		na

pa		ya		sha		ksa
pha		ra		sha		tra
ba		la		sa		jna
bha		va		ha		
ma						

Kutaksara - heaped syllables

	ha	khsa	ma		bindhu
	la	va	ra	ya	nada
					visarga

Ten elements of the Kalachakra

Ya
Ra
Va
La
Ma
Ksa
Ha

7 letter monogram

LANTSA AND VARTU

In Tibet, the Ranjana script became known as Lantsa ('pleasant, delightful'). In the monasteries of Tibet, Lantsa serves as a sacred script used as decoration on murals, printed or signed on mandalas, and the chosen script to write mantras under the title of a Sadhana, that which has been translated from Sanskrit into Tibetan.

Tibetan monks also produced the closely related script called Vartu (vartula – round). It appears to be a more casual form of handwritten calligraphy, but the basic principles in the forms and calligraphy of the consonants are the same as in Lantsa. Vartu was in full use for newspaper print until the mid-20th century and is still used for newspaper headlines.

Lantsa and Vartu are two Dakini script styles which became the fundamental vehicle of Buddhist textual tradition in Nepal and Tibet. From the 8th century CE, in Buddhism, a 'terma' represents a form of hidden teaching. If the concealed or encoded teaching or object is a text, it was often written in a Dakini script.

In Tibetan Buddhism, Dakini, meaning 'sky walker', is a female spirit associated with the transmission of teachings to her disciples. Therefore, Dakini is a term used to describe the Brahmi script styles employed by Buddhist monks during the 11th century CE for making new copies of the Sutras in Sanskrit. The calligraphic excellence and diversity of the divine scripts created by Tibetan Buddhist monks stand shoulder to shoulder with the best from around the world.

Tibetan text pages, known as 'pecha', according to Tibetan tradition, are written by hand or printed from wood blocks. The text on the front page will have up to four lines written in a fancier style than the normal pages. The first line, the title in Sanskrit, is in Lantsa script, in black ink. In the second line, the same Sanskrit text will be rendered in Vartu script, also in black ink. The third line will be in a Tibetan script, usually in the Uchen style, in red ink. In the last line, the Tibetan translation of the Sanskrit text, written in a Naga script, appears in black ink.

a   aa   i   ii   u   uu   e   ai

o   au   ri   ree   li   lee   am   ah

ka   kha   ga   gha   nga   ca   cha   ja   jha   nya

tta   ttha   dda   ddha   na   ta   tha   da   dha   nna   pa   pha   ba   bha   ma

ya   ra   la   va   sa   sha   shha   ha   ksa

Lantsa

a   aa   i   ii   u   uu   e   ai

o   au   ri   ree   li   lee   am   ah

ka   kha   ga   gha   nga   ca   cha   ja   jha   nya

tta   ttha   dda   ddha   na   ta   tha   da   dha   nna

pa   pha   ba   bha   ma   ya   ra   la   va   shha   sha   sa   ha   kssa

Vartu / Wartu

UCHEN

Uchen, the national script style of Tibet, was created in the 7th century CE by Thonmi Sombhata, a minister of the first Tibetan Emperor, Songtsen Gampo (569-649 CE). Sombhata was sent to India by the Emperor to study the art of writing. On his return, he introduced his Tibetan script, whose letterforms were based on an Indic alphabet of that period, probably an eastern form of the Siddham script.

Gampo created Uchen, the most common form of formal script used for writing the Tibetan language. Uchen or 'dbu-can' means 'with a head'. As a script, it is characterized by its Nagari style, heavy horizontal lines and tapering vertical lines. It is used to write entire sutras or Buddhist texts, while other Tibetan scripts (Ume) are more frequently used to write a single phrase or saying. Because of its exceptional clarity, it became the model for letterpress and digital type, establishing Uchen as the international script of Tibet.

HORYIG

Horyig is a Tibetan form of Asian square script calligraphy where the letters are arranged vertically in columns or horizontally in lines, used to write Sanskrit, Mongolian, Chinese and Tibetan during the 13th century. The script style is derived from Basiba, a Chinese script used for making seals.

The Tibetan word 'Horyig' translates as 'Mongolian Writing'. Tibetans use Horyig as a decorative script for seals and temple inscriptions, written in various widths, wide and narrow, with the letters arranged in a single vertical column.

Horyig was adapted from the Mongolian square script known as the 'Phags-pa script, named after a Tibetan lama called Bio-gros rGyalantshan, who was better known by the title of the 'Phags-pa Lama. In 1250 CE, Kublai Khan commissioned him to create a new national script to replace the Semitic derived Uigur script commissioned by Genghis Khan.

ཨ ཨ ཨི ཨུ ཨེ ཨོ

a   aa   i   u   e   o

ཀ ཁ ག ང ཅ ཆ ཇ ཉ ཏ ཐ ད ན

ka   kha   ga   nga   ca   cha   ja   nya   ta   tha   da   na

པ ཕ བ མ ཙ ཚ ཛ

pa   pha   ba   ma   tsa/tza   tsha/tsa   dza

ཝ ཞ ཟ འ ཡ ར ལ ཤ ས ཧ

wa   zha   za   '   ya   ra   la   sha   sa   ha

Uchen

ka	cha	da	ma	zha	la	'a	qa	w
kha	ja	na	tsa	za	sha	i	xa	y
ga	nya	pa	tsha	-a	sa	u	fa	
nga	ta	pha	dza	ya	ha	e	gga	
ca	tha	ba	wa	ra		o	ee	

Wide

Narrow

Column

Horyig

Sacred Scripts (South)

From the 3rd century CE onwards, Brahmi script variants developed through the southern dynasties of the Kalingas, Kadambas, Pallavas, Cholas and others to evolve into the modern scripts of southern India.

Southern Brahmi scripts are generally rounded or cursive, which comes from the practice of writing with a sharp stylus on palm leaves that tend to split where straight lines are used, although some are distinguished by the use of long descenders and arched ascenders.

The most influential southern variant is Grantha, an important historical script with two variants, developed by the Pallavas to write Sanskrit and Pali throughout greater Tamil Nadu.

Between the 6th and 7th centuries, religion and trade carried the monumental form of Pallava Grantha to Southeast Asia, where it evolved into the national scripts of Burma, Cambodia, Laos, Thailand, Vietnam, Malaysia, Indonesia, Sumatra and the Philippines, adapted to write the native languages before the arrival of the Chinese, Roman and Arabic scripts.

GRANTHA

The Pallavas were a highly influential southern dynasty who practiced Hinduism and supported Buddhism. They ruled over modern Tamil Nadu and Andhra Pradesh from the 3rd to the 9th century. Grantha emerged as a distinct script during the 5th century.

In Sanskrit, Grantha literally means 'knot' – a word used to denote literary works and the scripts used to write them. This stems from the practice of binding inscribed palm leaves using a length of thread held by knots to form books. Some believe that when the Vedas were first written down in the 5th century CE, they were written in Grantha.

By the 6th century, it had developed a more rounded, ornate or decorative style called Pallava Grantha, not for everyday use, employed in rock inscriptions and copperplate engravings.

The exemplary features of the Pallava script are a florid and elaborate script with its combining of round and rectangular strokes, adding typographic effects such as notches as heads and space-filling tails. This made Pallava Grantha eminently suitable for civic and religious inscriptions, still having a monumental feel, yet more decorative.

Pallava Grantha is an archaic and ornamental form of calligraphy. It is distinct from other Grantha scripts, created by the Pallavas at a later date for the same purpose. The scripts of Tigalari, Malayalam, Sinhala and Tamil are descended from these later modern Grantha variants. It remained in popular use until the 19th century and is still in restricted use in traditional Vedic schools in the 21st century.

a   aa   i   ii   ai   e   o   u   au

ka   kha   ga   gha   na   ca   cha   ja   jha   na

ta   tha   da   dha   ma   ta   tha   da   dha   na

pa   pha   ba   bha   ma

ya   ra   la   va   sa   sa   sa   ha

Pallava Grantha (Monumental)

a   aa   i   ii   u   uu   ri   rii

li   lii   e   ai   o   au

ka   kha   ga   gha   na   ca   cha   ja   jha   na

ta   tha   da   dha   na   t   th   da   dha   na

pa   pha   ba   bha   ma

ya   ra   la   va   la   sa   sa   sa   ha

Modern Grantha / Tamil Grantha

During the 6th century CE, Hinduism, Buddhism and trade spread from south India's east coast, with priests, monks, scholars and traders taking the Pallava Grantha script to Southeast Asia, where it was to be admired, appreciated and emulated to become the earliest relic of writing in the region.

These early texts were written in Sanskrit and Pali, but the Pallava script was adapted to write local languages, becoming the parent script of modern Burma, Cambodia, Thailand and Laos. By the 8th century CE, Pallava Grantha had become the parent script of Java, Bali, Sumatra, Borneo and the Philippines, before the arrival of Arabic and Roman scripts.

OLD KHMER

Khmer is the name for a medieval kingdom that covered parts of modern Cambodia, Thailand and Laos. Its literary tradition goes back to the 7th century CE; its script is derived from Pallava script, first attested to in Old Khmer inscriptions dating from 611 CE.

In Thailand, Old Khmer is called 'Khom' (Phasa Khom). They consider the script to be extremely sacred and to possess magical power within the letters. It is used for sacred and religious texts, never for common speech or everyday matters. It is traditionally used when inscribing 'kathas' – Thai/Pali sacred prayers written on paper, cloth, metal or any other surface, including skin, for Sak Yant tattoos.

LANNA

Lanna was the name of an independent kingdom of northern Thailand (Chiang Mai) that existed between 1250 and 1558 CE. They spoke a Tai language that shares such strong similarities with Lao, to the point that Siamese Thais referred to it as Lao. Thai and Lao are mutually intelligible, being linguistically similar but written in two slightly different scripts.

Adapted during the reign of King Mang Rai and named after the kingdom, Lanna is a curvilinear script ultimately derived from Pallava, used to write the northern Thai dialect of Tai Muang, also called Tai Yuan. From the 13th century, it became a source script for several other Tai dialects.

Used for religious purposes to write Old Lao (Tai Noi, Lao Thom), it is found in old manuscripts and temples in northern Thailand. It is the only Tai script to have been inscribed in stone.

រូម៉ានេឡ្ងា កខគឃងจ ហากกณ

Modern Khmer (Cambodia) - Thai Siam - Hanacaraka or Javanese

g	kh	k	k	ng	j	ch	ch	ch	j	dt	th

dt	t	n	dt	th	t	t	n	b	ph	p	p

m	y	r	l	w	s	s	s	h	l

Old Khmer / Khom - script and superscript

k	kh	k	kh	ng	c	s	c	s	nga

t	th	t	th	n	t	th	d	th	na	p	ph	p	ph	m

j	r	l	w	ss	h	l	xx	kh	b	f	f	j	h	s

Lanna

Om / AUM – Seed Syllable Supreme

The symbol known as Om or Aum is probably the most important sacred symbol of Indic religion. Its variations are found in all of its major belief systems, where it is revered as the ultimate symbol of creation. Great importance was attached to the word in antiquity.

In Indian philosophy, Tantra, the science of the Divine Word, is based in the theory of sound vibration. This philosophy states that the universe is made of sound vibrations, created when the supreme consciousness, Shabda Brahman, resonated as the bija mantra 'om/aum' from which all other sound vibrations are manifest.

In the beginning was the Word, and the Word was with God. This is how the Bible describes the start of creation. In Indic religion, the Word was OM and God is the Singularity – The One – Brahman. OM is more than a word; it is a Bija Mantra, a sound vibration which caused heat, warmth or love to manifest itself as the Flame or Light, in order to illuminate the Darkness, the Void.

THE ETERNAL SYLLABLE / THE PRIMORDIAL SOUND

First mentioned in the mystical texts of the Upanishads, OM is the universal name of the Divine and has different spellings, such as AUM and AHM. OM is not a word but rather an intonation which, like music, transcends the barriers of age, race and culture. It is made up of three Sanskrit letters – A U M – when combined together they make the sound AUM or OM. It is believed to be the basic sound of the world and to contain all other sounds. Tantric Buddhism employs the independent vowel 'A' sign to represent OM.

From the supreme consciousness or Brahman is born the living cosmos. The cosmos evolves through three stages: creation, preservation and destruction. In the Hindu pantheon, Brahma, Vishnu and Shiva represent these three aspects, respectively. Together in their capacity as universal life itself, they are called the Trimurti. This triple aspect of creation is also symbolized in the mantra called OM, in which the three individual sounds A U M correspond to the three stages and gods of the Trimurti, respectively.

Since OM is the expression of the highest faculty of consciousness, these three elements are explained accordingly as three planes of consciousness. 'A' as the waking consciousness or Jagrat, 'U' as the dream consciousness or Svapna, and 'M' as the consciousness during deep sleep or Susupti. OM as a whole represents the all-encompassing cosmic consciousness or Turiya, on the fourth plane, beyond words and concepts, the consciousness of the fourth dimension.

आम आँ आँ अँ अँ

| a u m | au m | au m | aum | om |

Theoretical evolution of Aum/Om

M
Shushupti
destroyer
deep sleep state

Turina
absolute transendental point

Maya
illusion

A
Jagrat
creator
waking state

U
Swapna
preserver
dream state

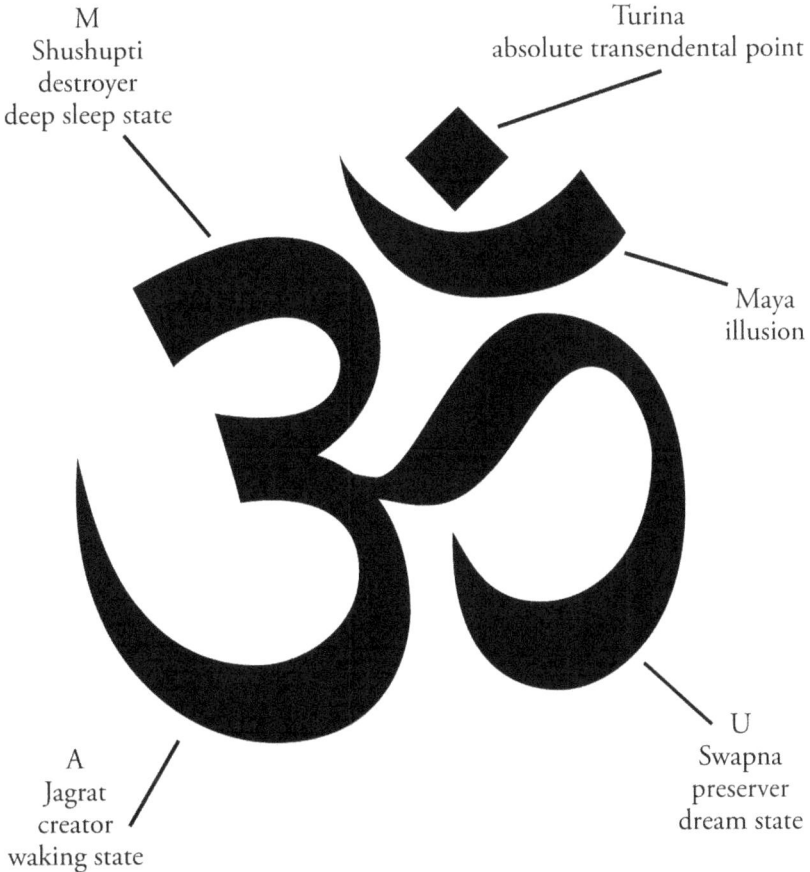

The Bija AUM (Akaram Ukaram Makaram)

Omkara Yantra
Grraphic represemtation of the primordial seed sound Aum/Om,
symbolizing the whole cosmos.

The symbolic meaning of OM remains the same, no matter which calligraphic variant OM is written in. Its image is found at the head of letters, at the beginning of mantras, in yantras, on pendants and enshrined in every temple and family shrine. The syllable occurs in English in words like omniscience, omnipotent and omnipresent. Thus, OM is used to signify divinity and authority and is akin to the word 'Amen'.

HOW AUM CREATED THE COSMOS

Om is the power of sound that brings forth the material world, the concrete universe, composed of the collective sounds of the letters of the Sanskrit alphabet. In the beginning, the mass of the entire creation was contained in one primal star, sometimes referred to as the Singularity – The One. This primal star was undivided awareness and consciousness. Love was the motivation that caused the first movement within the plasma of the star.

The spinning mass of (Sirius B) generated this first sound as it moved into its elliptical orbit at the center of the primal star. Without movement, there is no sound (love was God's motivation). The first sound in the creation was/is the first sound of Aum, the A, pronounced as A in America, on the tone F. This first movement and its sound continue to exist as Sirius B and its elliptical orbit. The counter point to Sirius B, counter spin, exists in Sirius A and its elliptical orbit, and generates the second sound of Aum, U, in the tone F". The third sound of Aum, M, is generated by the double helical spiral vortex that extends from the center of the primal star to the top and the bottom. This double helix flow form was generated by and tuned to the movements of Sirius A and B at the center of the primal star in the tone of G.

When the internal vortex motion and the resulting sound generated by Aum and the F, F", G, tri-tone reached full resonance, the primal star suddenly expanded into the infinite detail of the created universe, in the event known as the Big Bang. Aum radiates from the stars of Sirius A and B. Or, in simple terms, sound vibration created heat that created light.

Stroke order

	Devata	Seed Mantra	Element	Subtle element	Vital air in the subtle body
	Subhadra	Slim	water	taste	Apana
	Balbhadra	Hlim	earth	smell	Prana
	Jagannatha	Klim	fire	sight	Samana
	Sudarsana	Plim	ether	sound	Udana
	Sirhhasana	Dhlim	air	touch	Vyana

Aum/Om is split into five shapes to represent the entire universe, resolved into five cosmic principles.

Hindu Devanagari — Jain Bangala — Mahayana Buddhism Siddhamatrka — Sikhism Gurmukhi

Aum/Om religious calligraphy

Bengali — Grantha — Kannada — Malayalam — Tamil

Ranjana — Uchen — Javanese — Balanese — Hanzi

Om/Aum written in various scripts

Varnamala of Bija – Mystical Alphabet

Varnamala and Aksaramala are common Indian terms used to denote their alphabet. In simple terms, they both translate as 'garland of letters' and represent the alphabet in terms of gross speech. It is the traditional way of arranging the Sanskrit letters according to the phonetic principle laid down by ancient grammarians.

Parallel to the development of the Brahmi writing system was an elaboration of Sanskrit's mystical significance. The 51 sounds of Vedic Sanskrit were perceived as the Varnamala of Bija, the title of the necklace worn by the goddess Kali, who uses them to destroy and re-create the universe. The 50 sounds also form the body of the goddess Kundalini, and as such, appear on the lotus petal of the chakras of the human body; they are the sound patterns that create and maintain our organ system. These are the forms in which the mystical or esoteric knowledge of the Vedas is encoded within the Indian alphabet.

Tantric philosophers have devoted a large portion of their vast literature to the explanation of sacred sound, symbol and worship. In Mantra Shastra, the Vedic theory of Universal Creation through Sound is called Shabda. The primordial sound Om (Shabda Brahman) generates the cosmic energy, which spreads like ripples through a pond and becomes the immediate progenitor of the universe. This is possible because the primordial vibration returns as primordial variations or Nada Brahman. Creation proceeds from the subtle to the gross as cosmic vibrations (nada). The degree of vibration varies in concentration and wavelength, giving birth to what we perceive as light, volume and structure. Shabda Brahman is the Father, and Nada Brahman is the Mother, the Matrika.

Hindus believe that Vedic Sanskrit is a language of dynamism, that the 51 sacred sounds are three-dimensional fractal sound formulas that can resonate into being all the possible constructs and processes in creation. All physical forms are vibratory sound resonance fields and are contained within the 51 astral sound forms of the goddess language. The goddess creates the cosmos with these 50 sounds and their combinations. Aum, the Sri Yantra, the goddess and her language are one thing.

The Varnamala of Bija consists of fourteen vowels or svara, all coloured red. They contribute Matra or meter and timing to the words and the mantras. Within the 36 aksara, vyanjana or consonants, the vowel/consonants 'am' and 'ah' are blue. The 25 mute consonants, called sparsa, are the five vargas beginning with ka, ca, ta, tta, and pa are all coloured black. The ya-varga is coloured green, and the sa-varga is coloured purple.

The single ligature or samaksara, ksha, is white – bringing the total number of letters in the alphabet to 51. Om is red, making 52.

अ अा इ ई उ ऊ ऋ ॠ
a   aa   i   ii   u   uu   ri   rii

ल ॡ ए ऐ ओ औ आं आः
li   lii   e   ai   o   au   am   ah

Red - vowels / svara   Blue - vowel consonants / vyanjana

क ख ग घ ङ
ka   kha   ga   gha   nha

च छ ज झ ञ
ca   cha   ja   jha   jna

ट ठ ड द ण
tta   ttha   dda   ddha   nna

प फ भ म व
ta   tha   da   dha   nna

त थ ढ ध न
pa   pha   ba   bha   ma

Black - mute consonants / sparsa - ka, ca, ta, tta, pa vargas

य र ल ब   श ष स ह
ya   ra   la   va   sa   ssa   sha   ha

Green - mute consonants / sparsa   Purple - mute consonants / sparsa
ya varga   sa varga

क्ष   ॐ

White - ksha - ligature / samaksara   Red - Om / AUM

Varna - colour, shade, class, group

As Sarasvatti is the goddess of speech and Vak is the goddess of the voice, Kali is the keeper of the mother tongue, the Sanskrit language and its letters, its words, mantras and shastras. Kali's large, red, protruding tongue represents the mother tongue.

The 51 sacred sounds are shown as 51 different postures of the goddess, symbolizing the written forms of the Vedic sounds. Each sound represents a form of divine feminine energy, a form of Shakti (matrika Shakti). Called matrikas, 'little mothers', they are the individual goddesses that together make up the body of the mother goddess. The matrikas represent the universe of names and forms, that is speech (shabda) and its meaning or object (artha). This is why the goddess Kali wears the Varnamala of Bija.

The Varnamala of Bija is a necklace of skulls or severed heads, each having one of the 51 letters inscribed upon it – together, they represent infinite knowledge. As a garland, it represents the interconnectedness of all creation. Different names are used to describe it.

As the Mundamala, Kapalamala or Rundamala, it is the Garland of Skulls or Severed Heads, numbered at 108, an auspicious number in Hinduism – representing dominion over, and the power of words and thoughts, of all knowledge. A characteristic of the fierce aspect of the mother goddess and the god Shiva, in Tibetan Buddhism wrathful deities wear it. It has the same number of beads as a Japamala or rosary used for counting repetition in mantras.

As the Varnamala of Bija, it is symbolic of the origin of sound, signifying that Kali is Sabda Brahman, the source of creation, representing victory over Time and Death, the continual creation and destruction cycles of human existence. The Sanskrit word 'kal' means 'to count' or 'to measure'. The name Kali is the feminine of Kala, or Time. Hence Kali can be understood as 'action through time'. Time is the womb from which all creation occurs. From this womb, Kali Ma as the mother goddess brings forth all of creation.

Therefore, Kali devours all Time or Kala, and then resumes her own dark formlessness; that is, the names and forms that the letters signify, the dualism in consciousness, which is creation, vanish. There is neither 'I' (Aham) nor 'This' (Idam) but the one non-dual Perfect Experience which Kali in her own true nature (Svarupa) is. In this way, her Garland is understood, wearing the sounds which she as the Creatrix bore and she as the Dissolving power takes to herself again.

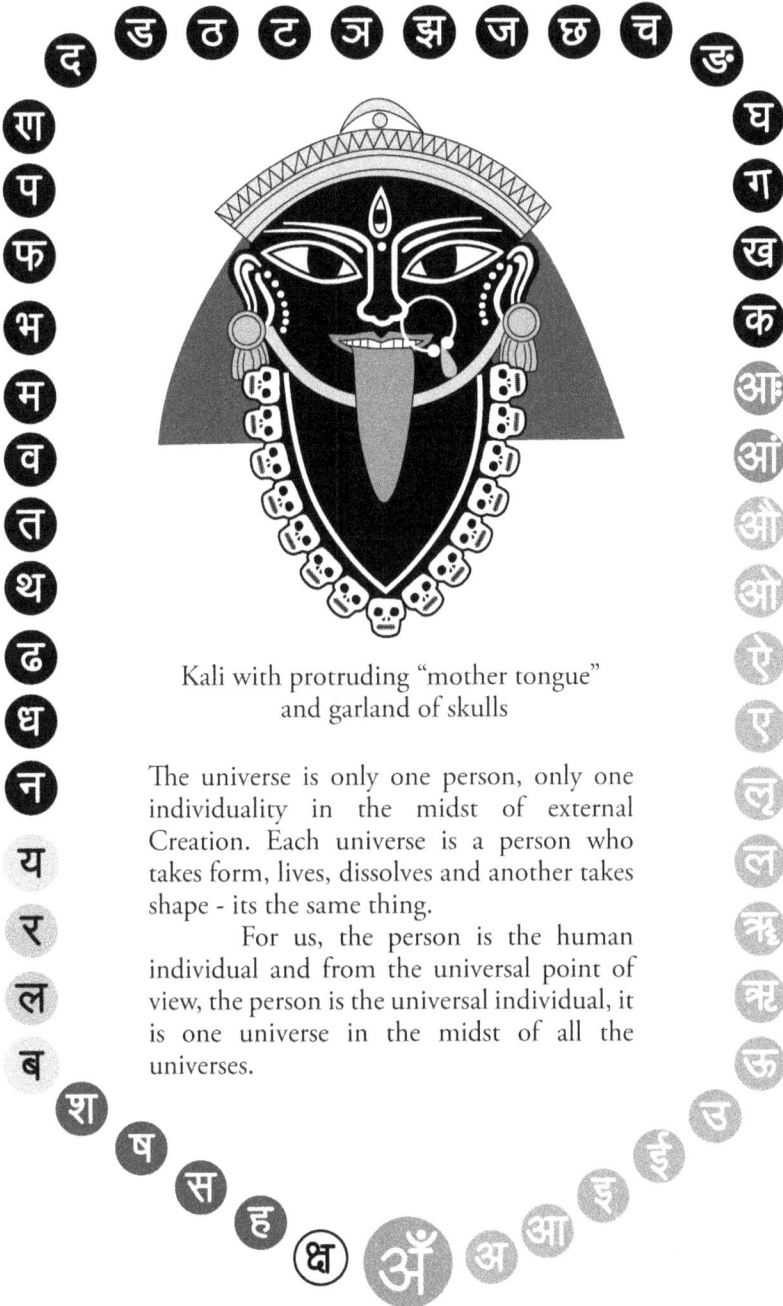

Kali with protruding "mother tongue"
and garland of skulls

The universe is only one person, only one individuality in the midst of external Creation. Each universe is a person who takes form, lives, dissolves and another takes shape - its the same thing.

For us, the person is the human individual and from the universal point of view, the person is the universal individual, it is one universe in the midst of all the universes.

Along with ancient Egyptian, Hebrew, Tibetan and Chinese, Sanskrit is one of the five holy languages of man, the root language of all Indo-European tongues. Hindus and Buddhists believe that all words in Sanskrit are derived from root syllables called bija. They conceive the Sanskrit alphabet as a matrix, used as a collation tool for the assembly of written information into a standardized order. Their system is ideal for forming new words, eliminating the need to borrow words or scientific terms from other languages.

Sanskrit is considered to be a goddess language, and there are several common Indian terms that are confused when used to describe its letters. The term 'bija' relates to the seed sounds that are the basis of mantra. The term 'matrika' refers to the cosmic feminine energy or Shakti that is the subtle form of gross speech or varna. The terms 'varna' and 'aksara' are used in relation to the classification of the gross form of the sounds of the Sanskrit language or speech.

The difference between varna and aksara is that varnas cannot be split; 'a' and 'k' or vowels and consonants are varnas. Aksara are syllables, combinations like 'k' and 'a' to make 'ka'. Once a syllable is shaped, it is indivisible. The situation is further confused by the use of compound terms such as Bijaksara and Matrikaksara, used to denote the written form. Varna and aksara are classified into two types: Svaraksara or vowels, usually shortened to svara, and Vyanjanaksara or consonants, shortened to vyanjana. Svaraksara are also known as Pranaksara – i.e., they are the main sounds in speech. The Ayogavahah, 'am' and 'ah', are considered to be svara as well as aksara; they are vowel-consonants.

VARNA

The purest vibrations are the varna, the imperishable letters (aksara), which are revealed to us, imperfectly, as audible sound (dhvani) and visible form (rupa). These sounds and forms are provisional, a reflection of the immutability of the varna. Varna are to ordinary sounds and letters as atoms are to matter. The varna are identified with God's Primal Energy (Om), 'The gods are the seed of the world', the letters developed from the seeds. It is the varna that bring about Life.

According to the Mantra Shashtra, varna or articulated speech (meaningful sound) is visual in that it can be seen in colour. Generally, the term varna can mean 'the separation of the sun's rays or energies', used to describe the shape, sound and colour of the letters of the Sanskrit alphabet. Their varna (colour - class, category) is determined by the guna or quality associated with the sound. Guna is not to be confused with gana.

Commonly, the units of vak or speech are referred to as varnas. This means that they are the basic sounds, the phonemes; they are the units of speech. On a deeper level, the varnas are the units of shape or form, units of colour, and they are the units of sound that appear as aksara, letters/phonemes, to our ears.

There are seven basic varnas – a, e, u, ae, o, am, ah. These seven flavours are the primordial variations of the Nada that originate in Muladhara as vak or speech. They are the basic forms of sounds. They do not need any intervention of the tongue to be produced. The other vowels – ai, ou, au – are combinations of these.

SVARA

Svar is the name of the sun, the shining light; svara are the shining sounds. Vowels or svara are both varna and aksara. Svara are the speech sounds that can form a syllable and can be pronounced independently. Within the svara, there are two groups of 'bouquets of mantra' – the Hrusva svara 'a i u ru lu E O' are lunar, and the Deergha svara 'A I L U ai ou am ah' are solar – they are the seeds of creation from whom manifest the moon and the sun, Am and Ah respectively, giving rise to light, air, and space, and also the five great elements: strength, potency, enlightenment, power (Shakti) and resources. These are the rays emanating from the goddess.

AKSARA

Svara are solar symbols, aksara are lunar symbols – the reflected light of the sun. Aksara or akshara means 'imperishable, entity' or 'atoms of speech'. The imperishable aksara seeds each letter of the alphabet and becomes manifold. These voiced syllables, structured into words and sentences, give rise to action or Aksara Brahma. The point or Bindhu is the basis of all creation and the goddess as mantra – rupinis – appear as the Aksara Brahma. Almost a million mantras are formed from these syllables, each with a specific power, creating, sustaining, dissolving and merging.

The term 'aksara' is commonly used to denote the whole alphabet, some may confine that to just 34 consonant syllables, others confine their number to 25, the number of mute consonants or sparsa, the reflected sounds that form a 'magic square' of Sanskrit phonemes. The remaining consonants, the semivowel or anthastha, represent the bija mantra of the lower four of the seven chakras. The sibilants, sha, sha and sa are Shakti, the energies that manifest the universe; their consorts are Brahma, Vishnu and Shiva. Ha is the bija mantra of the throat chakra.

In ancient India, the Sanskrit alphabet was intimately connected with stories of creation and with early models of cosmology. One starting point of the system was the five fundamental elements (ether, air, fire, water and earth). This evolved into a complex system. The 14 vowels were spirit, and the 36 consonants were matter. These 36 consonants (thirty-four vyanjana and two ayogavahah) became linked with 36 elements (tattvas) and associated with the 12 solar signs.

Key combinations of vowels and consonants became seed letters (bija) and linked with the 7 chakras in the body, the seven planets, the 7 days of the week, etc. This idea formed a starting point for oriental cosmology.

TATTVAS

According to ancient Indic philosophy, the universe is made up of 36 elements known as tattvas. Tattva means reality, truth, an element or aspect of reality, conceived as an aspect of a deity. The number of tattvas varies; together they are thought to form the basis of all our experience. Samkhya has 25. Shivaism has 36. Tamil Siddha has 96. Hindu Tantra has 5, and in Buddhism they are the list of Dharmas that constitute reality.

In Shivaism, the 36 consonants (thirty-four vyanjana and two ayogavahah) of Vedic Sanskrit represent the 36 tattvas. The 14 vowels are Shakti – the whole being the universe as sound – the 36th tattva being Shiva/Shakti. The universe begins with the Shiva tattva; within it are five energies which are encoded within the vowels of Sanskrit.

The first energy of the highest (anuttara) consciousness is represented by the vowel 'a'. The second energy is the blissful state of ananda, represented by 'aa'. The third state is the subtle state or iccha, represented by 'i'. The gross state of will is represented by 'ii'. The fourth is the energy of knowledge or janna, represented by 'u'. The 'uu' refers to the appearance of a lessening. The fifth energy of the Shiva tattva is kriya, the energy of action, represented by the last four vowels: e, ai, o, u, representing degrees of vividness.

The tattvas are the five gross elements: earth, water, fire, air and ether, which are assigned the Ka-varga. The Ca-varga contains the five senses or Tammatas of sound, taste, form, touch and smell. The Tta-varga are the five motor organs: generation, evacuation, ambulation, grasp and speech. The Ta-varga are the five organs of sense: ears, tongue, eyes, skin and nose. The Pa-varga are limited experience: mind, ego, buddhi, prakriti, purusha.

VARNA SHIKSHA

The magical symmetries of the Sanskrit alphabet are found in various Hindu and Buddhist texts. The Hindu correspondences come from a very old Sanskrit text found by accident, unlabelled and mis-catalogued in a university in Mysore. Named Varna Shiksha, it describes a number of qualities of letters of the Sanskrit alphabet previously lost, making the Varna Shiksha a precious jewel in the treasury of knowledge.

In the mislabeled Varna Shiksha, the letters of the Sanskrit alphabet are categorized into gender – male, female and neuter – and divided into 'qualities' called 'gunas', used by Hindus to categorize behaviour and natural phenomena.

There are three gunas: sattva, rajas and tamas. Sattvas have the positive qualities of balance, harmony, goodness, purity, etc., and are white in colour. Rajas are red in colour and have the active qualities of passion, moving, dynamic, ego, etc. Tamas are blue/black and have the negative qualities of imbalance, disorder, chaos, viciousness, ignorance, etc.

The vowels, a, i, u, e, o, am, are male; aa, ii, uu, ai, au, ah, are female. Aa, ai, o, au, are sattvic. A, ii, ri, rii, lri, e, am, ah, are rajas. I, u, uu, are tamas. The consonants are categorized into gender depending on their position in their varga. The first and the third letters, ka, ga, ca, ja, ta, da, ta, da, pa, ba, of the vargas, plus sha and ksa, are male. The second and fourth letters kha, gha, cha, jha, tha, dha, tha, dha, pha, bha, of the vargas, plus ssha and sa, are female. The last letter of each varga, na, na, na, na, ma, the four letters of the ya-varga, ya, ra, la, va, plus ri, lri, ha, la, are neuter.

GUNAS

The Sanskrit word 'guna' means string, thread, strand or virtue, merit, excellence or quality, peculiarity, attribute or property. The concept of gunas originated in Samkhya, one of the six Astika schools of Hindu philosophy. It is most related to the Yoga school of Hinduism. This dualistic philosophy records the universe as consisting of two realities, Purusa – consciousness, and Prakriti – mother. Jiva, a living being, is that state in Purusa bonded to Prakriti in some form.

This fusion led to the emergence of Buddhi – intellect, and Ahankara – ego consciousness. Samkhya also describes the universe as one created by Purusa/ Prakriti entities infused with the various permutations and combinations of various enumerated elements, senses, feelings, activity and mind.

During the state of imbalance, one or more of the constituents overwhelms the others, creating a form of bondage particular to the mind. The end of the imbalance is called liberation or Kalvalya.

Prakriti is the first cause of the manifest material universe – of everything except Purusa. Prakriti accounts for whatever is physical with mind and matter cum energy force. It is the first tattva or principle of the universe. It is composed of three escated characters or tri-gunas called sattva, meaning goodness, constructive, harmonious. Rajas means passion, active, confuses. Tamas means darkness, destruction and chaotic. All of these gunas are present in everyone and everything; it is the proportion that is different.

The Upanishads is one of the earliest texts making reference to the relationship between the Trimurti and the three gunas as creative/activity, preservation/purity, and destroyer/recycler. The idea that three types of guna, innate nature and forces that together transform and help in changing the world is, however, found in numerous earlier and later texts.

As Shiva's wife, Kali, is the embodiment of the three gunas or 'principles of nature' – sattva, rajas and tamas. She creates with sattva – goodness and purity; preserves with rajas – passion and action; and destroys with tamas – ignorance and inertia. Her white teeth symbolize sattva or serenity. Her red tongue symbolizes rajas or activity, and her drunkenness as tamas or inertia – meaning tamas can be conquered by rajas and rajas by sattva.

The three gunas are used to understand or interpret natural objects, beings or occurrences. For example, a large stone or a person with destructive tendencies is viewed as tamasic. A thunderstorm or a naturally agitated person is thought to be rajasic. A fresh orange or a naturally peaceful individual is considered sattvic. If the individual feels the pull of one guna more than another, it is believed that, as humans, one has the ability to change its level through meditation, lifestyle choices and spiritual practices.

Letter	Sound	Gender	Guna/ Quality	Deity	Colour
अ	a	M	rajas	all deities	red
आ	aa	F	sattva	Parasakti	white
इ	i	M	tamas	Vishnu	black
ई	ii	F	rajas	Maya Sakti	yellow
उ	u	M	tamas	Vaatsu	black
ऊ	uu	F	tamas	Bhumi Devi	black
ऋ	ri	N	rajas	Brahman	yellow
ॠ	ree	N	rajas	Sikhandi	yellow
ल	lri	N	sattva	the Asvins	white
ए	e	M	rajas	Virahadra	yellow
ऐ	ai	F	sattva	vital essence of speech	-
ओ	o	M	sattva	One supreme god	light
औ	au	F	sattva	Adi Shakti	white
आं	am	M	rajas	the Great Lord	red
आः	ah	F	rajas	Kalarudra (time)	red

Shiksha correspondences for the a-varga or svara (vowels)

Letter	Sound	Gender	Guna/ Quality	Deity	Colour
क	ka	M	rajas	Prayapati	yellow
ख	kha	F	sattva	River Ganges	white
ग	ga	M	rajas	Ganesha	red
घ	gha	F	sattva	Bhairava (Shiva)	white
ङ	na	N	-	Time	black
च	ca	M	tamas	Candra du dra	black
छ	cha	F	tamas	Bhadrakali Ma Diva	red
ज	ja	M	rajas	Jambhaha	red
झ	jna	F	tamas	Ardhanansam	black
ञ	na	N	rajas	snake deveta	yellow
ट	tta	M	rajas	Bhrngisam	red
ठ	ttha	F	sattva	Moon	white
ड	dda	M	raja	One-eyed	yellow
ढ	ddha	F	raja	Yama	blue
ण	nna	N	raja	Nandi	red
त	ta	M	sattva	Vastu Devata	white
थ	tha	F	sattva	Brahman	black
द	da	M	raja	Durga	black
ध	dha	F	raja	wealth-bestowing	yellow
न	na	N	sattva	Savitri	crystaline

Shiksha correspondences for the ca, tta and ta vargas

Letter	Sound	Gender	Guna/Quality	Deity	Colour
प	pa	M	sattva	Porjonya (rain)	white
फ	pha	F	-	land of cattle	black
ब	ba	M	raja	Trimurti	red
भ	bha	F	raja	Bhorgava	red
म	ma	N	tamas	God of Love	black
य	ya	N	tamas	Vayu (air)	black
र	ra	N	rajas	deveta of vehicles	red
ल	la	N	rajas	Prithiri (earth)	yellow
व	va	N	sattva	Varuna	white
श	shha	F	rajas	Lakashimi	gold
ष	sha	M	rajas	dvadasatma	red
स	sa	F	rajas	Shakti	red
ह	ha	M	sattva	Shiva	white
ळ	la	N	raja	Atma (self)	red

Shiksha correspondences for the pa, ya and sa vargas

1) Vasini अ आ इ ई उ ऊ ऋ ॠ ल ए ऐ ओ औ आं आः

2) Kamesvara क ख ग घ ङ

3) Modini च छ ज झ ञ

4) Vimala ट ठ ड ढ ण

5) Aruna त थ द ध न

6) Jayini प फ ब भ म

7) Sarasvatti य र ल व

8) Kali श ष स ह ळ

Goddesses of the eight vargas

Matrika – Mother Letters

The Sanskrit word 'Matrikas' means 'little mothers'. In Hinduism, they are portrayed as a collection of female deities who always appear together in groups of various sizes: 1, 7, 8, 14, 16, 34, 50, 51 and 52. They originated in pre-Aryan Indus folklore as local goddesses, extensions of the Mother Goddess. In Devi lore or goddess worship, they all converge together to project one Great Mother Goddess – Mahadevi.

At some point in time during the Mauryan Empire, they were seen as hindering the process of birth and child growth. In the Kushan era, they became entwined with the myth of Skanda. During the Gupta era, this link was reinforced further when Gupta warriors adopted Skanda, and the goddesses associated with him gained prominence.

In the Purana manuscripts of the Gupta era, the Matrikas were warrior goddesses who emerged from the various parts of the Devi, to help her in the fight against demons. They were seen as a dangerous group of female spirits or goddesses with a malevolent nature, somewhat similar to that of the goddess Kali, also described as a Matrika.

In the philosophy of Mantra Shastra, Shabda Brahman (Om) emanates the primordial vibration that returns to him as primordial variations in the form of his wife Nada Brahman, her body being the cosmos formed by the 51 vibrations that are the sounds of Vedic Sanskrit, each sound being an individual aspect of the Mother Goddess or Matrika (Mother). She is said to be the source of everything made of words, mantras and shastras.

In Tantra, the 51 sounds of Vedic Sanskrit, from A to Ksha of the Varnamala of Bija, have been described as the Matrikas themselves. Together, they constitute the body of the goddess in the form of sound. The Matrikas represent the universe of names and forms; that is, speech (shabda), and its meaning or object (artha).

The Matrikas are the subtle (mystical) forms of varna or articulated speech. The term Matrika can also mean a storehouse of sound syllables, and logos, as the Mother of the spoken word (vak-devi). All we think, imagine, desire, aspire, and dream begin here.

In Tantra, the embodiment of feminine forces or Shakti is called Matrika, referring to groups of Mother-like deities, the personified energies of the goddess or Deva-Shakti. A diagram, a posture of herself, represents each goddess. The 51 Vedic sounds are shown as 51 different postures of the goddess, symbolizing Matrika, the goddess form of Vedic Sanskrit – together, the sound and the diagram are Matrika.

अं आं इं ईं उं ऊं ऋं ॠं

Am	Aam	Im	Iim	Um	Uum	Rum	Ruum
a	aa	i	ii	u	uu	ri	rii

लृं लॄं एं ऐं ओं औं अं अंः

Lrum	Lruum	Em	Aim	Om	Oum	Amm	Aha
li	lii	e	ai	o	ou	am	ah

Vowels

कं खं गं घं ङं चं छं जं झं ञं

Kam	Kham	Gam	Gham	Nham	Cam	Cham	Jam	Jham	Jnam
ka	kha	ga	gha	nha	ca	cha	ja	jha	jna

टं ठं डं ढं णं तं थं दं धं बं

Tam	Tham	Dam	Dham	Nam	Ttam	Ttham	Ddam	Ddham	Nnam
ta	tha	da	dha	na	tta	ttha	dda	ddha	nna

पं फं भं मं नं   यं रं लं वं

Pam	Pham	Bam	Bham	Mam		Yam	Ram	Lam	Vam
pa	pha	ba	bha	ma		ya	ra	la	va

शं षं सं हं क्षं

Sham	Sham	Sam	Ham	Ksham
sh	sha	sa	ha	ksha

Sapatmatrika - seven groups of consonants

Ashtamatrika - eight goups of vowels and consonants

It is believed that the letters of the Sanskrit language emanated from the Mother, and she takes her name in every one of them. For the purposes of daily recitations, each of the 51 letters/matrika is extended, in the given order, into the name of a Devi. Matrikas are the binding energies that make it possible to understand words or symbols strung together as language.

SAPTA AND ASHTA MATRIKA

Depending upon the philosophy, Matrikas can denote a single character or the entire collection of characters or alphabet. In southern India, they are worshipped as the 'Saptamatrikas' or 'Seven Mothers'. In Nepal and Tibet, they are venerated as the 'Ashtamatrikas' or 'Eight Mothers'.

The number of Matrikas is determined in the structure of the Sanskrit, which is arranged into seven and eight individual groups of letters called varnas. First is the 'A' group containing vowels. The Matrikas can be identified with 14 vowels, plus the anusvara and visarga, making their number 16. The Saptamatrikas or Seven Mothers correspond to the seven consonantal groups headed by Ka, Cha, Ta, ta, Pa, Ya and Ksha. If the vowel group is added, they become the Ashtamatrika or Eight Mothers.

MATRIKA NYASA

During the ritual worship of the Mother, her presence is invoked in the body of the Sadhata through a procedure known as Anga-Nyasa or consecration of different parts of the body. The invoking of the Mother – Matrika Nyasa – along with the five elements is a significant ritual. It is meant to emphasize that you belong to the Mother and that you are sanctified by her presence in you.

In Matrika Nyasa, the letters of the Sanskrit alphabet are placed on the body – head, face, hands, anus and legs. As this is done, the practitioner uses various hand gestures (mudras). The letters are prefixed with Om and suffixed with Namah. A more specialized installation of Matrika Nyasa combines the installation of the most powerful set of all letters with the bija HRIM of the goddess known as Ada Shakti or Durga, the supreme body of the universe, the consort of Shiva. This ritual differs from Kundalini Yoga, in which certain letters are grouped together with each one of the chakras, the six psycho-physical centers on the human body.

Matrka Nyasa

a - Amrita
aa - Aakarshini
i - Indrami
ii - Iishani
u - Urdhava-keshini
e - Ekapandini
ai - Aishvari
o - Omkarini
au - Aishadhantika
am - Ambika
ah - Aksharatmika

ka - Kalarati
kha - Khatita
ga - Gayatri
gha - Ghantadhari
nha - Nanatmika
ca - Chanda
cha - Chaya
ja - Jaya
jha - Jhankarini
jna -Jnanaupa

ta - Thankahasta
tha - Thamkorum
da - Damri
dha - Dhamkarini
na - Naminit
ta - Tanasi
ttha - Thamini
dda - Dakshayani
ddha - Dhatri
nna - Nanda

pa - Parvati
pha - Phatkarini
ba - Bandhini
bha - Bhadrakali
ma - Mahakaya
ya - Yashasvini
ra - Rakta
la - Lambobosti
va - Varada, Shashini
sa - Sarasvatti
ha - Hamsavathi
ksha - Kshamavathi

Goddess names of the Matrikas

Bija – Seed Syllable

In Indian philosophy, the Vedic language has its roots in a divine primordial language. This root language consists of single-syllable sounds called 'bija', pronounced 'beej', meaning 'seed' or 'germ'. Bija have multiple meanings and indications depending upon their intonation and the intention with which they are used. These seeds cannot be translated into a literal meaning but have the power to create great transformative growth and expansion in humans at the physical, emotional and spiritual levels.

Out of the bija or root language arises the language of the Vedic texts, which is already differentiated, though not fully, into nouns and verbs. When they are written, they are referred to as Bijaksara, the visible form of a deity. In general, the bija of all deities ends with the Anusvara (M) or Visarga (H).

A bija is a basic mantra, usually of one syllable, which is understood to be the audible form of a deity, OM being the Supreme Bija and Mantra. Generally, a bija-mantra consists of a single letter 'A', but sometimes it constitutes several syllables, 'AUM'. Some bija-mantras are made up of compound letters, such as the mantra HREEM. There are words that do not quite fit the definition of a seed syllable, called Samput, but which function in more or less the same way. SVAHA – comes from Vedic ritual and is used at the end of Buddhist mantras. PHAT – a very ancient Indian magical word. Their meaning is subtle and mystical.

The form of the bija-mantra is the form of the deity signified by it. There are four great goddess bija-mantras that govern the prime forms of energy as magnetic force, electrical force, heat, and delight. This is a Tantric teaching that reflects the Vedic word and the four main Vedic deities.

HRIM (pronounced as Hreem) is the primary mantra of the Great Goddess, and awakens the soul to the force of divine love and truth. KRIM (pronounced Kreem) is the great mantra of Kali, the goddess of energy and transformation. HUM (pronounced Hoom) is a Shiva mantra but also a mantra of Chandi, the fierce form of Kali. It is used to destroy negativity and creates great passion and vitality. SHRIM (pronounced Shreem) is a mantra of love, devotion and beauty, relating to Lakshmi, the goddess of beauty and divine grace. The bija of the five elements are HAM – ether, YAM – air, RAM – fire, VAM – water, and LAM – earth.

ह्रिं

Hri

ह्रीं   ह्रीः

Hrim   Hrih

Bija - Seed Syllable   Bija-Mantra

स्वाहा   फट्

Svaha   Phat

Bija Words

ह्रीं   क्रीं   श्रीं   हूं

Hrim - Durga   Krim - Kali   Shrim - Lakshmi   Hum - Shakti

4 Great Goddess Bija Mantras

हं   यं   रं   वं   लं

HAM   YAM   RAM   VAM   LAM
ether   air   fire   water   earth

Bija of the five elements

Written in the proper way with the proper spirit, the concentrated power of bija is capable of manifesting the latent Devas or Buddhas within the practitioner. Without proper knowledge, the letters are nothing more than profane markings. It is said that those who have mastered bija may dispense with all texts, mantras or images, as they can see the world of Buddha in a single letter.

Bija can be written in any Brahmic script, but they are generally written in Devanagari by Hindus and in Siddhamatrika, Ranjana and Uchen by Mahayana and Vajrayana Buddhists. As well as being spoken, bija can be written on the body or in mandalas and yantras using a pen, brush or coloured sand.

A AS OM

As mystical Buddhism established itself outside of India with non-Sanskrit-speaking peoples, the complex philosophies of Hindu Tantra and the esoteric significance of the Sanskrit alphabet were incorporated into Tantric Buddhism with several changes. The letters were perceived as 'exploding' from the emptiness or Sanyota, rather than originating from Shabda Brahman, meaning that the letters were 'uncreated', existing according to natural principles and learned through insight. Strict adherence to classical Sanskrit pronunciation of mantras was disregarded as Buddhism spread outside of India. The letter A replaced Om as the Seed Syllable Supreme of Mahavairocana, the Great Buddha of Light, and meditation on this letter became an important esoteric practice.

HEART SUTRA BIJA

The Heart Sutra is one of the most famous Buddhist sutras, with a mantra that can be condensed into a single syllable – the bija Dhrih. Dhi is the Vedic root of 'Dhih', which incorporates a range of meanings, including to perceive, to think, to reflect, understanding, intelligence, knowledge and wisdom. Dhrih is sometimes combined with 'mma', resulting in the complex syllable 'Dhrihmma' associated with the Heart Sutra.

HUM (HOOM)

HUM is frequently the last syllable of a mantra. The diagram of HUM shows how it is put together in a single stack from various elements that are more or less the same in all Brahmic scripts.

आँ

Devanagari

अं

Siddham

अं

ॐ

Ranjana

AMH - Seed Syllable Supreme

A as OM

Uchen

वि

Dhi bija

वि:

Dhih
bija mantra

Dhihmma
complex syllable

Heart Sutra Bija

M

H

U
long vowel

ether
wind
fire

water

earth

Architecture of HUM (hoom)

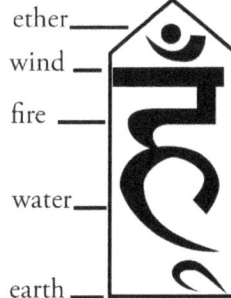

Chakra Bija – Seed Syllable Wheel

In Hindu mythology, Brahma the creator first showed himself as a golden embryo of sound. He was a vowel, vibrating outward; the sound echoed back upon itself and became water and wind. In Tantra, this power is called Matrika Shakti, the inherent feminine creative energy behind the letters that make up words. It is said that each letter of the Sanskrit alphabet has a corresponding sound vibration, both in the subtle energy channels of our bodies and in the cosmos. When these sound vibrations resonate with a corresponding vibration within us, they create thoughts; then these thoughts gradually manifest the grosser forms of feelings, and then speech. The Matrika Shakti resides in our energy body and rises of its own volition into consciousness, manifesting as our thoughts.

Mantras sounded in the Sanskrit language are designed to create sounds that literally vibrate the body. In Vedic healing, specific monosyllable seed sounds or bija-mantra were developed to create balance and harmony in the human body, mind and soul. Each and every part of our body functions at a specific rhythm and pulse, and when our systems are balanced and tuned with each other, we experience perfect harmony and health. An imbalance in our bodies could lead to mental, physical or emotional disease.

The sounds and syllables emitting from the different parts of the body are shown in diagrammatic presentations. In the Tantric ritual of Matrika Nyasa, the Matrikas (letters) are assigned to positions of the human body; the practitioner touches the appropriate area as he recites the alphabet. In Kundalini Yoga, certain letters are grouped together with each one of the Chakras – the 7 centers of transformation of psychic or mental energy into spiritual energy of the human body.

KUNDALINI

Kundalini is the form of the Goddess resting in Muladhara as a coiled serpent. As long as this energy remains dormant, the student will engage in an outward, sensuous life and live an ordinary life like any unconscious animal. When Kundalini is activated, it turns inward, and the student takes to a spiritual path.

When creation takes place, it is said that reversed coition of Shiva/Shakti takes place, and Bindhu or seed is deposited in Prakriti, resulting in the birth of the Kundalini goddess in the nature and form of letters. Kundalini is represented as a coiled serpent with 51 coils, which are the subtle forms of the sounds of Vedic Sanskrit.

7. Crown Chakra
Sahasrara Chakra - violet
1000 petals inscrbed with the
combinations of all letters of the alphabet,
seed syllable OM.

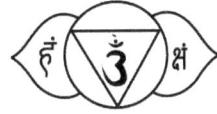

6. Brow Chakra
Ajna Chakra - indigo
HAM, KSAM,
seed syllable short (half) AM.

5. Throat Chakra
Vishuddha Chakra - blue
AM, AM, IM, IIM, UM, UUM,
RM,RRM, LM, LLM, EM, AIM,
OM, AUM, AMM, AMH,
seed syllable HAM

4. Heart Chakra
Anahata Chakra - green
KAM, KHAM, GAM, GHAM,
NAM, CAM, CHAM, JAM,
JHAM, NAM, TAM, THAM,
seed syllable YAM

3. Solar Plexus Chakra
Manipura Chakra yellow
DAM, DHAM, NAM, TAM, THAM,
DAM, DHAM, NAM, PAM, PHAM,
seed syllable RAM

2. Sacral Chakra
Svadhisthana Chakra - orange
BAM, BHAM, MAM, YAM,
RAM, LAM,
seed syllable VAM

1. Base Chakra
Muladhara Chakra - red
VAM, SAM, SAM, SAM,
seed syllable LAM

This sound evolves from Para state at Muladhara to Vaikari state in the Vishuddha chakra, the throat center where articulate speech comes from. One coil is Bindhu, two coils is Prakriti-Pirusa, three coils are three shaktis – iccha, jnana and kriyan, and the three gunas – sattvas, rajas and tamas, representing will, knowledge and action.

The coiled energy of the serpent goddess Kundalini, when activated, rises from the base of the spine to the point just above the head through ritual use of the chakra energy system. The practice of performing this ritual is called Kundalini Yoga – just one of the many forms of yoga, all derived from the same source. Most forms of yoga use meditation and chanting of bija-mantra to expand one's consciousness and help in healing the mind, body and spirit.

CHAKRAS

The concept of a chakra system emerged sometime between 1150 and 500 BCE and features in the tantric and yogic traditions of Hinduism and Buddhism. The ancient spiritual Indian texts refer to various systems, with variations in the number of chakras and their locations. Most commonly known is the more recent system with seven main chakras, dating to around the 8th century CE.

The Sanskrit word 'chakra' translates into 'wheel' and can be thought of as a vortex that both receives and radiates energy. They are the seven major energy centers in the human body that run from the base of the spine to the crown of the head. Emotions, physical health and mental clarity affect how well each chakra can filter energy. This in turn dictates how pure the energy is that is emitted from the body. Chakras are not materially real – they are to be understood as situated not in the gross body but in the subtle or etheric body. Repositories of psychic energies, they govern the whole condition of being.

Chakras are usually represented as lotuses. Each of the 50 petals of the first six chakras is associated with one of the letters of the Sanskrit alphabet. At the center of each chakra is a bija-mantra, the symbolic representation of the energy pattern of each chakra – its essence. When performing these mantras, the individual resonates with the particular chakra. Each chakra is characterized by a category of sounds, by a special colour of inner light, and by special forms of transcendental awareness.

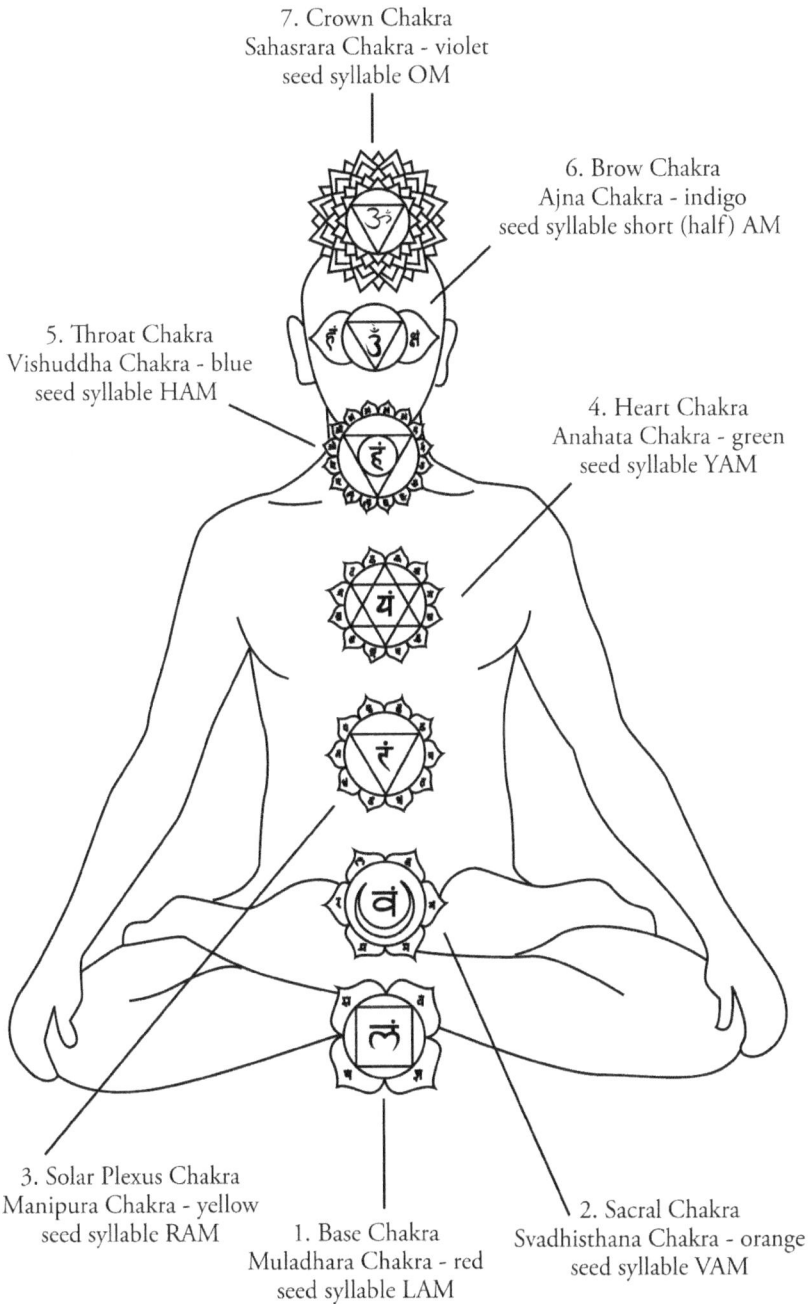

7. Crown Chakra
Sahasrara Chakra - violet
seed syllable OM

6. Brow Chakra
Ajna Chakra - indigo
seed syllable short (half) AM

5. Throat Chakra
Vishuddha Chakra - blue
seed syllable HAM

4. Heart Chakra
Anahata Chakra - green
seed syllable YAM

3. Solar Plexus Chakra
Manipura Chakra - yellow
seed syllable RAM

1. Base Chakra
Muladhara Chakra - red
seed syllable LAM

2. Sacral Chakra
Svadhisthana Chakra - orange
seed syllable VAM

Mantra – Thought Machine

Mantra is an organic language in which sound and meaning correspond as sound-ideas. The spiritual expression of sound is found in poetry and music, which are synthesized in the one profound and all-embracing vibration of Om – the sacred syllable or bija-mantra. In Tantra, everything in creation is formed from air that resonates as sound. This sound is called the 'Word'. This is not ordinary words or Shabda, of which speech is composed; it is mantra or 'instrument of thought' which creates a mental picture with its sound.

In India, not only the Word but also every sound of which it consists, every letter of the alphabet, is looked upon as a sacred symbol. The letters of the alphabet are mantras or sacred prayer syllables, linking the practitioner to a particular divine principle. Each letter is charged with energy that creates vibrations in the inner consciousness of the devotee. Mantras are tools for thinking and worshipping. Meditating on mantra shapes the mind and makes it pure.

Mantra is a sacred utterance, a magical sound. A syllable, word or group of words spoken or written in Sanskrit, believed to have psychological and spiritual powers. The earliest were composed in Vedic Sanskrit in India and are at least 3000 years old. They are now found in various schools of Hinduism, Jainism, Buddhism and Sikhism, and their equivalent can be found in Zoroastrianism, Taoism, Christianity and elsewhere.

Mantras are masculine (solar), feminine (lunar) or neuter. A female mantra is called a Vidya, meaning 'knowledge'. Solar and neuter forms are called mantras. A mantra can only work if it is received from a guru who has received it in an unbroken line from its first Rishi. Only then do they have life, according to the tradition. There are, however, exceptions to this, according to some Tantras which prescribe methods of purification for mantras received in dreams. In general, mantras are usually written from left to right using the Devanagari, Siddhamatrika, Ranjana and Uchen scripts, but they can be written in any of the Brahmi-derived scripts of Asia.

BIJA-MANTRA

Bija-mantra reflect the archetypical vibration behind all phenomenal objects, the vibration of the Divine Word itself. This is not a religious belief but the vibrational energy of cosmic intelligence that forms all things.

हूं हां हीं हूं हैं हौं हः

hum   hram   hreem   hraim   hroom   hroum   hrahada

Bija-Mantra - Devanagari

Green Tara Mantra - High / Honourific Uchen

Dainichi Mantra - Siddham

Kalachakra - Siddham

The most effective mantras are the seed syllables or bija – single or combinations of sounds containing the sum total of the divinity. The greatest of all these is Om, the Pranava Mantra, the source of all bija and mantra, the mother of all sounds. Om is the manifestation of Bindhu, the creative impulse of the cosmos – composed of the elements A U M – signifying the Trimurti, the creation, preservation and dissolution of the world.

Bija, like mantra, are spoken with the mind and heard by the heart. Bija-mantra do not have to have any literal meaning; they are mystical words – they can be spoken, sung and chanted individually, or strung together to form mantras. In Vedic terms, the bija-mantra SHRIM is a Soma mantra. It gives love, joy, bliss, beauty and delight. It has the light of the moon, and governs the mind and the realm between the atmosphere and heaven. It purifies and integrates the various aspects of our nature and renders them into ambrosia.

WRITTEN MANTRA

Written mantras add to the spiritual power of the spoken mantra. The Avira mantra 'Om All Pervading, Imperishable One' is the mantra of the Great Buddha called Damichi in Japan and Mahaircana in Tibet. Written in Siddhamatrika, the mantra is arranged in the form of a Stupa or temple and read from the bottom upwards.

Om Mani Padme Hum is probably the most famous Tantric mantra, particularly associated with Tibetan Buddhism. The mantra of the Boddhisattva called Avalokitesvara, the Mahavaircana, the compassionate aspect of Buddha. It is written from right to left in any of four script styles.

The Kalachalra mantra can be condensed into a complex syllable called The Powerful Ten. It is formed of seven syllables, Om, Ha, Ksa, Ma, La, Va, Ra, Tam, plus the visarga, bindhu and nada to make ten. It is formed using a technique called Kutaksara or 'heaped syllables' in which seven syllables have been arranged on top of each other to create a mystical monogram or magic sigil. It has been written in both Siddhamatrika and Ranjana scripts.

Bija and mantra such as Hum and Om Mani Padme Hum are written in a circlular arrangement referred to as Mantra Chakras (thought wheels), and can be composed of one-letter bija-mantra forms, or from the bija of one or more deities, especially Boddhisattvas.

Ranjana (Nepal)

Lantsa / Ranjana (Tibet)

Vartu / cursive Ranjana (Tibet)

Honourific Uchen (Tibet)

Mantra - OM MANI PADME HUM

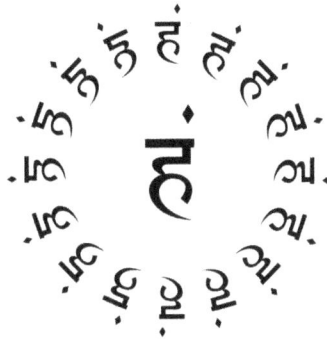

Hum - Devanagari

Bodhisattvas - Lantsa

Om Mani Padme Hum - Uchen

Mantra Chakra

Yantra – Instrument

Used in conjunction with each other to form powerful combinations, mantra, yantra and mandala are three basic tools of Tantra. Yantras are meant to inspire inner visualization and experience in the worshipper.

Meaning 'instrument' in Sanskrit, a yantra is a geometrical diagram which can represent a deity or divine figure, making the process of evolution conscious to the adept of Tantra. All primal shades of a yantra are psychological symbols corresponding to inner states of human consciousness, the sacred symbols of the process of involution and evolution.

Generally they are made of several concentric figures (squares, circles, lotuses, triangles, point). The point (bindu) at the center of the yantra signifies unity, the origin, the principle of manifestation and emanation. When these concentric figures are gradually growing away from its center (bindu) in stages, this is a symbol of the process of macrocosmic evolution. When they are gradually growing towards its center, this is a symbol of the process of microcosmic evolution.

The Sanskrit syllables inscribed on yantras are essentially 'thought forms' representing divinities or cosmic powers, which exert their influence by means of sound-vibration. In the Dharmic traditions, all phenomena are essentially the 'formation of vibration and resonance'. All form arises from the bija-mantra OM.

Bija and mantra are frequently substituted for anthropomorphic images on yantra because their concentrated natures make them more potent than coarse images. Commonly, the letters of the alphabet are placed on the outer rim or edge of the yantra and the mantra and bija within. Recitation of those divine powers inherent in the letters is sound to anchor the meditator in the world of the Supreme.

SRI YANTRA

Cymatics is the study of the interrelationship of sound and form, and the study of cymatics has proven that the visual form of Om is the Sri Yantra, the Divine Plan. Hans Jenny discovered that when Om is spoken (aum), the pattern of circles and triangles of the Sri Yantra appears in sand on a resonator plate or in an electron vibration field sensor called a Tonoscope. Jenny also discovered that when the sounds of the Vedic alphabet are spoken, the written form of the letter appears. The sound of the letter is the vibratory form of that letter. Images of the Sri Yantra have always shown that the 50 sounds of Vedic Sanskrit are distributed throughout the diagram of the Sri Yantra.

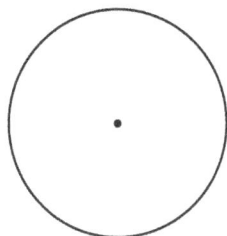

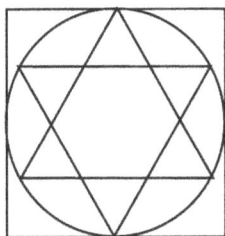

Bindhu   square, circle, triangle   wheel, lotus petals, gates

Basic geometric shapes, pictorial and abstract forms used
in yantra construction

Sri Yantra

Simple and Complex Yantras

MATRIKA YANTRA

The Matrika Yantra is the divine plan (Sri Yantra) of the universe expressed in words and syllables of the 51 letters of Vedic Sanskrit; accompanied in the rays of the light as Kala (sun), they sustain the universe. The vowels are 16 aspects (15 of night and one transcendent) of Soma (moon). The remaining consonants from 'ka' to 'bha' are the 24 aspects of the sun, and the consonants from 'ma' to the last are ten aspects of fire (agni).

The Matrika Yantra is to be drawn with saffron (kesara) for Shakti worship, and with ashes (bhasma) for Shiva worship. It contains all the 51 Matrikas and is used in the first of the ten rites to purify a mantra (samskara) after it has been received from a guru. On the petals of the yantra are the consonants, while the vowels are in the eight spokes. In the center is the syllable Hsauh, while in the cardinal directions is the Bam bija, and in the intermediate directions the Tham bija-mantra.

KALI YANTRA

The Kali yantra is used in Tantra to represent the goddess and embody her power of destruction and rebirth. The yantra is composed of a Bindhu, indicating its energy and its extreme concentration at the center. The circles symbolize the cyclical nature of both birth and death, representing the ongoing process of transformation. The lotus petals represent the lotus blossom, the eight chakras and Kali's role of nurturer. The inverted triangles may symbolize Shakti, the divine feminine energy.

The yantra is believed to possess occult power, capable of neutralizing negative influences, protecting against adversity and promoting spiritual growth.

It is used in meditation and worship of Kali, serving as a focus point to connect with Kali's energy and cultivate a deeper understanding of transformation and spiritual liberation.

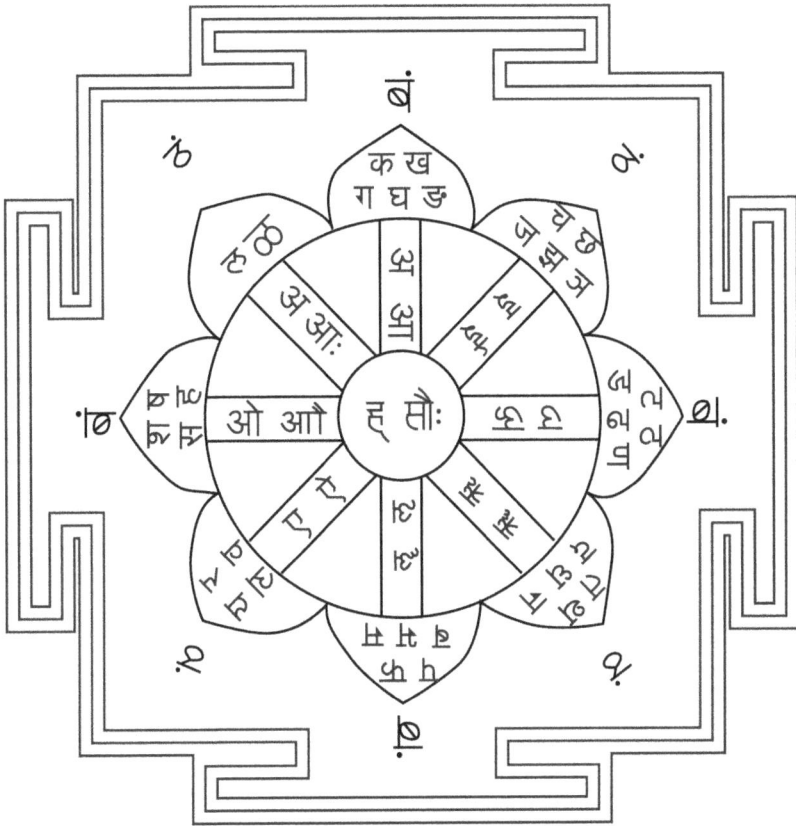

Matrika Yantra

Two forms of the Kali Yantra

Mandala – Circle

Mandala, meaning 'circle' in Sanskrit, is a sacred, symbolic diagram, a visual aid to attain desirable mental states. A mandala can be defined in two ways: as a schematic representation of the universe – or internally, as a guide for several psychological practices that take place in many Asian traditions, including meditation.

A traditional mandala is a simple or complex blueprint of a 'temple of the gods', as well as the entire universe. It is an integral part of Hindu and Buddhist tradition. They are not to be confused with yantra, which are mainly geometric. Simplistically speaking, Buddhists use mandalas, and Hindus use yantras.

Hindu mandalas are also superficially similar to Rangoli – pretty, traditional, freestyle designs that differ stylistically across India. Celebrated in local festivals, Rangoli are mainly drawn and coloured using dyed rice flour, and also sand, brick dust and flower petals.

In Tantric Buddhism, there are four types of mandalas. The Maha Mandalas depict the Buddhas and Bodhisattvas in human form. Somaya Mandalas show them as objects. Dharma Mandalas show them as bija. Karma Mandalas are three-dimensional sculptural mandalas like Angkor Wat.

PAINTING

Mandalas are objects of devotion in Hindu and Buddhist tantra, and they are also used in Jainism. They can be painted on paper, wood, stone, cloth, or even on a wall. They are painstakingly created with coloured sand, entirely by hand. From tracing the outline design to filling the sand, grain by grain, they can take weeks to build. This labour-intensive method is both an artistic and spiritual practice, and once the mandala is complete, it is followed by its ceremonial destruction. It is swept away into a jar and emptied into a nearby body of water as a blessing. The act of destruction is there to remind us of the impermanence of life – a powerful metaphor for the creative process.

In temples and monasteries, monks are taught the three lessons of mandala creation: maintaining discipline, perseverance and letting go. In the beginning, monks are not allowed to use coloured sand, working only with white sand to perfect and hone their skills. Any mistakes and the mandala is wiped away and begun again. When the process of maintaining discipline has manifested, the next lesson begins.

Perseverance is essential to the completion of any creative endeavour; things will not always run smoothly. Ego, creative block, forgetfulness, veto of ideas and sabotage, along with a host of other gremlins, will obstruct the completion of a project.

geometric

pictorial

Hindu

spoked

graphic

Maha Mandala

Buddhist

Somaya Mandala

Dharma Mandala

Only when the task is complete can the monk move on to the final lesson of letting go. Everything is in the past, let go and focus on the next task in hand. This is the way in which monks are taught to maintain creative flexibility and enjoy the work involved in the creative process.

SYMBOLOGY

Some mandalas are associated with a symbolic palace. In the center of the mandala lies the palace, which has four gates associated with the four quarters of the world and is located within several layers of circles that form a protective barrier around it. Each layer embodies a quality (e.g., purity, devotion, etc.) that one must obtain before accessing the palace.

Depending upon the tradition it belongs to, inside the palace, the mandala has symbols associated with different deities or cultural symbols, such as the male thunderbolt symbol, the female bell symbol, a wheel, the symbol of the Buddhist Eightfold Path, or a diamond – a symbol of a clear mind, amongst others.

On other occasions, mandalas can represent a particular deity or group of deities, which could number a few or thousands. In these cases, the deity or main deity is placed at the center of the mandala, while other deities are placed around the central image. The main deity is considered the generative force of the mandala, and the secondary deities are seen as manifestations of the power of the core image.

In many traditions in which mandalas are used, the practitioner, at least metaphorically, establishes a dialogue with the symbol or deity at the core of the mandala by moving progressively from the outside inward, towards the center. Once within the center, the practitioner is able to perceive all manifestations as part of a single underlying whole and gets closer to the goal of enlightenment or perfect understanding.

DHARMA MANDALAS

Dharma mandalas with only bija are regarded as the most sublime, the vision of one who is totally awake. Outside of India, the esoteric practices related to Sanskrit script, especially the writing and recitation of mantra, remained widespread, but in general there was a simplification of the incredibly complex Indian tantric doctrines in China and Japan. Emphasis was placed on seed syllables, especially in conjunction with mandalas.

In China, the sound mattered less than its written form. In fact, nothing in China had any real value unless put in writing. This led to the creation of large, complex mandalas by Chinese and Japanese Buddhists that viewed the cosmos in the form of Buddhas represented as bijaksara.

Great Protective Circle
Radiates the mandala's
infinite colourful light

Buddha of Compassion
Represented by lotus flowers

64 Lotus Petals
Represents the
purified state
of mind

Gate with 11 levels
Represents
the states leading to
enlightenment

Circular Beam
of Vajras
Represents
indestructibility

Cresent
Moon and
Half-Vajra
Symbolises
the Buddha's
body, speech
and mind

Precious Umbrella
Provides protection
from suffering

Entrance
Indicates entrance to the
mandala's eastern quadrant

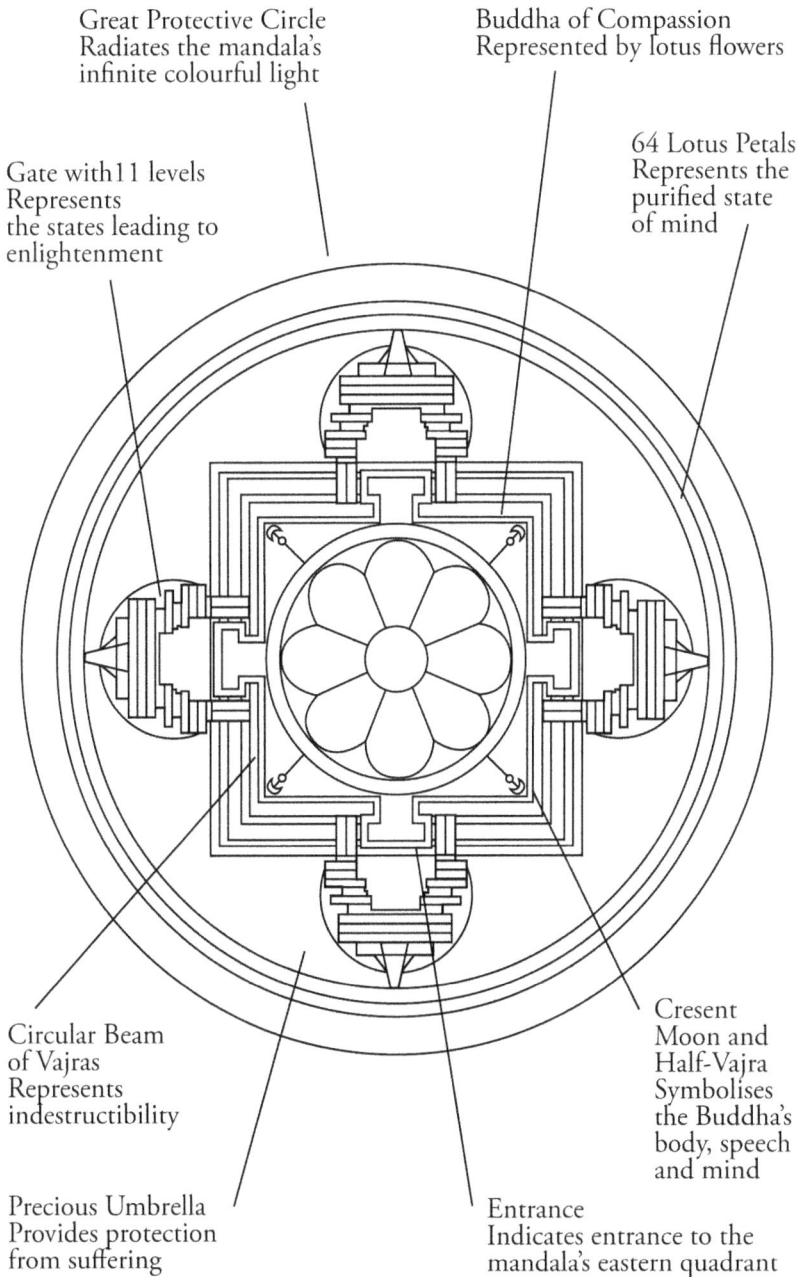

Anatomy of a Tantric Buddhist Karma mandala

Graphic variety in mandala design

Hrih - Om Ah Hum Tram

Hokke - Lotus Sutra mantra

Fudo Myoo

Amida (Amitabha)

Amitabha (Amida)

Five Buddhas of the Vajradhatu

Eight deities of the Garbhadhatu

Dharma Mandala

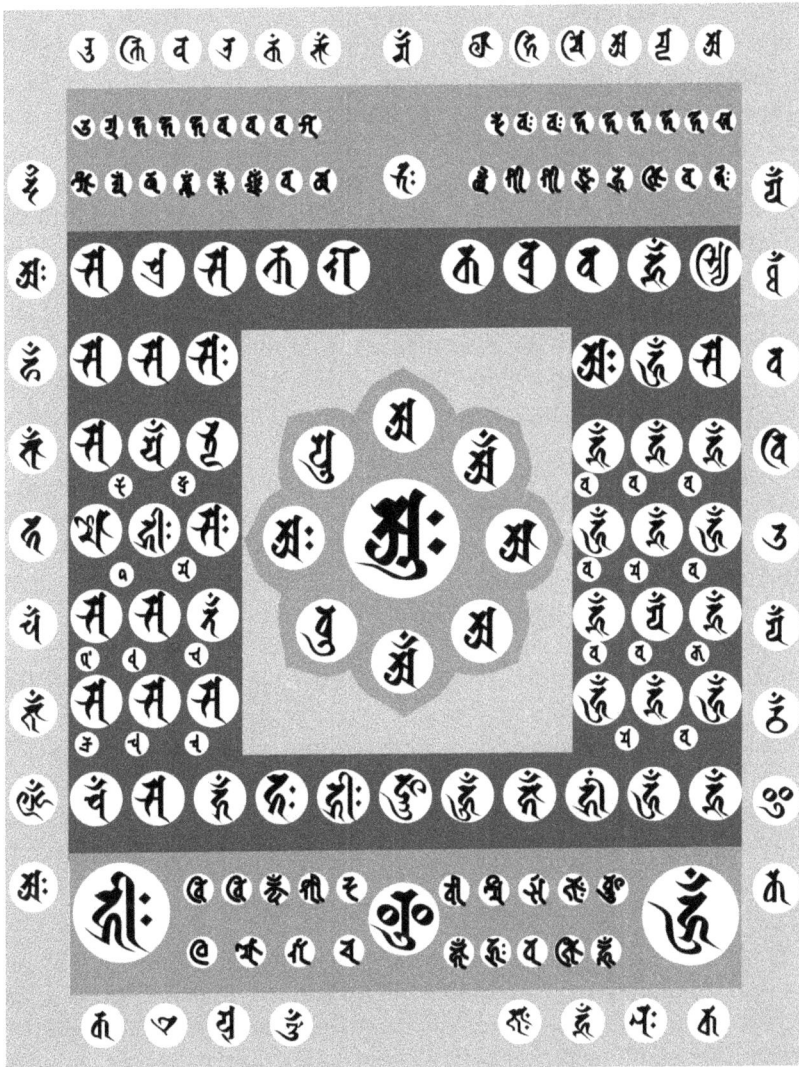

Shinji or Seed Syllable Mandala
(detail of center pannel)
deities symbolized by their individual bija

Sak Yant – Tattoo Yantra

Sak Yant is a form of tattoo art that originated with the Tai tribes of southwest China and northwest Vietnam over 2,000 years ago. Sak means 'tattoo' and Yant means 'yantra' in the Thai language. A form of mystical diagram used in Dharmic religion, they are considered to be sacred designs that offer power, protection, charisma and other benefits to the wearer. While the tradition of tattooing originated with indigenous tribal animism, it became closely tied with the Hindu-Buddhist concept of mystical geometric patterns used in meditation. The designs consist of several graphic elements, including pictorial and abstract renderings of Buddha and other deities, sacred animals called Himapant, and Pali phrases written in various sacred scripts.

Himapant animals are mystical animals from the ancient mystical Indian forest of Himapant. They include insects, fish, birds, reptiles, mammals and hybrids like mermaids, dragons, griffins and demigods, representing elemental powers and Bodhisattvas.

The scripts used for Yant designs vary culturally and geographically. In Thailand and Cambodia, both the Old Khmer and its modern variant are used. The Old Khmer script is considered to be an especially powerful magic script. In northern Thailand and Myanmar, the Lanna and its variant scripts are employed in Yant design. In Laos, they use the Lao Thai script. These scripts are used to spell out abbreviated syllables from Pali incantations.

In the 21st century, Sak Yant is mainly practiced in Thailand and, to a lesser extent, in Cambodia, Laos and Myanmar. Their popularity among the masses, fuelled by Western celebrity endorsement, has turned many modern-day Thais to view Sak Yant as nothing more than stylish amulets and talismans or good luck charms – so much so that some are asking for a complete ban of any tattoo of religious figures like Buddha.

YANT GRAO PAETCH (DIAMOND ARMOUR YANTRA)

The Thai Buddhist monk called Luang Phor Porn, who was ordained in 1895, found the hidden mystery of the Yant Grao Paetch or Diamond Armour Yant/ Kata. It consists of the kata called the Eight Direction Mantra. It is said that if chanted consistently and regularly without fail, it can make one immensely wealthy. Its powers are said to be an invincibility spell, as well as providing an extensive set of Buddhist blessings for luck, karma improvement, prosperity, and protection against all ailments and dangers, as well as providing a wealthy future. Along with the Gao Yord Yant, it is one of the fundamental Yant designs. Without the Grao Paetch Yant, it would be impossible for many other Yant to exist, due to the fact that many other Yant contain the same kata inscribed in the structure.

Yant Grao Paetch / Diamond Armour

Yant Hah Taew / five sacred lines

YANT HAH TAEW (FIVE SACRED LINES)

This Yant dates back over 200 years to the ancient kingdom of Lanna in northern Thailand. The Buddhist monk Kruba Kam designed the Yant around 1296, the same time as the city of Chiang Mai was founded. It is a series of five magic spells or katas written in Old Khmer script; the original lines have been completely replaced over the centuries. They are chanted 108 times before entering a higher state of meditation.

YANT JIN JOK SAWNG (TWO-TAILED GECKO YANTRA)

A Himapant yantra, the two-tailed gecko is inscribed with a kata or mantra down the middle of its back. Considered lucky, it is used by shopkeepers for business and general finances, and also by gamblers. It is often made with metal or on cloth.

YANT GAO YORD

Also called Yant Kru or Master Yant, the Gao Yord is a most sacred Buddhist yant with very wide-ranging powers of protection. It is quite possibly the most important of all available yant designs, because of its universal power. It is the first yant design given to a follower of a yant master, tattooed before other personal designs are added to the body. There are three main variations of the basic design which represents the nine peaks of mount Meru, the abode of Lord Brahma and other deities in Hindu mythology. In Buddhism, the mountain is known as Sumeru.

The spiral designs are called Unnalome, indicating the earthly distractions we encounter in our daily lives. As we grow older and wiser this spiral gradually decreases until it becomes a straight line pointing upwards. This signifies the path to Nirvana or true enlightenment. The set of three ovals called Ong Pra (Buddha's body) are a representation of the Lord Buddha. The Gao Yord Yant has nine Buddha's each bestowing special powers or spells.

In some versions of the yant, there is a mantra/kata, Buddhist Psalm or incantation written at the base of the design, in various scripts, Khmer, Shan, Lanna, and gives the abbreviations for the names of these Buddhas – a, song, wi, su, loe, pu, sa, pu, pa. It does not say anything as it is a chant, it is not a phrase as such but rather the use of syllables to represent certain elements involved with Buddhist magic.

Other versions of the yant design feature a central patchwork of small squares, a magic box, although the lines are not shown in some designs. Each square contains an abbreviation, written in Old Khmer, for the names of the protection spells the yant will bestow. The number of small squares varies according to the design.

Himapant
Yant Jim Jok Sawng Haeng
Two-tailed Gecko

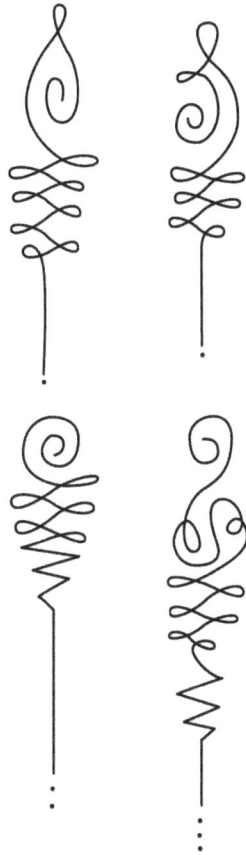

Unalome

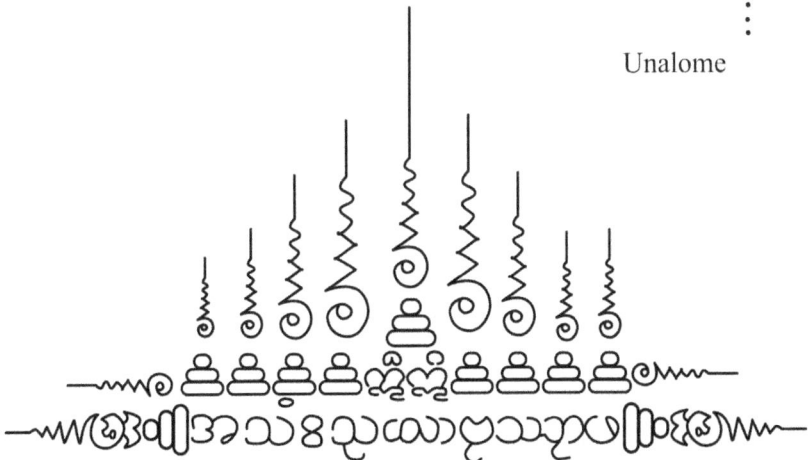

Yant Gao Yord

Bodhisattvas – Mind of Awakening

In Buddhism, Bodhisattva is a Sanskrit term for anyone who, motivated by great compassion, has generated Bodhicitta, which is a spontaneous wish and a compassionate mind to attain Buddhahood for the benefit of all sentient beings. In early Buddhism, the term Bodhisattva was primarily used to refer specifically to Gautama Buddha in his former life. It comes from the Jataka tales, in which Bodhisattva originally referred to the pre-enlightened practitioner of austerities.

Mahayana Buddhism is primarily based on the path of a Bodhisattva, in which life in this world is compared to people living in a house that is on fire. People take the world as reality, pursuing worldly projects and pleasures without realizing that the house is ablaze, due to the inevitability of death. A Bodhisattva is someone who is determined to free sentient beings from Samsara and its life cycle of death, rebirth and suffering. Bodhisattvas take the Bodhisattva vows in order to progress on the spiritual path towards Buddhahood. This type of mind is known as the 'mind of awakening' (Bodhisattva).

TAIZOKAI / GARBHADHATU

As mystical Buddhism established itself outside of India with non-Sanskrit-speaking peoples, the complex philosophies of Hindu Tantra and the esoteric significance of the Sanskrit alphabet were incorporated into Mahayana and Vajrayana Buddhism, specifically in Tibet, China and Japan, with several changes. One of these changes was that Buddhas and Bodhisattvas replaced the Deva and Devi of the Hindu pantheon, although the seed syllables of the Buddhas were formed in patterns similar to that of the Devas; e.g., HRIM, the seed syllable of Amitabha Buddha, consists of H – karma, R – passion, I – calamity, M – removed, epitomizing Buddha's vow to free his followers from all evils.

In Tantra, each Bodhisattva is associated with a seed syllable. From emptiness comes the seed. From the seed, the concept of an icon develops – and from that conception, the external representation of the icon is derived. Awareness of emptiness is transformed into a seed; the seed develops into a Buddha which may then be portrayed as an image. Written in the proper way with the proper spirit, the concentrated power of the seed syllable is capable of manifesting the latent Buddha within us. Without such proper knowledge, the letters are nothing more than profane markings.

The 13 Buddhas are often grouped together. The list is comprised of the 13 Buddhas and Bodhisattvas who are venerated on special days following a believer's death.

12. Mahavairocana
Tathagata.
Dainichi Nyorai

7. Bhaisajya
Tathagata.
Kushi Nyorai

1. Acala Vidyaraja.
Fudo Myoo

8. Avalokitesvara
Bodhisattva.
Kanzeon Bosatsu

2. Sakyamuni
Tathagata.
Shaka Nyorai

9. Sthamaprapta
Bodhisattva.
Seishi Bosatsu

3. Manjusri
Bodhisattva.
Monju Bosatsu

10. Amitabha
Tathagata.
Amida Nyorai

4. Samantabhadra
Bodhisattva.
Fugen Bosatsu

11. Aksobhya
Tathagata.
Ashuku Nyorai

5. Ksitigarbha
Bodhisattva.
Jizo Bosatsu

13. Akasagarbha
Bohisattva.
Kokuzo Boastsu

6. Maitreya
Bodhisattva
Miroku Bosatsu

Taizokai / Garbhadhatu - The Thirteen Buddhas and Bodhisattvas

A different deity is honoured on the 7th, 27th, 37th, 47th, 57th, 67th, 77th and 100th days and on the 1st, 3rd, 7th, 13th and 33rd year anniversaries. Although they are linked in a sequence, they also stand alone and can be written separately.

SANZON (THE THREE HONOURED ONES)

A Buddha or Bodhisattva is often shown together with two attendants. The attendants complement the principle symbolized in the central figure. For example, Amida attendants are Seishi or strength, and Kannon or skilful means – they are the two vehicles that bring their masters' unlimited compassion to sentient beings.

AMIDA
hrih

SEISHI   KANNON
sah   sa

Amida Sanzon

氣

CHINESE MYSTICISM

Chinese Mysticism

China is sometimes referred to as 'San Jiao' or 'the land of three teachings', referring to Daoism, Confucianism and Buddhism, the major faiths of China, where religion and philosophy overlap. There are no distinct divisions between the secular and spiritual aspects of life in the way that there are in many Western traditions. Knowledge of the cosmos was a shamanic one, and the origins of Daoism can be traced back to shamanic practices – and such thoughts and beliefs still influence Chinese mystic practices today.

Daoism begins with the 'Wu', the ancient shamanic priesthood, but it and later contemporary Confucianism did not emerge until 600 BCE. Neither was formalized until much later – Daoism in the 3rd century CE; Confucianism by the neo-Confucianists in 1150, when it was adopted as the Chinese imperial religion until Communism replaced it in 1911.

The differences between them are that Daoism advocates the use of meditation, yoga and alchemy to rise above human existence and gain immortality, and Confucianism seeks to improve the quality of life in a strictly material world.

'Dao' translates as 'the Way/Path' and its cosmology is uniquely devoid of symbolic deities, focusing instead on energetic and elemental principles such as yin-yang and chi.

It is a simple and workable philosophy of how the universe is put together, how it functions and our place in it. It seeks to understand and align with the Dao through practices like meditation and the cultivation of internal alchemy. By using its principles, we can learn to flow more harmoniously with nature instead of being in opposition and fighting nature.

Confucianism is not primarily concerned with mysticism, but it does emphasize ethical conduct and social responsibility, seen as a path to inner harmony and a mystical experience of the natural world.

The core of Daoist texts are found in three books: Tao Te Jing (Yi Jing/I-Ching), Zhuang Zhi and the Daozang. The Confucian Canon is a collection of books consisting of the five classics, which include the I-Ching and the four books of neo-Confucianism.

Chinese folk religion blends elements of Daoism, Confucianism and Buddhism, incorporating ancestor worship, the veneration of deities and practices like divination and exorcism.

Originating during the Tang dynasty, Chen/Zen Buddhism is a blending of Indian Buddhist thought and Daoism. It developed from Mahayana Buddhism, emphasizing meditation (zen or dhyana) to directly realize one's true awakened nature and the interconnectedness of all existence, rather than relying on scripture and deities.

Wu ritual and dancing

Shamanic spirit

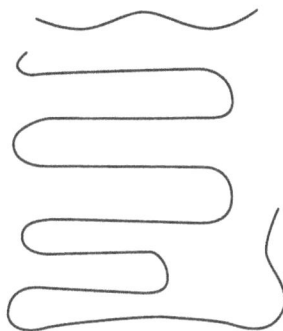

Talisman to 'scatter clouds'

Yin-Yang / Tai Chi

Dao / Tao - the Way / Path

Traditional Beliefs

Chinese metaphysics is a philosophy based on the universal life force known as chi and a harmony between the five elements and yin and yang. This ancient system of cosmology and philosophy is intrinsic to Chinese cultural beliefs, centering on the dynamic balance of opposites, the creative forces of ever-changing opposites.

Its principles have existed for thousands of years; examples are Neolithic wood-henges for timekeeping, oracle bone script for divination, and zodiacs for astrology. It is based on precepts handed down thousands of years ago in the Chinese classics such as the I-Ching, concerned with divination, and the Li Shu or Book of Rites, concerned with order, the harmony of heaven and earth.

The oldest and deepest elements within Chinese metaphysics have been in use since at least the Shang dynasty (circa 2200 BCE), within the influence of ancestors, divinities, feng shui, calendars, almanacs, zodiacs and fortune-telling; with the addition of number astrology and divination, it was complete by 200 BCE. Around 100 BCE, ancient metaphysics emerged in the later Daoist texts with Buddhism, Tantra and Zen, merging from 400 CE to the present. The notion of internal alchemy blossomed between 400 BCE and 1600 CE.

WU SHU – FIVE ARTS / STYLES

Within the discipline of Chinese metaphysics is the Wu Shu or the Five Arts/Styles. They are Yi-Medicine, Xiang-Appearance, Ming-Destiny (astrology), Pu-Divination, and Shan-Mountain (spirit) and have guided Chinese people throughout the ages. They are considered the biggest gift from Chinese ancestors to all human beings on earth. The content of each of the five arts is complex and difficult to master. As such, practitioners focus on just one or two of them and may only do one or two of the disciplines within each art.

Derived from the I-Ching or Book of Changes, they are the five fields of study that form an essential foundation for ancient discussions surrounding space, time, the universe and its laws, channelling the concept and reasoning of yin and yang. They are used to teach enlightenment or the Dao, being rooted in Daoist principles, with early Daoist studies contributing to their development.

The five arts studied encompass a diverse collection of practices, including medicine, diet, alchemy, fortune-telling, geomancy, astrology, divination, physical and mental well-being, martial arts, calligraphy and talismanic writing. The use of tools such as the bagua, magic squares and cosmic boards is a prime feature of the Wu Shu.

Lao Tzi   Seal of Lao Tzi   Robe

Daoist symbols

Kongfuxi / Confucius   Water (life force)   scholar / enlightenment seal script

Confucian symbols

Chi Tze - Laughing Buddha
Chan/Zen - Chinese Buddhism

Shen - god, deity, spirit

Daoist Cosmology

Chinese cosmology emphasizes a holistic view of the universe as a single interconnected organism with a focus on the interconnectedness of heaven, earth and humanity. It differs from Western cosmologies by emphasizing the cycles of yin and yang, the five phases and the concept of chi or vital energy. The universe is believed to arise from a primordial chaos, evolving through these cycles and phases.

PANGU

Chinese myth tells that, in the beginning, the universe was nothing but chaos, and the heavens and the earth were intermingled in the form of a black egg. The god Pangu was born inside the egg and slept for 18,000 years, during which time, matter and spirit or yin and yang balanced as he grew.

When he awoke, he realized he was trapped inside the egg. He cracked it open and began to push it apart, essentially splitting yin and yang. The upper half of the shell became the sky above him; the lower half became the earth beneath him.

Pangu feared that the earth and the sky would meet again, and the longer he held them apart, the thicker they became and the taller he became; pushing them apart by precisely 10 feet per day, he became wiser than the sky and stronger than the earth.

After another 18,000 years, Pangu died; his body formed the various parts of the world and all its elements. Today, he is held responsible for the weather.

DAOIST COSMOLOGY

Every spiritual tradition has a defined or implied cosmology – a story about the origin of the universe. In Daoism, cosmology is uniquely devoid of symbolic deities, focusing instead on energetic and elemental principles.

WUJI AND YOUJI

According to Chinese philosophy, 'the Limitless' or 'Wuji' produces the delimited 'Youji', and this demarcation is equivalent to 'the Absolute' or 'Taiji – Tai Chi' (the two opposing forces in embryonic form).

TAIJI / TAI CHI

The Tai Chi produces two forms named yin and yang, which are called 'Liangyi' or the 'manifest opposing forces'. The Chinese have a deep belief in chi, and it is incorporated into every aspect of their life. Chi is the life force that is everywhere; it penetrates the living and the land and may be divided into Sha (negative/yin) or Yun (positive/yang).

WU XING – FIVE PHASES

The first thing that chi generates are the five elements. Daoist cosmology is structured on five elements: fire, earth, metal, water and wood. Everything on earth and in heaven, including the colours of the spectrum, is characterized by the constant interplay among the five elements, which is always moving, unstable and changeable, like yin and yang.

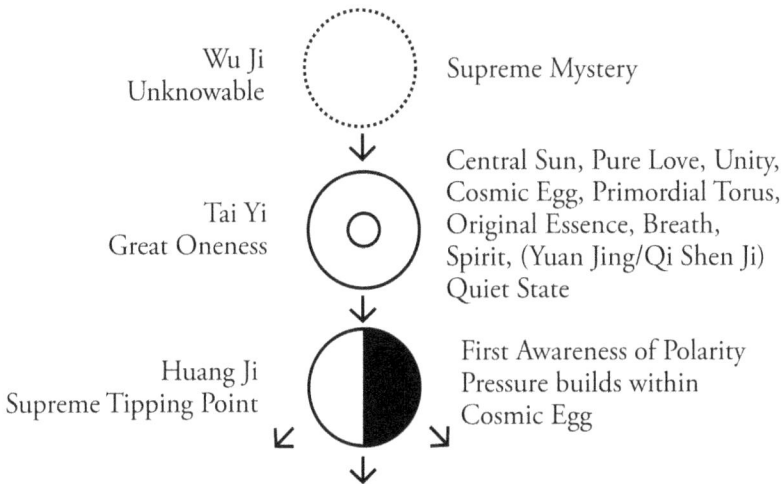

Wu Ji
Unknowable

Supreme Mystery

Tai Yi
Great Oneness

Central Sun, Pure Love, Unity, Cosmic Egg, Primordial Torus, Original Essence, Breath, Spirit, (Yuan Jing/Qi Shen Ji) Quiet State

Huang Ji
Supreme Tipping Point

First Awareness of Polarity Pressure builds within Cosmic Egg

Egg cracks open, Creation begins, 3 Pure Ones Regulate Yuan Jing/ Qi Shen Ji seperate, 8 trigram forces express

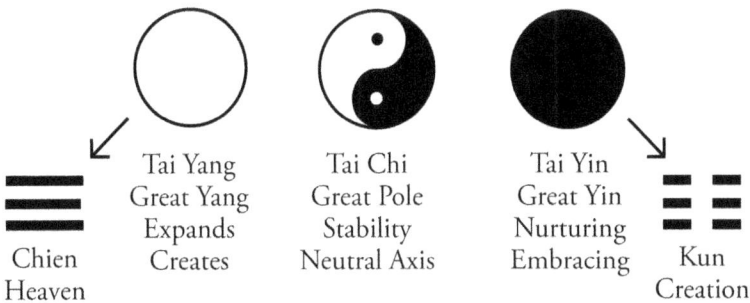

Tai Yang
Great Yang
Expands
Creates

Chien
Heaven

Tai Chi
Great Pole
Stability
Neutral Axis

Tai Yin
Great Yin
Nurturing
Embracing

Kun
Creation

GAU / TRIGRAMS

The Five Phases are pictured inside an octagon surrounded by the pre-celestial bagua (8 trigrams) representing the conjunction of heaven and earth. The trigrams were conceived as images of all that happened in heaven and on earth. At the same time, they were held to be in a state of continual transition, one changing into another, just as transition from one phenomenon to another is continually taking place in the physical world – the fundamental concept of the I-Ching. The creation of these lines is explained in the traditional yin-yang philosophy as the Taij producing two forms named yin and yang, which are called Liangyi or the 'manifest opposing forces'.

TEN HEAVENLY STEMS

Except for the sun and the moon, there are five planets in the ancient Chinese solar system. These five extremely bright planets move forward and away from the earth periodically, with different influences and powers. The approaching earth phase is the yang, while the departing one is the yin. Each of the five planets is named after one of the five elements, and both planet and element have two phases; the 10 Heavenly Stems represent these phases. This enables the 10 Heavenly Stems to describe the five elements in more detail, each element having a yin stem and yang stem.

TWELVE EARTHLY BRANCHES

The circle pictures the post-celestial bagua encircled by the 12 Earthly Branches representing the years, months, days and hours. They also regulate the 10,000 things and are equivalent to the signs of the Chinese zodiac.

10,000 THINGS

From the five elements come the '10,000 things', representing all of manifest existence, all of the objects, inhabitants and phenomena of the world that we experience. Human beings are among the 10,000 things – combinations of the five elements in different combinations.

For Daoists, spiritual growth and change is a matter of balancing the five elements within the person. Unlike many religious systems, human beings are not regarded as something separate from the natural world, but just another manifestation of it.

Another way of describing this process is to say that these stages represent the descent of energetic consciousness into physical forms. Daoist mystics, using various Nei Dan or inner alchemical techniques, are said to be able to reverse this sequence of events, to return to the energetic, blissful realm of Dao. To practice Dao is an attempt to perceive the presence and workings of the universal Dao in the 10,000 things and to live in balanced accordance with it.

Yin-Yang flows in 5 phases
Creation cycle (wu xing)

10 Celestial Stems
regulate the 5 seasons that
shape the worldly destiny
of each human soul
Prenatal human Jing/Qi/Shen
balanced with single
androgynous (male/female) soul.

Ren Lei
Humanity

12 Earthly Branches/Animals
regulate 100,000 things (Wan Wu)

12 Human vital organ spirits
regulate heart-mind (Xin)
Jing/Qi/Shen polarize into male
and female body. This inspires
greater creativity to complete our
world destiny (Ming) and spiritual
self-realization (Xing)

Taijitu – Yin-Yang Symbol

The ancient Chinese believed in a non-personal creative energy that brought the universe into existence. Before this, only chaos existed; harmonizing the two complementary forces of yin and yang formed order and creation.

They believed that harmony and order was the natural way of things because disorder only had bad effects, so they sought to implement the simple philosophy of balancing opposites in as many aspects of their lives as possible – sweet and sour food is an example of this. This simple but profound concept is expressed by the symbol called Taijitu (Great Eternal).

In the Christian religion, light overcomes darkness. In Chinese philosophy, life is a mixture of light and dark, warmness and coolness. The Taijitu is the perfect example of the proper mixture in the right proportions. At the center of the cosmological system is Unity or Wu Ji, symbolized by a circle – this developed into Tai Chi. The yang half contains the seed of yin, and the yin half contains the seeds of yang. The aim is to obtain a life-giving and sustaining balance.

YIN-YANG FORMS

The Tai Chi produces two forms named yin and yang, known as Liangyi or the 'manifest opposing forces', complementary and interacting energies of nature such as male and female, dark and light, that have to be balanced to live in perfect harmony.

Over the millennia, Chinese philosophers have employed graphic symbolism to express the nature of yin and yang. Because yin is earth and yang is heaven, the two concepts are associated with the square and the circle, respectively. In Chinese metaphysics, yang is the warm, impregnating southern side of a hill; yin is the fertile, shady, northern side of a hill. In Feng Shui, yang represents hills, and yin is symbolic of valleys.

When yin and yang are combined, they form a perfect circle – the Taiji. The I-Ching refers to it as the 'Taijitu' or 'Diagram of the Supreme Ultimate', of which there have been various designs throughout the millennia. The Taijitu should always be shown with the yin to the right, indicating the cardinal compass directions. The light yang is at the top, representing summer and the south; while the dark yin is at the bottom, representing winter and the north.

CORRESPONDENCES AND ATTRIBUTES

Yin and yang are at the root of the Chinese view of the universe. Yang represents the male aspect of the cosmic Dao; it is symbolic of light, assertion, creation and all things positive. Yin is the female aspect of the cosmic Dao, symbolic of yielding, night and negative phenomena.

Yin Creation	Yang Heaven	Yin Matter Dark Earth Female	Yang Spirit Light Heaven Male

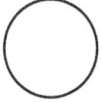 

Geometric shapes   Unigrams

  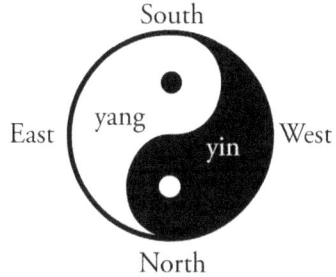

Taijitu   North

Wu Wi	Tai Ji	Wu Ui	Yin	Yang

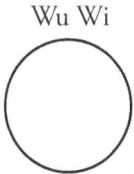    

Heaven   Human   Earth   Inactive   Interactive

Aspects of the Taijitu

Young Yang Yang Resting	Old Yang Upmost Yang	Young Yin Yin Unresting	Old Yin Upmost Yin

East Spring Wood Morning Birth	South Summer Fire Midday Growth	West Autumn Metal Evening Aging	North Winter Water Night Death

Four images of the Taiji

In the beginning, there was nothing except infinite space – the cosmos or Taiji/ Tai Chi. Out of this infinite space came two fundamental principles that govern everything: matter and spirit. Matter is dark and solid and known as yin. Spirit is seen as light and ethereal and is known as yang. At a simple level, they are the female and male principles, respectively – man and woman, husband and wife, light and dark, sweet and sour. Yin governs earth and all that is negative, female, dark, water, soft, cold, death or still. Yang derives from heaven and all that is positive, male, light, fiery, hard, warm, living and moving.

The combination and permutation of yin and yang forms the rest of the universe, whose life and breath is chi. The two breaths of nature, or two types of chi, are essentially one breath. They make up the male and female principles. When they unite, they constitute the beginning or birth of things; when they disperse, they cause decay, dissolution and death. At a more universal level, they are negative and positive, 0 – zero, and 1 – one.

All lives are born out of, and come back to, the earth. The four seasons change under the moon and the sun. So, the sun and the moon together constitute a Taiji, which contains both yin and yang and corresponds to the earth on the ground. Then the five elements are formed.

WU XING / FIVE ELEMENTS

The Taijitu also incorporates into its design the five elements or Wu Xing. They are arranged on the Taijitu to cover all eight of the compass points. Metal is found at north and northwest, and water is in the west and northwest – both are yin; metal is lesser yin, and water is greater yin. Wood is positioned in the east and northeast, and fire is in the south and southeast – both are yang; wood is lesser yang, and fire is greater yang. Earth is both yin and yang, and that is why it is shown as occupying the center of the Taijitu or other such symbols. In Feng Shui, Earth is positioned at west-southwest, between fire and metal.

HUMAN BODY

The Taijitu also represents the human body – the head at the top representing spirit or yang, and the body below representing matter or yin. Yang or male is the left side of the body, while the right side is yin or female. Illness can be seen as a result of an imbalance of yin and yang. The abilities of the human body are seen as yang, while food, the energy source, is seen as yin. Chinese herbalists and acupuncturists classify diseases, ailments and the human body and its internal organs according to their yin and yang qualities.

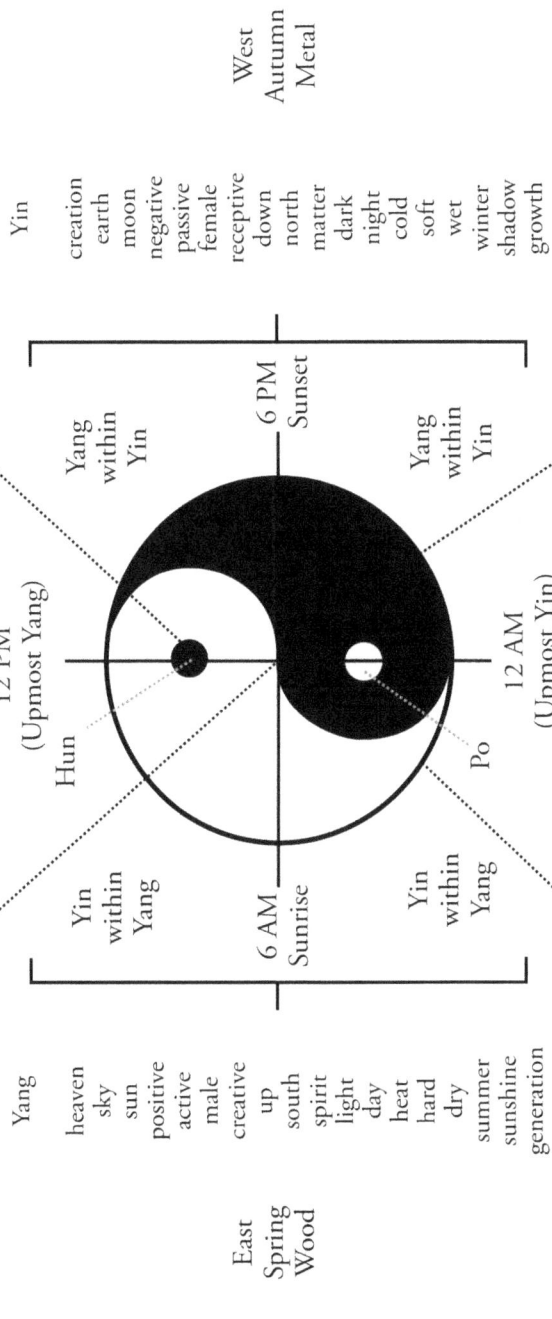

These dots indicate that there is no absolute yin or yang, each contains the germ of each other

The Wuji or Still Point. The calm in the midst of the storm. Stillness in movement

Moving around the circle shows the natural cycle from yin to yang and back to yin again

The outer circle indicates that all things are made up of yin and yang

Correspondences for the Taijitu

Yin

creation
earth
moon
negative
passive
female
receptive
down
north
matter
dark
night
cold
soft
wet
winter
shadow
growth

West
Autumn
Metal

Yang within Yin

6 PM
Sunset

South
Summer
Fire
12 PM
(Upmost Yang)

Hun

North
Winter
Water
12 AM
(Upmost Yin)

Po

Yin within Yang

6 AM
Sunrise

Yang

heaven
sky
sun
positive
active
male
creative
up
south
spirit
light
day
heat
hard
dry
summer
sunshine
generation

East
Spring
Wood

TAIJITU DESIGN

After observing the universe from the sun/moon perspective, Chinese philosophers found that the universe changes every day, and it has seasonal and annual cycles. From these cycles, the unchanging rules are created. In general, the Taijitu is a Chinese representation of the entire celestial phenomena. It contains the cycles of the sun, the four seasons and the 24 segments of chi – the foundation of the I-Ching and the calendar.

When observing the cycle of the sun, the ancient astronomers used an 8-foot-long pole, posted at right angles to the ground, to record the positions of the projected shadows. Using six concentric circles, marked by the 24 segmented points, they divided the circle into 24 sections and recorded the length of the shadow every day. By noting the sunrise and the position of the Big Dipper constellation, they found that the length of a year is around 365.25 days, with the shortest day on the summer solstice and the longest day on the winter solstice.

Connecting each line and drawing the yin part from the summer solstice to the winter solstice creates the solar chart or Taijitu. Yin begins at the summer solstice, and yang begins at the winter solstice. Therefore, a small yin circle is marked on the summer solstice position, and a small yang circle is marked on the winter solstice. Called Hun and Po, they represent the seed of yin within yang and the seed of yang within yin – the idea being that neither can exist without the other.

TAIJITU VARIATIONS

In modern Chinese, 'taijitu' is commonly used to mean the simple 'divided circle' form (tai chi/harmony), but it may refer to any of the several schematic diagrams that contain at least one circle with an inner pattern of symmetry representing yin and yang. There is one basic form with several variants, conceived around the idea of two interlocking spirals, commonly described as two snakes or two fishes resting head-to-tail against each other, with each spiral featuring an inverse dot. There is no official standardized rendition, but various portrayals have appeared through the millennia, with many 'artistic' variations created in the 20th and 21st centuries.

The credit for drawing the first Taijitu is traditionally given to Emperor Fu Xi, or Lao Tzu, the founder of Daoism. The earliest evidence for a yin-yang symbol is found on Chinese pottery circa 2600 BCE. One old manuscript visualized yin-yang as formed from two snakes. This may be related to Fu Xi and his wife Nuwa, who are portrayed as half-human, half-snake deities. Fu Xi was in charge of painting the sky; Nuwa was in charge of decorating the earth.

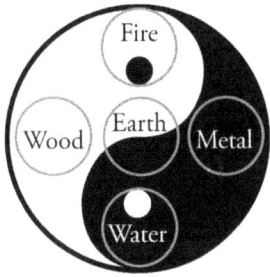

Five Elements

Head
Yang

Mind
Yin

Womb
Yin

Sexuality
Yang

Human Body

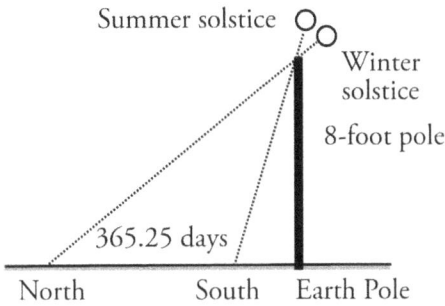

Summer solstice

Winter
solstice

8-foot pole

365.25 days

North   South   Earth Pole

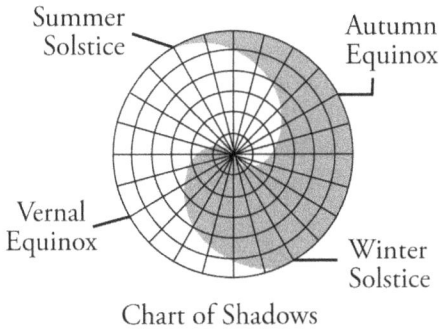

Summer
Solstice

Autumn
Equinox

Vernal
Equinox

Winter
Solstice

Chart of Shadows

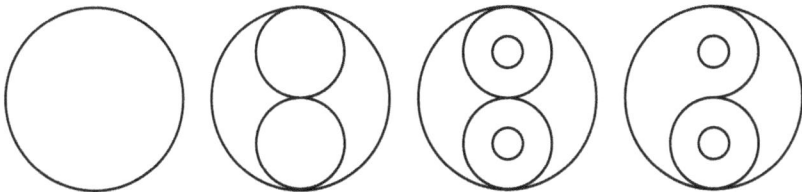

How to draw the Taijitu

The original Daoist Taijitu was drawn with the yang portion on top and the yin portion at the bottom. By rotating the sun chart and positioning the winter solstice at the bottom, it forms the modern vertical symbol. The first taijitu to feature the classic 'two fishes' design appeared during the Song dynasty, in a book written in 1135 CE by Mr. Chang, the earliest teacher of the Early Heaven Bagua diagram, from which the 'two fish shapes' symbol is derived. The dots were introduced in the later Ming dynasty (16th century), replacing the droplet shapes used earlier by Zhao Haigan.

Confucian philosopher Zhou Dunyi (1017–1973 CE) popularized the circular diagram referred to as the Taijitu Tushuo, named after the text called 'Explanation of the Diagram of the Supreme Ultimate', the cornerstone of Neo-Confucianist cosmology. In this taijitu, the empty inner circle represents Wuji, and the outer circle represents Taiji, comprised of three concentric circles, halved and filled with alternate black or white sections to represent yin and yang as broken and unbroken lines. An older design from the Tang dynasty follows early Daoist principles, originally coloured red and black for fire and water.

Zhao Haigan (1351–1395) was the first to popularize the swirling variant. When the diagram is combined with the eight trigrams, it is called the Hu Te or Natural River chart, spontaneously generated by heaven and earth. In Zhao's original schematic, Hun and Po are droplet-shaped before being replaced by dots in the later Ming period. An early Ming dynasty book contains a yin-yang diagram called the Zhou Yi Taijitu. The text mentions the I-Ching, yin-yang and Bagua philosophy. By the end of the Ming period, the diagram had become a widespread representation of Chinese cosmology.

Introduced into Chinese philosophy during the Ming dynasty (16th century CE), Lao Zhide's design is similar to the 'Gankyil' symbol of Tibetan Buddhism that has three or four swirls. Lao Zhide's has two swirls, terminating in a central circle that represents Wuji, with a center point, Tanyi, the world embryo.

Fu Xi - snake

Ancient - fish

Modern - fish

Taijitu Tushuo
11th c.

Zhou Haigan
14th c.

Taijitu variants

Lao Zhide
16th c.

Pre-celestial sequence

Post-celestial sequence

Yinyangyutu - Ba Gua Motif

Qi / Chi – Life Energy

Pronounced 'chee', Qi is the standard Chinese spelling. Ch'i is the pinyin spelling, with modern variants including Chi, Khi, Ki, Ke, He; and Ki, Gi, Khi in Japanese, Korean and Vietnamese.

Qi translates as 'air' and figuratively as 'energy, life force or energy flow'. The practice of cultivating and balancing Qi is called Qigong. The terms Shang Qi and Sha Qi describe positive and negative energy types.

Concepts similar to Qi can be found in many cultures: 'prana' in Hinduism, 'lung' in Tibetan Buddhism, 'ruah' in Judaism, 'mana' in Hawaiian, and 'manitou' in Native American. In Western philosophy, 'pneuma' in ancient Greece and 'energia – elan, vital, vitalism' are purported to be similar.

Qi is an uncommon Chinese character, mostly found in Daoist talismans. Historically, Qi was written using three horizontal lines until the Han dynasty (206–120 BCE), when its traditional 'Hanzi' form replaced it. The Japanese and Korean glyphs are the same as the Chinese Hanzi form.

The ancient Chinese believed Qi permeated everywhere and linked their surroundings together. Qi was also linked to the flow of energy around and through the body, a vital force forming part of any living entity. By understanding the rhythm and flow of Qi, they believed that they could guide exercises and treatments to provide stability and longevity.

According to traditional Daoist theory, there are three different types of Qi energy which affect everything in the universe: Ten Qi – heaven, Ki Qi – earth, and Nin Qi – human being. Together, they form Qi – the underlying principle in Chinese traditional medicine, Feng Shui and Chinese martial arts.

In Chinese acupuncture, needles are inserted into specific parts of the body to balance the flow of Qi. Feng Shui is based on calculating the balance of Qi interacting between the five elements, yin-yang and other factors. Notable martial arts that are Qi-focused include Baguazhang, Tai Chi Chuan, Aikido, Kendo, Hapkido, and Aikijujitsu. Demonstrations of Qi in martial arts include the 'unraisable body' and the 'unbendable arm'.

Qigong involves coordinating breathing, movement and awareness. It is traditionally viewed as a practice to cultivate and balance Qi. With its roots in traditional Chinese medicine, philosophy and martial arts, Qigong is now practiced worldwide for exercise, healing, meditation and training for the martial arts. Typically, a Qigong practice involves rhythmic breathing, slow and stylized movement, a mindful state and visualization of guiding Qi.

oldest form (air)　　　　oracle bone script　　　　bronzeware script

large seal script　　　　small seal script

Ancient forms of Chi

Small seal
script

Hanzi
standard

Hanzi
simplified

Printed
character

Shinjitai
Japan

Hangul
Korea

Standard forms of Chi

Philosophically, Qi is more of a multi-meaning or multi-compound concept than a specific matter, energy or function, containing all forms of Qi. Yuan Qi or Parental Qi has its roots in the kidneys and spreads throughout the body. It is the transformation of all the yin-yang energies of the body. It is the dynamic force that motivates the functional activity of the internal organs.

Zhong Qi or Center Qi is energy generated from the spleen and stomach, whose function is to transport Qi from food into the chest, where it combines with the Qi of the heart and lungs. Gu Qi or Food Qi is the energy that transforms food into a used form by the spleen. Qing Qi or Clear Qi, also known as Yang Qi, is the purest energy from the Gu Qi. Shuo Qi or Turgid Qi is the un-pure, energetic essence of Gu Qi to be further refined and excreted. With Zong Qi or Gateway Qi, the spleen sends Gu Qi to the lungs where, with the assistance of Yuan Qi, it combines with air and transforms into Zong Qi.

With Zhen Qi or True Qi, Zong Qi originates in the lungs; it is then transformed into Zhen Qi with the catalytic action and refinement of Qi. It is the Qi that circulates in the channels and also outside the body and maintains the organs. Zhen Qi has two different forms: Ying Qi and Wei Qi. Ying Qi or Nutritive Qi is the Qi activated by the insertion of acupuncture needles – nourishing the internal organs and whole body. It is closely related to the emotions, since it is directed by thought. Wei Qi or Proactive Qi, is fast-moving, 'slippery' and more yang than Ying Qi, flowing underneath the skin and in between the muscles to protect the body from harsh weather conditions, microorganisms, harmful emotions and evil spirits. Zheng Qi or Upright Qi, also known as Righteous Qi, is a general term to indicate the various Qi protecting the body from invasion by Xie Qi or Pathogenic Qi.

Hou Tan Zhi Qi or Postnatal Qi is the energy from food, drink and air cultivated after birth. Postnatal Qi depends on Parental Qi, Yuan Qi, for development. Both form the foundation for the body's vital energy. Zang and Fu Qi or Organ Qi is the energy responsible for the functioning of the internal organs. The Yang Fu, hollow bowels, produce Qi and blood from food and drink. The Yin Zang, solid viscera, stores vital substances.

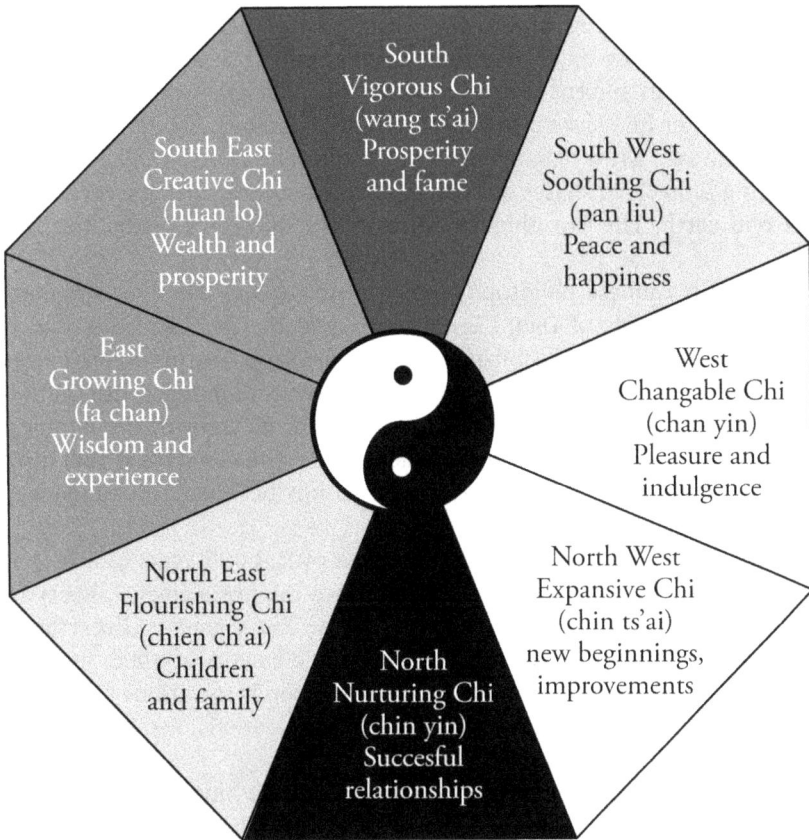

South
Vigorous Chi
(wang ts'ai)
Prosperity
and fame

South East
Creative Chi
(huan lo)
Wealth and
prosperity

South West
Soothing Chi
(pan liu)
Peace and
happiness

East
Growing Chi
(fa chan)
Wisdom and
experience

West
Changable Chi
(chan yin)
Pleasure and
indulgence

North East
Flourishing Chi
(chien ch'ai)
Children
and family

North
Nurturing Chi
(chin yin)
Succesful
relationships

North West
Expansive Chi
(chin ts'ai)
new beginnings,
improvements

Chi energies, direction, names and attributes in
Western '8 Aspirations' Feng Shui

Wu Xing – Five Phases / Elements

The theory of Wu Xing or the five elements has been central to Chinese philosophy since Han times, developed at the same time as the four elements were conceived in ancient Greece. Western elements are seen as the building blocks of matter in a system in which they are balanced. By contrast, Chinese elements are seen as ever-changing, in a constant state of flux – and a translation of Wu Xing is the 'Five Phases or Changes'. The four Greek elements are air, fire, water and earth. The five Chinese elements are wood, fire, earth, metal and water.

Wu Xing is Chinese philosophy's attempt to explain how life is organized through the concepts of Dao, Chi, yin-yang and the five elements. Dao is a composite of everything, the intrinsic order of all things. The life breath of Dao is Chi. Yin-yang and the five elements describe the way we interact with Dao, with nature. Yin and Yang symbolize the creation process through the interaction of bipolar forces – the passive and the active. The five elements model further differentiates this dynamic into the relationship between five fundamental powers.

The five elements theory is reputed to be over 4,000 years old. It is said that as heaven and earth interact, they produce the five elements. Everything between heaven and earth is influenced by the five elements. Everything in creation can be categorized within the five basic elements of wood, fire, earth, metal and water. Therefore, each element corresponds to various factors, such as colours, shapes, foods, internal body organs, emotions, activities, seasons, directions, numbers, etc.

The trigrams are related to the five elements of Wu Xing, used by Feng Shui practitioners and in traditional Chinese medicine. The Kan and Li trigrams correspond directly with the water and fire elements. The element of earth corresponds with the trigrams of Kun/earth and Gen/mountain. The element of wood corresponds with the trigrams of Xun/wind and Zhen/thunder. The element of metal corresponds with the trigrams of Qian/heaven and Du/lake. They all have correspondences in astrology, geology, geomancy, anatomy, the family, and others.

Wu Xing - 5 elements

Fire
火

Wood
木

Earth
土

Water
水

Metal
金

Productive (circle) and Destructive (pentagram) cycles

Qian	Li	Kun	Gen	Kan
wood	fire	earth	metal	water

Productive sequence

Qian	Kun	Li	Gen	Kan
wood	earth	fire	metal	water

Destructive sequence

These elements have predictable, observable relationships to one another. The dynamic interplay between each of the elements forms the impetus involved in life and change. This birth and transformation is the process of Dao.

In the five element theory, the very fact that there are five elements creates a continual imbalance. This is essential to the Chinese philosophy of Yi or continual change.

PRODUCTION AND DESTRUCTION SEQUENCES

The elements may be arranged in a number of sequences. The basic principle of the five element theory describes two cyclical patterns – productive and destructive – with no beginning and no end. They are the cycle of creation and the cycle of destruction.

In the productive sequence called Sheng, each element is created by its preceding element and creates or nourishes its following element. Wood burns and so produces fire, which leaves behind ash, and so creates earth, which produces metal, which melts like ice to produce water, which nourishes life to produce wood. As water is the mother of wood, this process describes distinct phases from birth to death.

In the cycle of destruction, each element controls or is destroyed by another. This cycle is necessary to enable change and a dynamic of movement through changing polarity and, therefore, ultimately a balance of power. In the destructive sequence, each element destroys the next-but-one of the productive sequences. Wood destroys earth by drawing strength from it. Fire melts metal. Earth pollutes water. Metal chops down wood. Water puts out fire.

In the Hetu and pre-celestial Bagua, the elements are sequenced as: fire brings water, water feeds wood, wood brings metal, metal brings fire – and reversely: fire melts metal, metal chops wood, wood drains water, water quenches fire. Whereas in the Luoshu and post-celestial Bagua, the elements are sequenced as follows: water feeds wood, wood brings metal, metal brings fire, fire brings water – and reversely: water quenches fire, fire melts metal, metal chops wood, wood drains water.

2. FIRE

1. WOOD

Greens & Blues
Plants & Flowers
All Woods
Column & Pillar
East
Dragon
Spring

Reds
Lighting, Candles
Fireplace, Sunlight
Animals, Leather, Wool, etc.
Triangle, Pyrmid, Cone
South
Phoenix
Summer

3. EARTH

Yellows
Earth tones,
Soil, Ceramics
Tile, Brick,
Stucco, Square,
Plateau
Rectangle
Center

Reduces
Makes
Feeds
Reduces
Consumes
Reduces
Extinguishes
Melts
Creates
Yin Yang
Reduces
Cuts
Dams
Reduces
Nurtures
Reduces
Holds

5. WATER

Black & Dark Colours
Water Features, Glass
Crystal, Mirrors,
Assymetry
North
Tortoise
Winter

4. METAL

Whites & Pastels
Rocks & Stones
All Metals
Arch, Circle, Oval
West
Tiger
Autumn

▲ Nourishing cycle

◮ Controling cycle

△ Reductive cycle

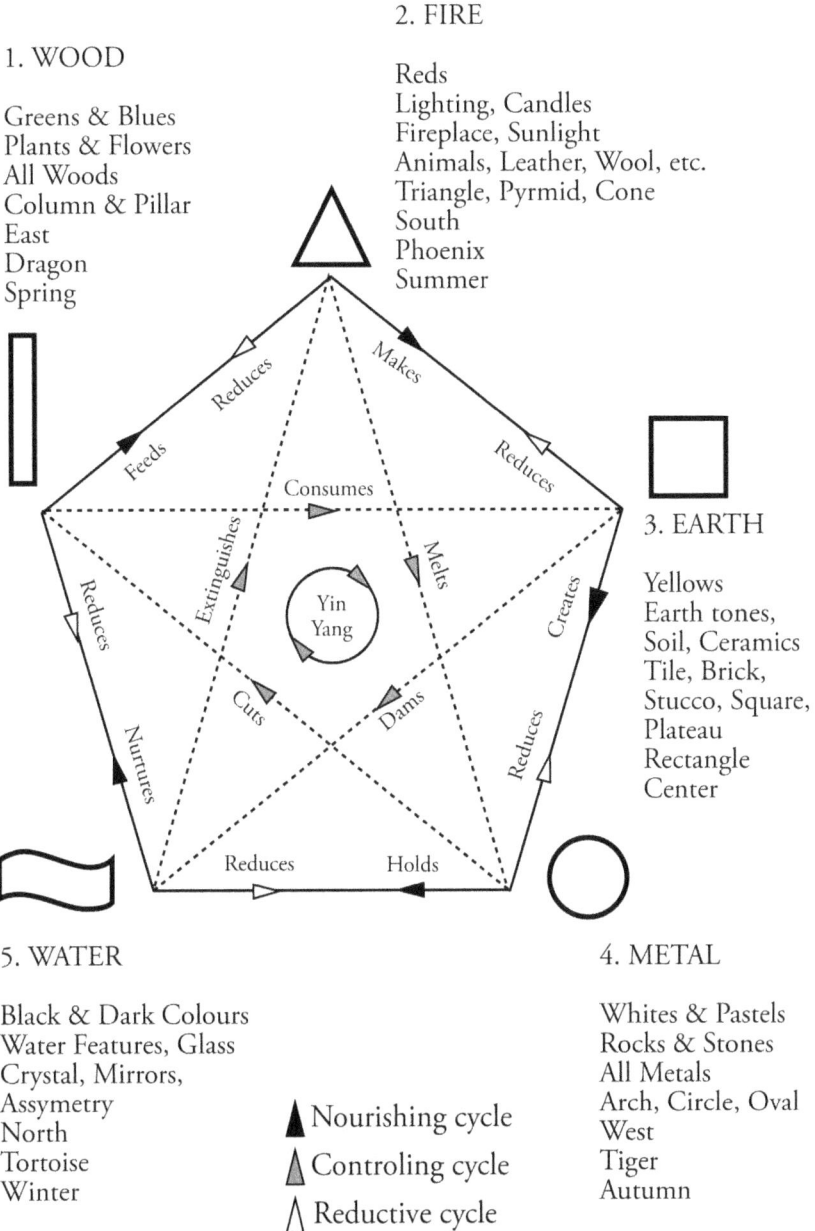

Feng Shui Wu Xing chart

Gau – Trigrams

The Chinese use their word 'gau', meaning 'divinatory symbols', to describe what Westerners call the trigrams and hexagrams of the I-Ching. The three-line glyphs or trigrams, and the six-line glyphs or hexagrams, are used in Daoist philosophy to represent the fundamental principles of reality. When the eight trigrams are combined with themselves and each other, they produce the 64 hexagrams of the I-Ching.

The trigrams were conceived as images of all that happened in heaven and on earth. At the same time, they were held to be in a state of continual transition, one changing into another, just as transition from one phenomenon to another is continually taking place in the physical world – the fundamental concept of the I-Ching. The creation of these lines is explained in the traditional yin-yang philosophy as the Taij producing two forms named yin and yang, which are called Liangyi or the 'manifest opposing forces'.

Daoist philosophers ascribed a single unbroken line to yang and a single broken line to yin as a form of shorthand. Using yang as south and yin as north, they combined the two lines to represent east and west, creating the Si Xian or four bigrams to represent the four cardinal points of the compass and the four seasons. These four new symbols produced another four, to make the rest of the inter-cardinal compass points and the mid-seasons. By adding a third yin or yang line to each bigram, the eight trigrams or 'ba gua' were created, incorporating the Daoist philosophy of heaven, earth, man. The top line represents the duality of heaven and creation – the yin/yang. The middle line represents heaven and creation coming together to create the four seasons and the cardinal points of the compass. The bottom line represents human beings.

Each trigram has a name, a number, and an opposite, and each trigram is associated with a direction, a feature of the physical world, and a quality that may be attributed to a physical action – heaven balances earth – the firm and the yielding. Wind balances thunder – the gentle and the arousing. Water balances fire – the mysterious and the illuminating. Mountain balances lake – stillness and joyfulness.

Over time, the eight trigrams came to have manifold meanings with correspondences in astrology, geology, geomancy, alchemy, anatomy, the family, and others – all representing certain processes in nature corresponding with their inherent character. They are usually listed with their Chinese name and its translation, season, direction and main attribute.

The term 'bagua' as opposed to 'ba gua', is used to describe the Daoist religious motif that incorporates the eight trigrams arranged in a circle, but most often octagonally, usually around a symbol called a Taijitu, denoting the balance of yin and yang. In Feng Shui, it is centered around a mirror. They can also be arranged as a quadrat for use as a 3x3 magic square.

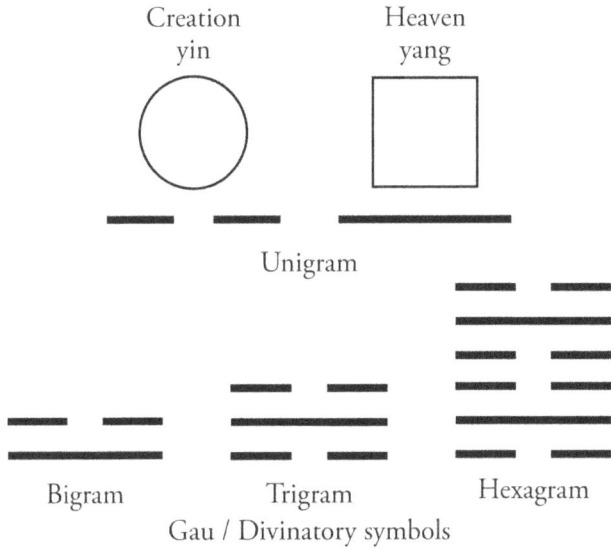

Creation
yin

Heaven
yang

Unigram

Bigram   Trigram   Hexagram

Gau / Divinatory symbols

Winter	Spring	Summer	Autumn	Winter
Old Yang	Young Yang	Old Yang	Young Yin	Old Yin

Si Xian - 6 bigrams

1. Kun   2. Gen   3. Kan   4. Sun   5. Zhen   6. Li   7. Dui   8. Qian

Ba Gua / 8 Trigram

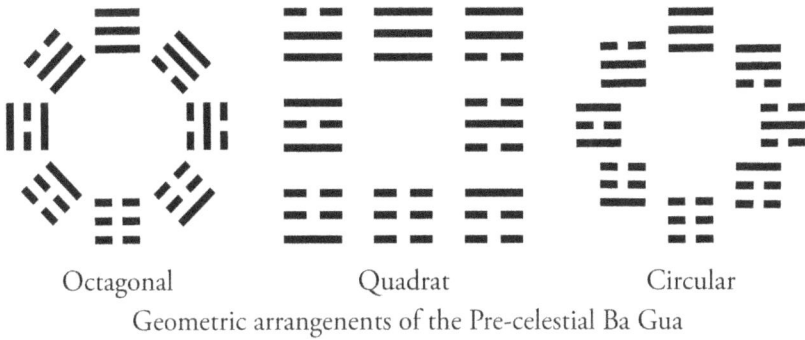

Octagonal   Quadrat   Circular

Geometric arrangenents of the Pre-celestial Ba Gua

The bagua symbolizes a miniature representation of the universe, a template or ruler within Daoist cosmology to track change. For the Chinese, it is seen as a very lucky symbol, representing as it does almost their entire spiritual and philosophical beliefs all in one image.

Originally used as an herbal and agricultural almanac, the trigrams represent the eight sectors of heaven derived from the eight compass points and their relationship to the five elements.

There are two arrangements of the bagua – the Xiantiantu or pre-celestial bagua, also called the Fu Xi sequence, and the Houtaintu or post-celestial or manifest bagua, also called the King Wen sequence – both said to be inspired by two ancient cosmological charts called the Hetu and the Luoshu, respectively. They are differentiated from each other by the numerical assignment and placement of the trigrams within their respective bagua motif.

COMPASS POINTS

One of the most noticeable things about the bagua as a compass is that north is at the bottom, south is at the top, east is on the left and west is on the right. The reason south is at the top and the east is on the left is because this is a map looking outward at the universe, like a sky map, which supposes that you are lying down, facing the sky with your feet in the north, head in the south, with the west to the right, and east to the left. An earth terrain map supposes that you are lying face down, facing the earth, so that east is on the right. However, if east were on the right of the bagua, then it could be interpreted as looking inward into universal energies within one's self. Bagua that have north at the top and south at the bottom are solely used by Westerners for convenience.

NUMBER SEQUENCES

There are different ways of interpreting the trigrams according to the numerical value assigned to them, aside from their inherent sequential number sequence based on the generation of the trigrams from the Wuji.

There are three further number systems: an inherent binary system that also produces a decimal code, plus a 'symbolic number' system. The trigrams can also be counted from the bottom line up (Sheng) or from the top down (Ko), depending on whether we read the trigrams as if we were looking in from the outside of the circle or outwards from the center.

Taijitu
(Wu Ji - centre)

Lang Yi

Yang Yi

Yin Yi

Tai Yang
(strong yang)

Shao Yin
(weak yin)

ShaoYang
(weak yang)

Tai Yin
(strong yin)

1	2	3	4	5	6	7	8
Yang	Yin	Yin	Yang	Yin	Yang	Yang	Yin
Chien / Qian	Tui / Dui	Li	Chen / Zhen	Xun / Sun	Kan	Ken / Gen	Kun
Heaven	Lake	Fire	Thunder	Wind	Water	Mountain	Earth
South	South West	East	North West	South East	West	North East	North
Metal	Fire	Fire	Water	Metal	Wood	Wood	Water
Father	3rd Daughter	2nd Daughter	1st Son	1st Daughter	2nd Son	3rd Son	Mother

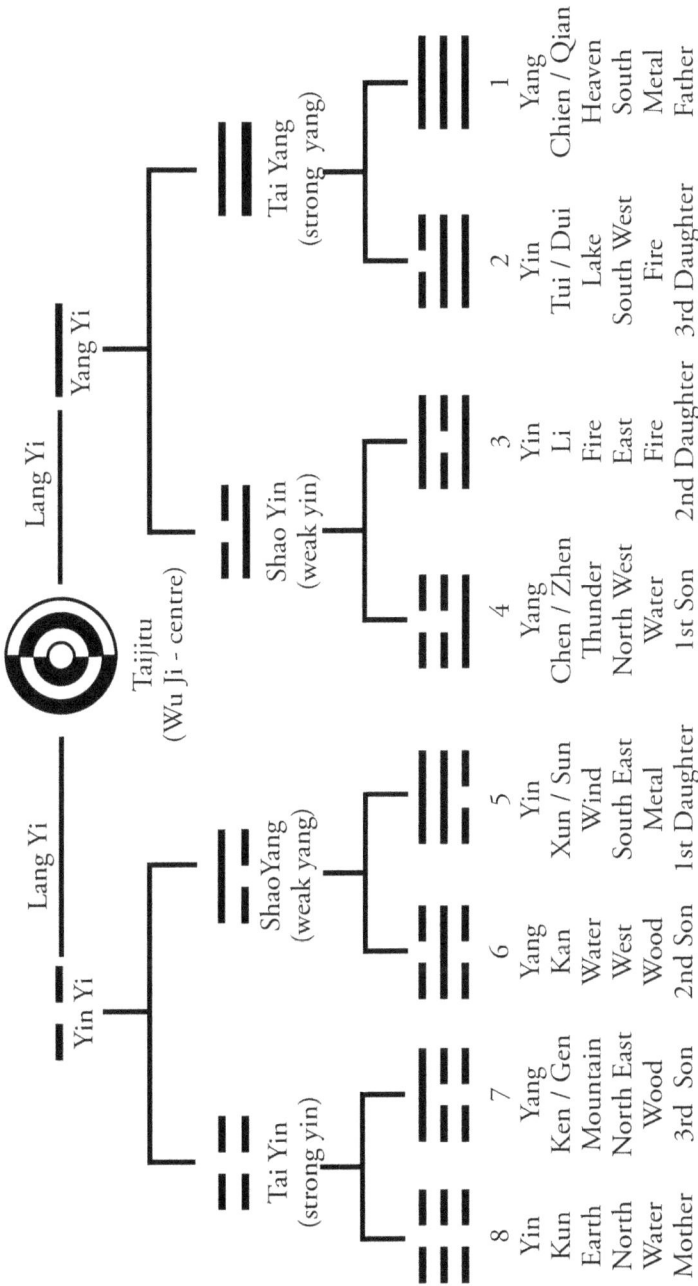

Number, Name, Meaning, Direction, Element, Spouse

Evolution of and names for the eight trigrams of the I-Ching in the Pre-celestial sequence

The eight trigrams are actually numbers written in binary code. Their numbers are in numerical order; as the trigrams rise one above the other, the number gets higher. The ancient Chinese conceived their binary code after realizing that nature itself is a binary phenomenon. All aspects of Chinese civilization were based on harmonious binary opposites.

Interpreting yin as 0 and yang as 1, so the trigram Kun is interpreted as 000 and Qian as 111, makes a binary interpretation of each trigram. This binary order is converted into a decimal order from 0 to 7, with Kun interpreted as 0 and Qian as 7. Both the binary order and decimal order of the trigrams are found in the pre-celestial bagua when read up from the bottom, around on the right, then up again on the left to the top. Both systems give a good approximation of the spiral pattern of light and dark of the Taijitu.

In 1789, German mathematician Gottfried Leibniz published a paper announcing his invention of binary code. 25 years later, a Jesuit missionary working in China sent him illustrations of the I-Ching trigrams and hexagrams. He then produced a second paper, crediting the Chinese with inventing the first binary code.

PANG TONG

In both the Fu Xi and the King Wen sequences, the trigrams are paired according to the Pang Tong, literally meaning 'linked principle', which means the yang lines in the first trigram of a pair turns into a yin line in the second trigram, and vice versa. The two trigrams are then placed opposite each other in the circle.

The pre-celestial bagua is made up of pairs of opposite trigrams that can be arranged in two ways: showing their lower lines closest to the center circle (as the ground upon which we stand), and the highest line positioned where the distant horizon meets the encircling heavens or outwards from the center.

The post-celestial bagua places the most dynamic trigrams in the most dynamic positions. A trigram is considered dynamic if it has a mix of yin and yang lines, especially if the yang lines are below the yin lines, so the yang and yin lines are moving towards each other. The dynamic nature of the trigram is further enhanced if the yang and yin lines are mixed, so as to reverse polarity twice, rather than just once, by going from yang to yin and back to yang, or yin to yang and back to yin. It seems as though the post-celestial sequence was contrived to include these properties – dynamic trigrams in dynamic positions, segregating male from female, bilateral and radial symmetry.

	0x1=1	▬▬	░░░	▬▬	░░░	▬▬	░░░	▬▬	░░░
2+4=6	1x2=2	▬▬	▬▬	░░░	░░░	▬▬	▬▬	░░░	░░░
	1x4=4	▬▬	▬▬	▬▬	▬▬	░░░	░░░	░░░	░░░
	Decimal	0	1	2	3	4	5	6	7

Sheng / top - down method

	1x4=4	▬▬	▬▬	▬▬	▬▬	░░░	░░░	░░░	░░░
1+2=3	1x2=2	▬▬	▬▬	░░░	░░░	▬▬	▬▬	░░░	░░░
	1x1=1	▬▬	░░░	▬▬	░░░	▬▬	░░░	▬▬	░░░
	Decimal	0	1	2	3	4	5	6	7

Ko / bottom - up method

	2x0=1	▬▬	░░░	▬▬	░░░	▬▬	░░░	▬▬	░░░
	2x1=2	▬▬	▬▬	░░░	░░░	▬▬	▬▬	░░░	░░░
	2x2=4	▬▬	▬▬	▬▬	▬▬	░░░	░░░	░░░	░░░
	Decimal	0	1	2	3	4	5	6	7
	Binary	000	001	010	011	100	101	110	111

Decimal to Binary conversion

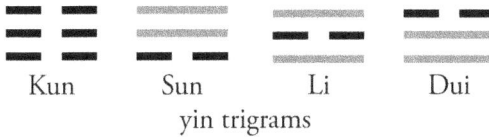

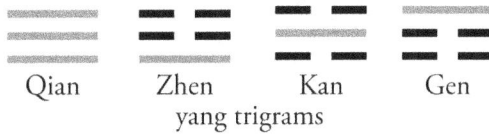

Kun   Sun   Li   Dui

yin trigrams

Qian   Zhen   Kan   Gen

yang trigrams

I-Ching yin yang sequence

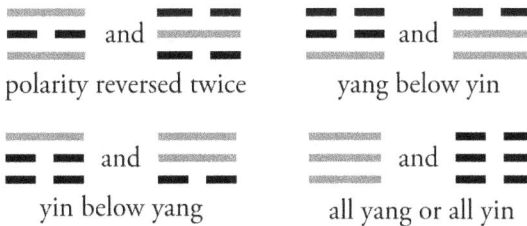

and   polarity reversed twice

and   yang below yin

and   yin below yang

and   all yang or all yin

Dynamic trigram pairings

Pang Tong Sequences

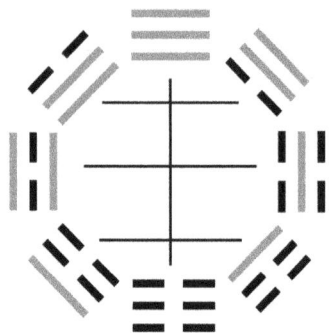

Bilateral symmetry of opposites   Radial symmetry of yin yang

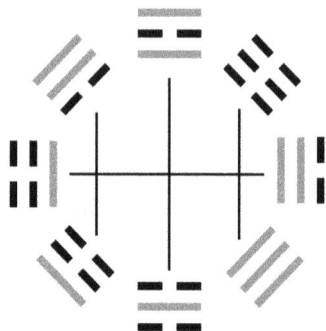

Pre-celestial sequemce

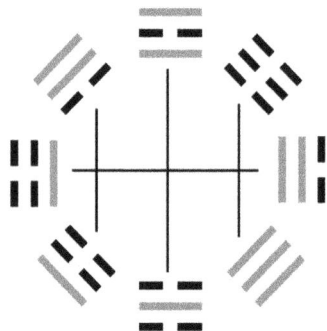

Bilateral symmetry of yin yang   Bilateral symmetry of dynamic pairings

Post-celestial sequence

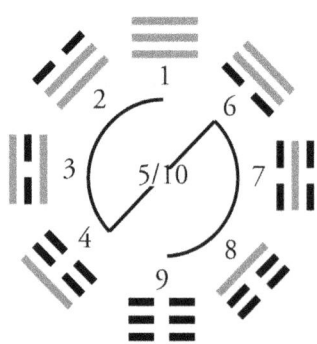

Hetu   Luoshu

Number sequence - Pre-celestial   Number sequence - Post-celestial

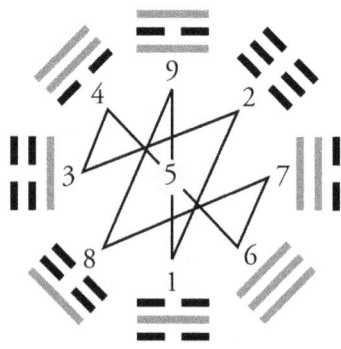

binary quadrat

quadratic taijitu

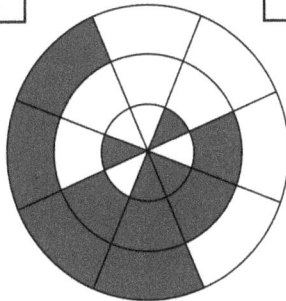

radial taijitu

Yin-Yang and the binary sequence

Binary Matrix

Pre-celestial Radial

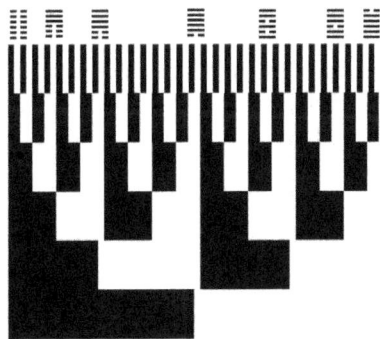

Shou Yong Precelestial

Binary Sequences

Gan Zhi – Stem and Branch

Gan Zhi or the Heavenly Stems and Earthly Branches system was invented in the time of Huangdi, the Yellow Emperor, around 2,600 BCE. It was used for reckoning time, to count and record the years, months, days and hours, based on astronomical data, to compile a lunar calendar. To achieve this, they developed two sets of celestial characters, ideographic signs, called Gan Zhi, meaning Stem and Branch.

These characters are most familiar to Westerners in the form of the 24 Mountains used as a directional guide on the Luopan or Feng Shui compass. They may also be familiar from their use in the Chinese astrological system called Ba Zi or Eight Characters. Daoist priests use them to represent the spirits of destiny in the creation of talismans to bring happiness and good fortune and exorcise evil spirits.

HUA JIAZI – SEXAGENARY CYCLE

Traditionally, Chinese time is divided into cycles – macro-cycles of many hundreds of thousands of years, and micro-cycles of hours, minutes and seconds. The sexagenary cycle of 60 is one such cycle – a constant repetition of a 60-second, 60-minute, 60-day, 60-month or 60-year cycle. Westerners still use the 60-second and 60-minute sexagesimal time measurements, as represented by the numerals 0-9 and their combinations.

In China, each measurement of sexagesimal time is represented by a cycle of 60 character terms. In its earliest use, during the Shang dynasty, the sexagenary cycle was applied only to the counting of days, as measured from one rising of the sun to the next. In time, the sexagenary system was applied to the counting of the years. Theoretically, the first such cycle began in 2,679 BCE, and 78 cycles have passed. The complex system was simplified by the introduction of the 12-year zodiac cycle. It replaced the unfamiliar numerals of the 12 branches with 12 animal signs, whose names best symbolized the hour or year. Each 12-year zodiac cycle corresponds to one of the five elements. When the zodiac cycle is completed five times (5 x 12 = 60), the cycle begins again.

GAN ZHI – STEM AND BRANCH

Used to measure time and direction, Gan Zhi – the 10 Heavenly Stems and the 12 Earthly Branches – are key categories in Chinese metaphysics.

The Gan Zhi duodenary system is used in the traditional Chinese calendar to designate the 12-year cycle in the sexagesimal system, the 12 double hours of the day and, eventually, the months and days. These four factors – years, months, days and hours – are the Si Zhu, or Four Pillars (of Destiny) of Chinese astrology.

甲　乙　丙　丁　戊

1. Jia	2. Yi	3. Bing	4. Ding	5. Wu
Yang	Yin	Yang	Yin	Yang
Wood	Wood	Fire	Fire	Earth

己　庚　辛　壬　癸

6. Ji	7. Geng	8. Xin	9. Ren	10. Gui
Yin	Yang	Yin	Yang	Yin
Earth	Metal	Metal	Water	Water

Shi Tian Gan - 10 Heavenly Stems

子　丑　寅　卯　辰　巳

I	II	III	IV	V	VI
Zi	Chou	Yin	Mao	Chen	Si
Rat	Ox	Tiger	Rabbit	Dragon	Snake
Yang	Yin	Yang	Yin	Yang	Yin
Earth	Earth	Wood	Wood	Wood	Fire

午　未　申　酉　戌　亥

VII	VIII	IX	X	XI	XII
Wu	Wei	Shen	You	Xu	Hai
Horse	Goat	Monkey	Rooster	Dog	Pig
Yang	Yin	Yang	Yin	Yang	Yin
Fire	Fire	Metal	Metal	Metal	Water

Shier Di Zhi - 12 Earthly Branches

Because 10 x 12 does not equal 60, the sexagenary cycle is made by pairing 5 of the stems with 12 of the branches: 5 x 12 = 60. The first year of the cycle is marked by the stem Jia and branch Zi, which, when taken together, make the year Jiazi – and like all the other years, it occurs every 60 years.

SHI TIAN GAN – 10 HEAVENLY STEMS

Except for the sun and the moon, there are five planets in the ancient Chinese solar system. These five extremely bright planets move forward and away from the earth periodically, with different influences and powers. The approaching earth phase is the yang, while the departing one is the yin. Each of the five planets is named after one of the five elements, and both planet and element have two phases – these phases are represented by the 10 Heavenly Stems. This enables the 10 Heavenly Stems to describe the five elements in more detail, each element having a yin stem and a yang stem.

The stems are considered to be associated with the myth and ritual origin of the '10 Suns'. This unit of 10 days, between the re-occurrences of the initial stem, formed a measure of time that would be the closest Chinese equivalent to the Western week. The oldest Chinese documents record the day according to a 10-day system, in which the days are measured using the Shi Tiangan or 10 Heavenly Stems, to identify each of the ten days by name and character. Every day also bears the name of one of the 28 constellations, with its ruling spirit for the day.

SHIER DI ZHI – 12 EARTHLY BRANCHES

Based on different meanings, six are yin and six are yang; the Shier Di Zhi or 12 Earthly Branches are not the names of constellations or any other celestial feature but numerals used to represent a repeated sequence of numbers: 1-12. Since the ecliptic is divided into 12 sections or houses, and there are 12 months in a year, the 12 Earthly Branches became obvious.

They are basically the same as the 12 zodiac animals, except that they are numerals employed to count years, months, days and hours. The 24-hour day was divided into 12 double hours that were represented by the 12 Earthly Branches. Months are reckoned according to the phases of the moon, as there are approximately 12 lunar months in the solar year. The months were also numbered by the branches and, subsequently, the days as well.

甲子　　甲戌　　甲申　　甲午　　甲辰　　甲寅

| 1. Jia-Zi Rat | 11. Jia-Xu Dog | 21. Jia-Shen Monkey | 31. Jia-Wu Horse | 41. Jia-Chen Dragon | 51. Jia-Yin Tiger |

乙丑　　乙亥　　乙酉　　乙未　　乙巳　　乙卯

| 2. Yi-Chou Ox | 12 Yi-Hai Pig | 22. Yi-You Rooster | 32. Yi-Wei Goat | 42. Yi-Si Snake | 52. Yi-Mao Rabbit |

丙寅　　丙子　　丙戌　　丙申　　丙午　　丙辰

| 3. Bing-Yin Tiger | 13. Bing-Zi Rat | 23. Bing-Xu Dog | 33. Bing-Shen Monkey | 43. Bing-Wu Horse | 53. Bing-Chen Dragon |

丁卯　　丁丑　　丁亥　　丁酉　　丁未　　丁巳

| 4. Ding-Mao Rabbit | 14. Ding-Chou Ox | 24. Ding-Hai Pig | 34. Ding-You Rooster | 44. Ding-Wei Goat | 54. Ding-Si Snake |

戊辰　　戊寅　　戊子　　戊戌　　戊申　　戊午

| 5. Wu-Chen Dragon | 15. Wu-Yin Tiger | 25. Wu-Zi Rat | 35. Wu-Xu Dog | 45. Wu-Shen Monkey | 55. Wu-Wu Horse |

己巳　　己卯　　己丑　　己亥　　己酉　　己未

| 6. Ji-Si Snake | 16. Ji-Mao Rabbit | 26. Ji-Chou Ox | 36. Ji-Hai Pig | 46. Ji-You Rooster | 56. Ji-Wei Goat |

庚午　　庚辰　　庚寅　　庚子　　庚戌　　庚申

| 7. Geng-Wu Horse | 17. Geng-Chen Dragon | 27. Geng-Yin Tiger | 37. Geng-Zi Rat | 47. Geng-Xu Dog | 57. Geng-Shen Monkey |

辛未　　辛巳　　辛卯　　辛丑　　辛亥　　辛酉

| 8. Xin-Wei Goat | 18. Xin-Si Snake | 28. Xin-Mao Rabbit | 38. Xin-Chou Ox | 48. Xin-Hai Pig | 58. Xin-You Rooster |

壬申　　壬午　　壬辰　　壬寅　　壬子　　壬戌

| 9. Ren-Shen Monkey | 19. Ren-Wu Horse | 29. Ren-Chen Dragon | 39. Ren-Yin Tiger | 49. Ren-Zi Rat | 59. Ren-Xu Dog |

癸酉　　癸未　　癸巳　　癸卯　　癸丑　　癸亥

| 10. Gui-You Rooster | 20. Gui-Wei Goat | 30. Gui-Si Snake | 40. Gui-Mao Rabbit | 50. Gui-Chou Ox | 60. Gui-Hai Pig |

Gan Zhi - Stem and Branch (sexagesimal cycle, 5 x 12 = 60)

Wu Shu – Five Arts

Guiding the Chinese people throughout the ages, the Wu Shu or Five Arts are a fundamental concept in Chinese metaphysics, referring to the five fields of study that form an essential foundation for the philosophical study of the universe and its laws. Derived from the I-Ching, the Five Arts cover ancient Chinese discussions surrounding time, space and the universe, channelling the concepts and reasonings of yin and yang.

As such, they are rooted in Daoist principles, with early Daoism contributing to their development. They are used to teach the Dao or enlightenment, and are quite difficult to master, so most practitioners only follow certain disciplines and may only do one or two of the disciplines within each art.

The Five Arts of the Wu Shu are Yi – medicine, Xiang – appearance, Ming – life, Pu – prediction, and Shan – mountain. The reason there are five arts is because only four would fit into the natal chart of a person, which leaves luck as the deciding factor.

The Wu Shu are considered the biggest gift from the Chinese ancestors to all human beings on earth. Yet Westernized Chinese are looking down upon ancient Chinese wisdom, the thoughts and teachings of their own ancestors, as superstition. Many Westerners are now developing a keen interest to learn and understand Chinese metaphysics, but most of the books are written in the Chinese language, and they are unable to learn the basics.

YI – MEDICINE

Yi is the art of healing and includes all forms of healing, both physical and mental, using Traditional Chinese Medicine (TCM) and the art of internal alchemy and cultivating the self. This includes medical prescription, soul healing, acupuncture, herbology and the Elixir of Life.

XIANG – APPEARANCE (PHYSIOGNOMY)

Xiang is the Chinese study of a person's physical appearance, which refers to the study of forms, meaning the study of the good or bad of a form. Well-known examples are palmistry, face-reading and mole-reading to infer character and personality traits. The study of Chinese names of a person also belongs to this group. The geomancy of Feng Shui, the study of the environment for the living and dead, also belongs to the study of appearance.

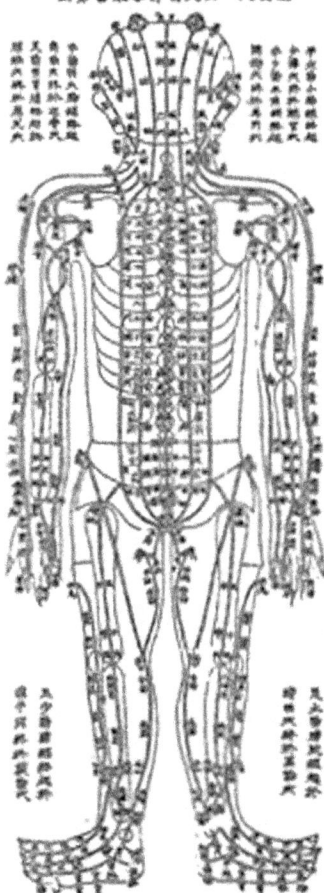
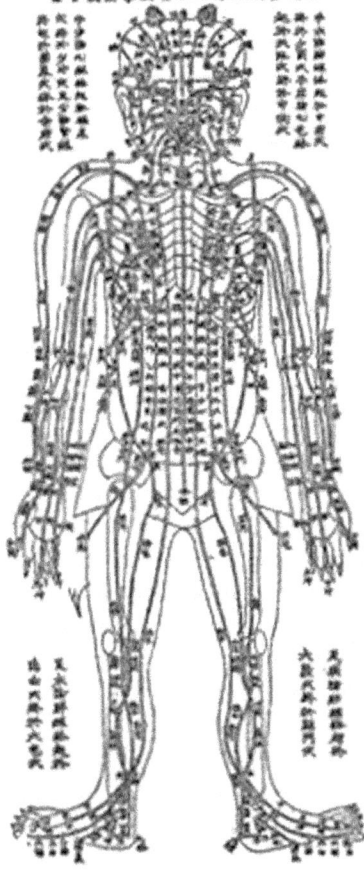

Yi - Medicine - illustrated acupuncture text

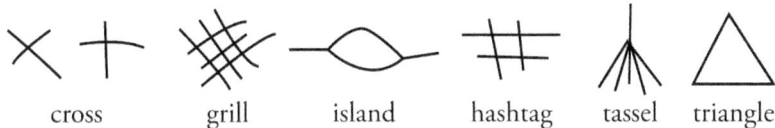

| cross | grill | island | hashtag | tassel | triangle |

Xiang - Appearence - some marks found on the palm of the hand

MING – LIFE (DESTINY/FATE/ASTROLOGY)

Ming is the Chinese art of destiny or fate. It focuses on understanding one's destiny, life or path and the influences that shape it, often through astrology, divination and the study of individual character.

The study of Ming includes several different methods of assessment using astrological systems such as Purple Star and Feng Shui, astrological systems including 8 Characters, Four Pillars and Flying Star.

PU – PREDICTION (DIVINATION)

This form of mysticism uses techniques like cosmic boards for divination, as well as other methods to gain insight into the future or understanding of hidden patterns.

The I-Ching is the most popular divination study. Others include Du Lui Ren, Tai Yi Shen Shu and Qi Mon Dun Jia – collectively known as the 3 Styles or the Shou Shi. They rely on numerical analysis to reveal one's past and future, to predict the outcome of incidents and events, divined from cosmic boards.

SHAN – MOUNTAIN (ALCHEMY OF IMMORTALS)

This cryptic-sounding subject is concerned with knowledge and skills that are learned and trained on the mountain. In ancient times, a person needed to go up a mountain to receive such knowledge through meditation and cultivation.

Shan is concerned with understanding the laws of the cosmos and nature, and the relationship between them. Studies that fall under this art include diet, physical health, martial arts, meditation and self-healing, which covers the thoughts and teachings of ancient Chinese sages. Qigong and Tai Chi, and the arts of Daoist sorcery, ritual, talismans and calligraphy belong to Mountain.

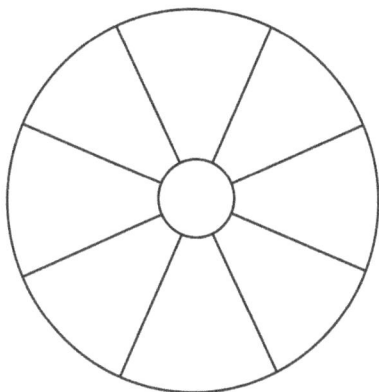

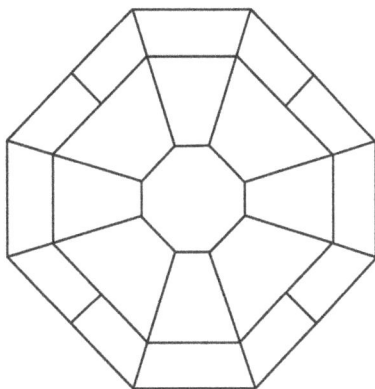

Feng Shui astrological cosmic boards (Shi)
Ming - Destiny / Astrology

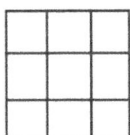

x3 square

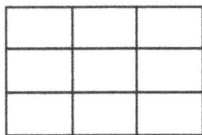

x3 horizontal rectangle

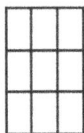

x3 vertical rectangle

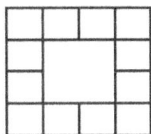

x12 horizontal rectangle
Shi - Cosmic boards
Pu / Divination

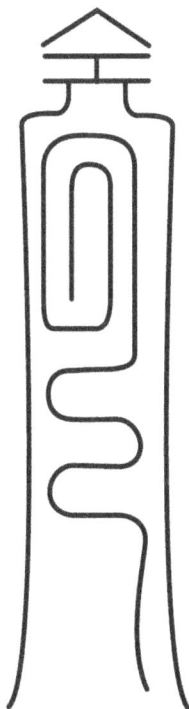

Fulu - Talismanic calligraphy
Shan / Mountain

Yi – Medicine

Yi is the art of healing and includes all forms of Traditional Chinese Medicine (TCM), including moxibustion, medical prescription and soul healing. The most common forms of TCM in the West are acupuncture, massage and herbal remedy.

In TCM, the body receives chi from the cosmos, and acupuncture involves releasing and connecting chi at 12 specific points throughout the body using tiny needles. Through the centuries, over 350 points have been identified on these meridians. Massage or Tui Na, literally meaning 'pushing and grasping', addresses the same acupuncture points using manual stimulation.

The nature and properties of plants were analyzed and given a classification, such as hot or cold, yin or yang, to create medicines, using different mixing and grinding techniques, accompanied by magic ritual, spellcasting, chanting and prayers.

THREE TREASURES

Chi – energy, Jing – essence, and Shen – spirit are referred to as the Three Treasures. Together, they form the foundation for understanding the human body and the healing practice of TCM, such as acupuncture, massage and herbology. Chi flows through the Jing Luo or meridians, which correspond to particular parts of the body. Jing is responsible for both the essential immaterial (soul) and essential physical (body) of a person. Shen is the yang portion of chi, responsible for regulating emotions. They also play a key role in the Nei Dan process of internal alchemy called the Circulation of Light.

FIVE FUNCTIONAL ENTITIES

According to TCM, the human body is a collective of interrelated yin-yang systems. When the yin-yang systems are in harmony, the body is healthy; where there is disharmony, there is illness. There are three major yin-yang systems that are crucial to health, known as the Five Functional Entities – they are responsible for performing five cardinal functions, which protect and maintain health within the body. They are actuation, warming, defence, containment and transformation.

The three major yin-yang systems are as follows:

1. The five vital or fundamental substances are chi/life force, Xue/blood, Jinye/bodily fluids, Jing/essence, and Shen/spirit.
2. Zang Fu are two sets of bodily organs that follow the Wu Xing cycles.
3. Jing Luo or meridians, although they are nonphysical, are the channels that connect the Zang Fu organs and regulate the flow of the fundamental substances throughout the body.

精

Jing - essence

氣

Chi - energy

神

Shen - spirit

3 Treasures

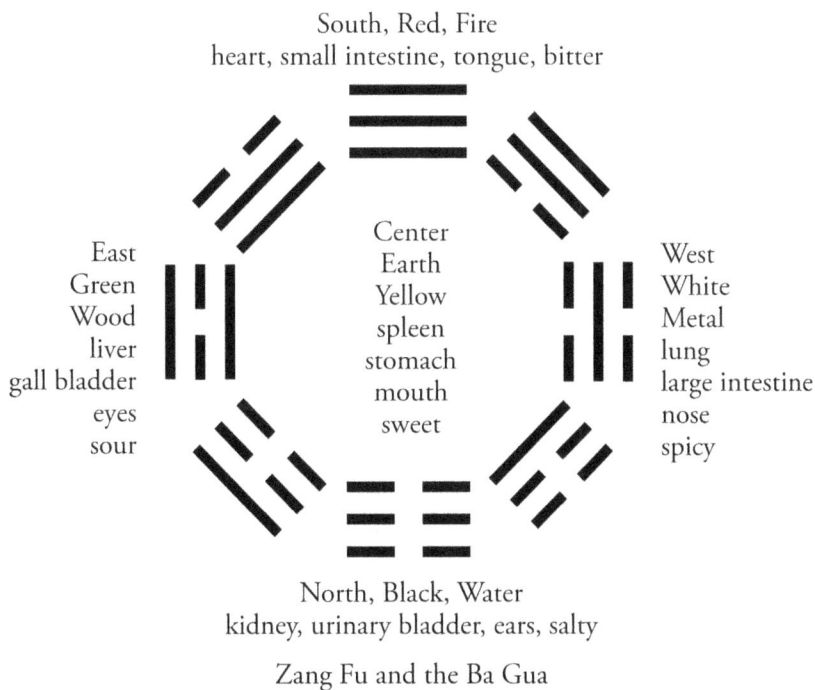

South, Red, Fire
heart, small intestine, tongue, bitter

East
Green
Wood
liver
gall bladder
eyes
sour

Center
Earth
Yellow
spleen
stomach
mouth
sweet

West
White
Metal
lung
large intestine
nose
spicy

North, Black, Water
kidney, urinary bladder, ears, salty

Zang Fu and the Ba Gua

ZANG FU ORGANS

Zang Fu is the name given to a collection of internal organs that produce and regulate chi within the body. They do not represent the anatomical structures but are seen as interconnected functions that explain how chi is produced in the body. There are 11 organs in all. The five Zang or yin organs are: heart, spleen, lung, kidney and liver. Their primary function is to produce and store energy (chi), blood, bodily fluids, essence (Jing) and spirit (Shen). The six Fu organs are yang: stomach, small intestine, large intestine, urinary bladder, gall bladder and sonjian (three cavities for the organs within the body's trunk). Zang Fu organs have a yin-yang pair and follow a Wu Xing cycle – meaning that each Zang Fu pair corresponds to one of the five elements, and they interact in a cyclical function with each other.

The internal organs of the body are associated with yin or yang and an element, and also the energy of a planet and a direction. The five elements are aspects of chi that flow between acupuncture points throughout the body via meridians or channels of energy flow. Each element has correspondences, associations with the seasons, body organs, colours, senses and emotions. These concepts inform the understanding of the body and its relationship to nature and the world in the world of traditional Chinese medicine. On an individual level, they help us to understand who we are, what illnesses we may be prone to and how to stay healthy.

MERIDIANS

Beginning in the chest, energy or chi is said to flow through the body in its yin and yang forms through pathways called meridians. This connects the chi to the yin and yang meridians in the hands and feet before returning to the chest. There are 20 meridians in all, the most important being the 12 regular meridians that connect to the internal organs and other parts of the body.

The 12 meridians on one side of the body are mirrored on the other side of the body. The 6 yin meridians are located in the inner region of the arms, legs, chest and torso. The 6 yang meridians are located on the outer region of the arms, legs, head and torso. The remaining 8 meridians store chi and blood for the 12 regular meridians, circulate a person's Jing 'essence' and defensive chi, and provide further connections between the 12 regular meridians. Among the 8 meridians are the Governing vessel 'Du Mou' and the Conception vessel 'Ren Mei', which are considered important because they contain certain points that are not on the 12 regular meridians.

YANG
Disease - acute, virulent, advancing, hasty, powerful, flourishing, patient feels hot skin hot to touch, high tempreture, feverish

Body - surface, back, spine, chi energy, clear body fluids

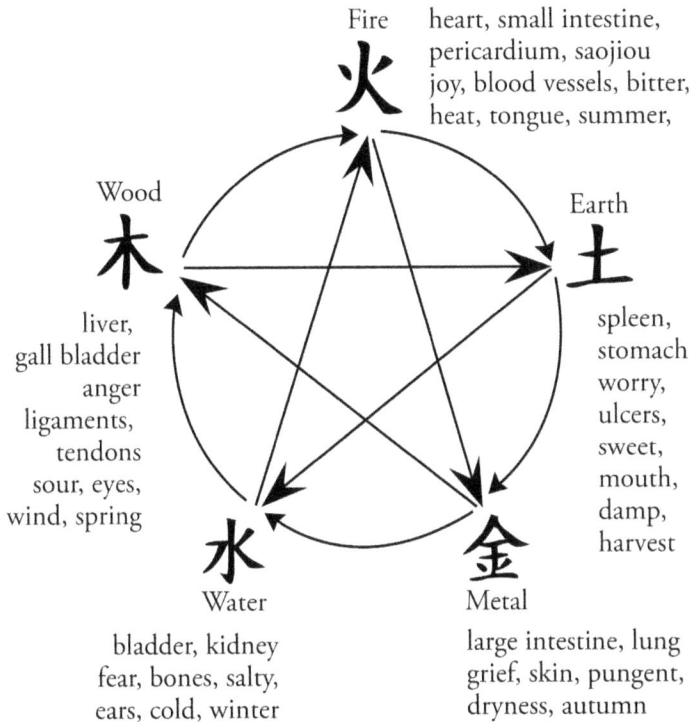

Fire   heart, small intestine,
火   pericardium, saojiou
        joy, blood vessels, bitter,
        heat, tongue, summer,

Wood   Earth
木   土

liver,   spleen,
gall bladder   stomach
anger   worry,
ligaments,   ulcers,
tendons   sweet,
sour, eyes,   mouth,
wind, spring   damp,
                        harvest

水   金

Water   Metal

bladder, kidney   large intestine, lung
fear, bones, salty,   grief, skin, pungent,
ears, cold, winter   dryness, autumn

YIN
Disease - chronic, non-activity, moist, retiring, lingering, weak, decaying, patient feels cold, skin cold to tuch, low tempreture, shivering

Body - interior, abdomen, chest, blood, cloudy body fluids

Zang Fu and the Wu Xing cycles

Nei Dan – Internal Alchemy

'Dan', meaning 'crucible' or 'elixir', is the Chinese word for what Westerners call alchemy. Chinese alchemy is based on doctrinal principles concerning the relation between the Dao and the Wan Wu or 10,000 things. Its teachings and practices focus on the idea of an elixir, or simply medicine, usually called the 'Golden Elixir of Life' or the 'Pill of Immortality'.

The first alchemists were seeking an elixir, which could be used to turn cheap metal into gold. This could be taken literally or be perceived as man being the base metal and his transformation through the internal alchemical process to become gold or purified and at one with the Dao.

Wai Dan, meaning 'external elixir', involves adding something to the body from outside, like diet and the use of minerals and herbs to promote long life. It is based on the ingestion of the compound of elixirs through the physical heating of natural substances in a crucible. Its texts consist of recipes, lists of ingredients, methods and passages concerned with the cosmological associations of minerals, metals, instruments and operations.

Thought to have developed from external alchemy, Nei Dan or 'internal elixir' doesn't involve external physical compounds but borrows a significant part of its vocabulary and imagery from Wai Dan. It aims to produce the elixir within the alchemist's person, body/spirit, according to two main models of doctrine and practice. First, by causing the primary components of the cosmos and the human body to revert to their original condition. Second, by purifying the mind of defilements and passion in order to 'see one's nature'.

FURNACE OF THE GOLDEN ELIXIR

In Daoist alchemy, external alchemy uses a physical crucible and ingredients, while in internal alchemy, the crucible, medicine or ingredients are symbols, and the creation of the elixir is a metaphysical process.

The Furnace of the Golden Elixir is described by Lao Tze in the I-Ching as "the process of internal alchemy that opens the gate to spiritual immortality." It is a metaphor for the order of practical spiritual work, symbolizing the method of creating the Golden Elixir, the Pill of Immortality, or true consciousness.

The aim is to reach transcendence and immortality through the firing process or illumination. The firing process is a matter of dissolving the lower self (yin – stripped away) and completing the higher self (celestial yang – pure). By retaining the yin and yang within, the firing is sufficient.

日丹 外丹 內丹

archaic	modern	Wai dan	Nei dan
	crucible	external alchemy	internal alchemy

Dan - crucible / elixir / alchemy

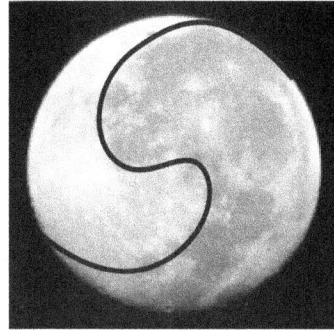

Taijitu spiral design on the face of the moon

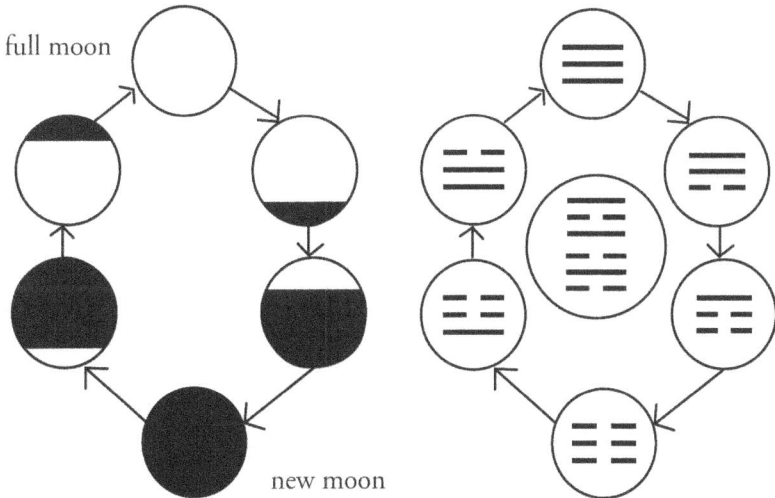

full moon

new moon

Furnace of the Golden Elixir
Lunar phases as represented by the trigrams of the I-Ching

MOON CYCLES

The furnace is a Daoist diagram in which six trigrams are arranged in a circle to form the furnace. The furnace shows how the trigrams of the I-Ching can be used to represent the yin and yang of the light of the moon as it passes through its phases. Beginning at the bottom with the new moon, the phases can be followed in a clockwise direction from right to left. The inner development of the elixir and the timing of its firing are no different from the ebbing and flowing of the lunar phases.

The new moon is mostly yin, dark and invisible, so its trigram is Kun, made up of three yin lines. Circling upwards to the left, the light of the waxing crescent moon is symbolized by the bottom yang/light of the trigram Zhen.

Dui, the trigram of bottom and middle yang lines and top yin line, represents the waxing gibbous moon phase. At the top are the three yang/light lines of Qian, as the full moon keeps the darkness of the night at bay.

As the moon wanes, the darkness creeps in, as shown in the last line of Xian in the waning gibbous phase. The waning crescent that is two-thirds dark is represented by the two lower yin lines of the trigram Gen. Coming full circle, we arrive back at Kun, the new moon. The remaining six trigrams remain associated with the 30-day moon cycle according to the Cantong Qi.

SIX ELEMENTAL TRIGRAMS

"The moon borrows light from the sun. The waxing moon represents the Yang Light of the Mind of Dao, which is conscious awareness, growing until it is full." The 2nd-century text called 'Cantong Qi – Triple Unity' speaks about the cycles of the sun and the moon representing the firing process of the furnace and matches them with the trigrams.

The 30-day lunar month is divided into six parts of five days, making six phases of the moon that represent the inner development of the elixir. The phases are represented by the six elemental trigrams that form the furnace used to illustrate the 'firing times' of the elixir.

Of the eight trigrams, two trigrams, Kun/water and Li/fire, symbolize the medicine or ingredients of the elixir – they are what are being fired and are not part of the firing times. The other six trigrams remain associated with the 30-day moon cycle according to the Cantong Qi.

The other six are the elemental trigrams, Qian, Kun, Zhen, Sun, Dui, Gen, and describe the stages of waxing and waning of the moon. They symbolize the firing times of the elixir within the body. Each of the six trigrams is associated with a yang line of the Qian hexagram, representing the gradual change of yin into yang; each yang line is also represented by the number nine and a dragon.

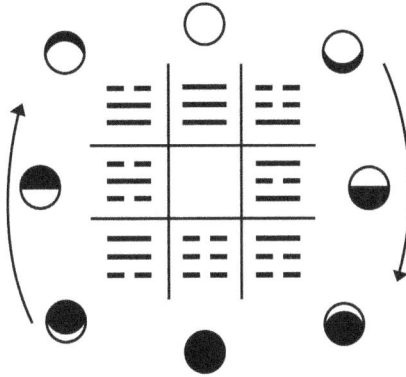

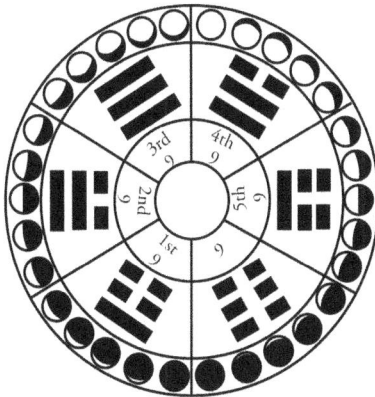

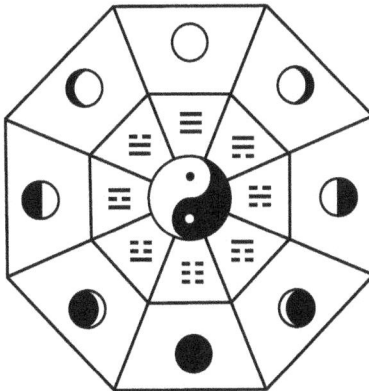

Pre-celestial arrangement and corresponding lunar phases

The trigrams Qian or heaven, and Kun or earth, are the father and mother trigrams; the remaining trigrams are their sons and daughters. In turn, they are matched with the 30-day moon cycle to symbolize the advancement of yang. This is because the elixir is the most precious treasure of the purest yang, and Qian or heaven is the trigram of the purest yang.

CIRCULATION OF LIGHT

In an ancient text called 'The Golden Flower' there is an account of a technique called the 'Circulation of Light' and its relationship with the hexagrams of the I-Ching. It is explained as depending entirely on the backward-flowing movement of chi, so that thoughts are gathered together.

The account tells a profound story of how light circulates together with the chi, where, from the bottom, they progress up the back of the body to the top of the head before their descent down the front, making a full circular orbit.

Hexagram 24, Fu/Return, represents the waxing of the moon, reaching the full moon at hexagram 1, Qian/the Creative Heaven, while hexagram 44, Gou/Coming to Meet, represents the first waning phase of the moon and ends with hexagram 42, Kun/Receptive Earth – and the circulation continues to complete a full circle or orbit.

Therefore, the Circulation of Light crystalizes all the energies of heaven and earth and of light and dark, represented respectively by Qian and Kun and the lines of the 12 Sovereign Hexagrams.

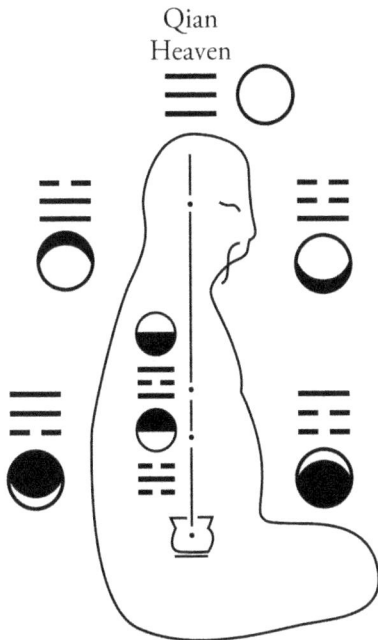

Qian
Heaven

Kun
Earth

Golden Elixir of Life
Pill of Immortality
(lunar)

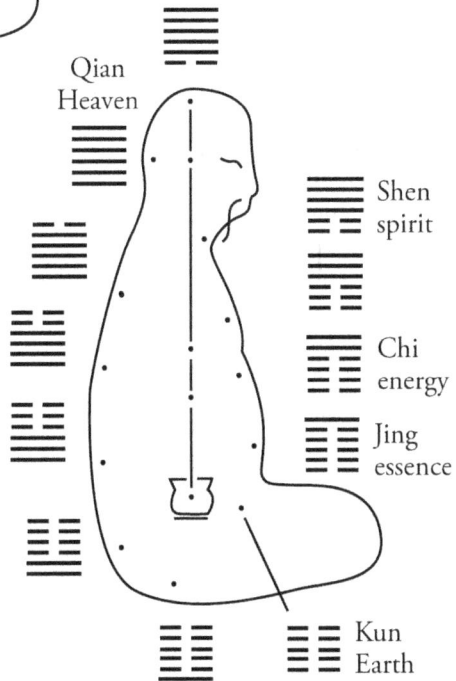

Qian
Heaven

Shen
spirit

Chi
energy

Jing
essence

Kun
Earth

Circulation of Light (solar)

Xiang – Appearance

Xiang is the study of physiognomy – the study of form, or the study of the good or bad of a form. Well-known examples are palmistry, face-reading and mole-reading. Feng Shui also belongs to the study of forms, as does the study of names of a person.

BA GUA SHOU XIANG – EIGHT TRIGRAMS PALMISTRY

One of the principal methods of Daoist palmistry or chiromancy involves the examination of the hands for trigram patterns formed by the lines themselves and utilizing the I-Ching for their interpretation. In addition, since Chinese script is more pictographic than alphabetic script, line formations that form themselves into clear and distinct Chinese characters could easily be read off from the hand. Later traditions of hand-reading made correlations with acupuncture points and meridians, and the five elements were utilized to classify hand shapes and other features.

The trigrams of the I-Ching were further incorporated into the system of hand analysis by allocating each one of the trigrams to specific areas of the hand, known as 'palaces' – much in the manner in which European chiromancers allocated astrological planets to the mounts of the hand. Each area of the palm was also accorded a connection with each of the seasons. In terms of Chinese medical palmistry, the eight trigrams system is based on readings of the colour and lustre and the sinking and bulging of each location, as well as any prominent blue veins appearing on the surface. Signs of both good and bad health are diagnosed via the ruling trigram of that area.

Bagua Shou Xiang is a system of Chinese palmistry, a formulaic imposition of the trigrams of the I-Ching onto the hand. The appearance of lines and markings are interpreted according to the post-celestial arrangement of the eight trigrams.

To help the reading, the bagua can be superimposed onto the palm or the back of the hand. In addition to providing confirmation of other signs on the hand, markings also offer clues to good and bad luck in different dimensions of one's life.

This is indicated by the governing trigram in different parts of the hand. The center square of the bagua is called the Ming Tang or Courtyard and indicates the overall well-being of the individual. It is diametrically opposed to the five elements system, meaning that they cannot be used at the same time.

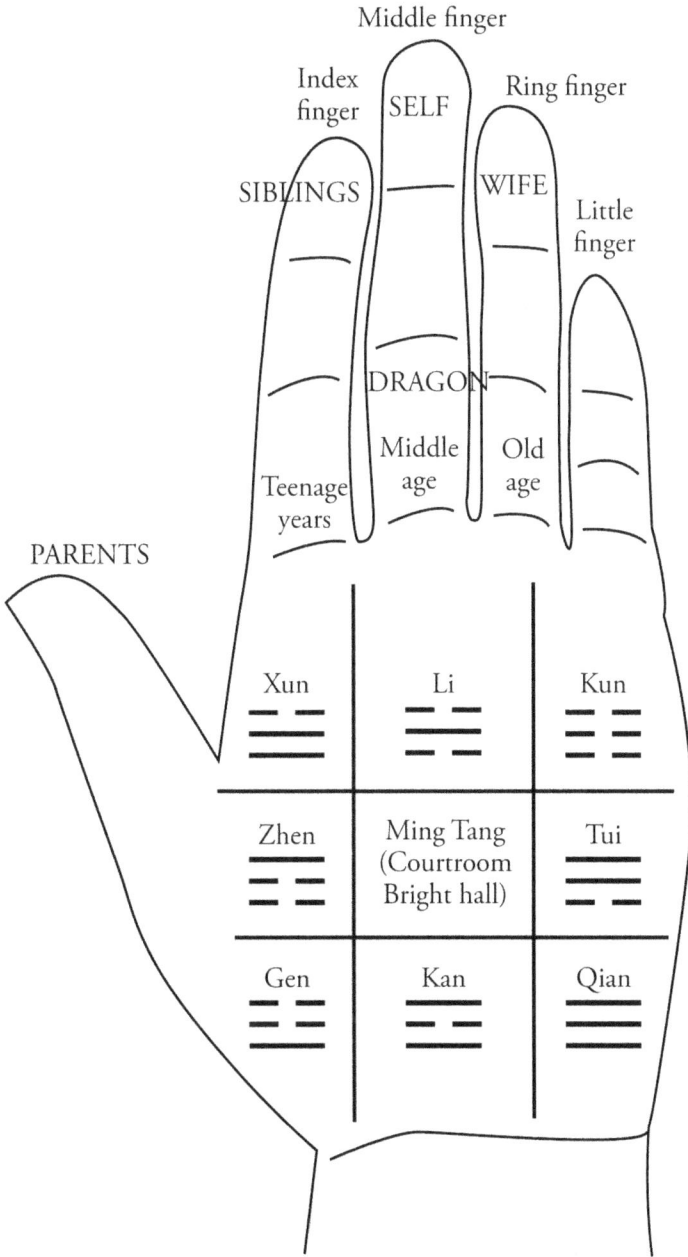

Post-celestial bagau used in palmistry

MIAN XIANG – FACE-READING

Mian Xiang or face-reading first appeared in the 8th century BCE, and by around 220 BCE, it had become a part of life for Chinese people. The method is used to study the personality and the past and future prospects of a particular person.

The art of face-reading is popular in Chinese medical practices as well. Chinese people believe that the face of a person represents his or her personality, health and fortune. They also believe that knowing this will help us live in peace with yin and yang and the five elements.

Based on shapes and colours, there are many methods in face-reading. 12 houses, 108 spirits, 3 quarters and 8 trigrams are just a few. Hexagrams are used to interpret facial expressions or emotional displays – open, joyful, sad, quiet – on a human face.

The hexagram is divided into three sets of two lines to help divide the human face into three constituent parts. The top two lines of the hexagram are assigned to the eyebrows and probability. The middle two lines are assigned to the eyes and opportunity. The bottom two lines are assigned to the mouth and event. Four hexagrams are also assigned to the facial expressions of intent.

MOLE-READING

The location of moles is greatly related to people's fortune. Generally, hidden moles, such as in the eyebrows, beard, or hair, are considered auspicious, whereas the obvious moles are considered inauspicious. The round and raised moles with good brightness in pure red or dark black are auspicious. Moles of any other colour are inauspicious.

Fire   Water   Earth   Gold   Wood
Face shapes and the elements

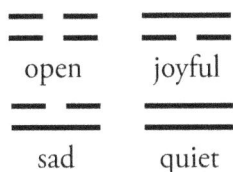

open   joyful

sad   quiet

Expressions
Bigram correspondences

eyebrows ⚊⚊) probability

eyes ⚊⚊) opportunity

mouth ⚊⚊) event

Division of hexagram for the
human face and correspondences

obligatory opportunity
is conceivable
probability of real
event

planned opportunity
is conceivable
probability of
feasible event

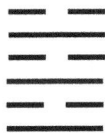

missed opportunity
is inconceivable
probality of
impratcical event

implict opportunity
is inconceivable
probability of unreal
event

Facial expression and social relationships

Feng Shui – Wind Water

Thought by some to be an adapted form of Vastu Shastra or Vedic geomancy, the traditional Chinese concept of Feng Shui, meaning 'wind-water', is the study of the form of the environment. It is concerned with the observation of appearances through formulae and calculation, linking the destiny of man to his environment, aiming to ensure that people live in harmony with their surroundings.

As a pseudoscience, it is mainly concerned with the study of yin and yang housing, or Yin Feng Shui for burial and Yang Feng Shui for the living environment. The Yin House or grave centers on predicting the fortune and decline of a deceased family. The Yang House or residence centers on predicting the fortune and decline of the living.

Originating from ancient Chinese astrology, some current techniques can be traced back to prehistory, with others added later. This long history begins with the Neolithic cultures of Yangshao and Hongshan over 3,500 years ago, when it was first used for the siting of graves, as it was most important to give the graves of ancestors a good place that would be unaffected by typhoons (wind) and floods (water).

In the Zhou dynasty (1122–770 BCE), astronomical correlations and Feng Shui principles were used to calculate the building of capital cities through the position of structures around the city. The structure of graves and dwellings seems to have followed the same rules. Beginning with palatial structures, all capital cities in China followed the rules of Feng Shui for design and layout.

The purpose of Feng Shui as the 'art of placement' is to enable the flow of beneficial chi or energy to the maximum in order to disperse, disrupt or remove obstructions to the free flow of chi. Both wind and water convey a sense of invisible energy, and the Great Wall of China was built with these principles in mind; the wall is curved to keep the chi moving.

Feng Shui discusses architecture in terms of 'invisible forces/chi' that bind the universe, the earth and humans together. As practiced today, the goal of Feng Shui is to situate the human-built environment on spots with good chi; the 'perfect spot' is a location and an axis of time.

Depending on the particular style of Feng Shui being used, an auspicious site could be obtained by reference to a local feature, such as a body of water, a star or a direction. The magnetic compass was specifically invented for use with Feng Shui, but until its invention, it relied on astrology to find connections between humans and the universe.

Feng (fung) - Wind. Shui (schway) - Water
Standard and Cursive scripts

Xiantiantu / Pre-celestial Ba Gua
Daoist Motif

Houtiantu / Post-celestial Ba Gua
Feng Shui Mirror

Yinyangyutu - Taijitu surrounded by the Ba Gua

The balanced blend of the five elements in Feng Shui creates a harmonious environment. These elements are allocated to the different shapes of the landscape, or rooms in a building, and to different objects in order to facilitate the flow of chi.

Chi is a moveable positive or negative life force. Polarity is expressed by yin and yang. The five elements are the forces essential to human life, the force fields of Feng Shui.

YUN AND SHA – POSITIVE AND NEGATIVE CHI

Feng Shui is about controlling the flow of Yun or positive chi, and Sha or negative chi, around and throughout a building. Mirrors are the most common means by which Yun Chi is enhanced and Sha Chi is deflected.

A bagua mirror consists of the eight trigrams surrounding either a concave, convex or flat mirror. Convex mirrors should be positioned in areas where the flow of chi comes to a dead end. Concave mirrors, intended to enhance the flow of chi, should be placed at an angle so that the path of chi is directed further along the way. Mirrors meant to counter Sha should reflect it straight back out of the house. Flat mirrors balance chi.

Sound is another way of deflecting Sha – wind chimes, running water or any melodic, pleasing sounds are all considered effective ways to deflect Sha. The presence of anything living – birds, dogs, cats and plants – helps to ward off Sha. Sha travels in straight lines, so straight objects such as fishing rods, armrests of chairs and bamboo poles can be positioned in a way to repel Sha.

Anything that moves in a breeze, such as flags, banners, mobiles and wind chimes, activates and disperses lingering Sha. The smoke from burning incense and gently flowing water also disperses Sha. Objects that are beautiful and enhance a sense of stillness and serenity, such as statues of Buddha, Kwan Yin (goddess of compassion and mercy), the Madonna, or even a piece of driftwood or a particular stone, can reverse intrusive Sha.

FENG SHUI TOOLS

Practitioners of the various Eastern and Western schools of Feng Shui employ a number of tools or instruments to chart and follow the movement of chi through space, environment, buildings and the human body. To help them do this, they use two versions of the bagua, the related Hetu and Luoshu charts, lunar and solar calendars, the Luopan or Feng Shui compass, and cosmic boards for astrology and divination.

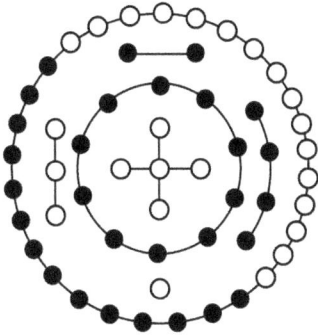

Hetu - celestial/stellar arrangement

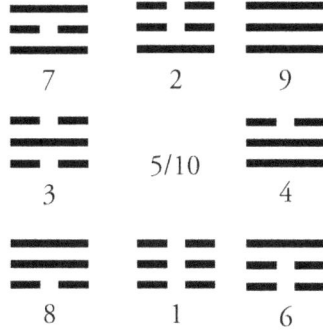

Hetu - trigram arrangement

Luoshu - ancient rendition

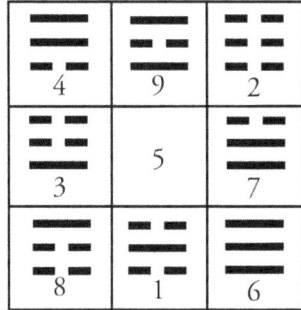

Luoshu Square - Nine Halls

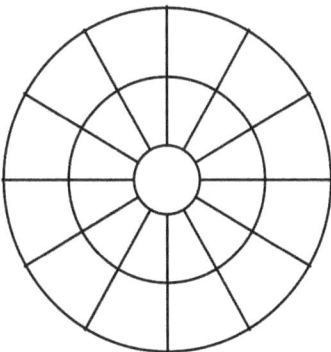

Liuren - Cosmic Board

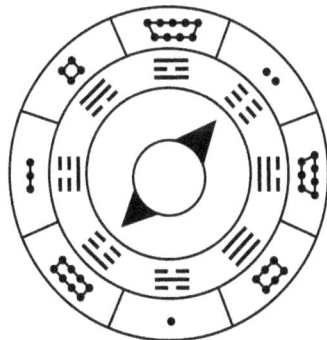

Luopan - Feng Shui compass

Feng Shui Tools

Pa Kua / Ba Gua – Eight Trigrams

Pronounced 'pah kow' (standard) or 'bah gwah' (pinyin), both terms translate into English as 'eight divinatory symbols'; the combined term 'bagua' is used to describe the Daoist religious motif that incorporates the eight trigrams of the I-Ching arranged octagonally, usually around the Taijitu symbol, denoting the balance of yin and yang or a mirror in Feng Shui.

Said to have been invented by legendary sage king Fu Xi (circa 2600 BCE), the bagua is linked to the compass points, the directions, the five elements, the seasons, animals, organs, family members and the Eight Immortals (Xian).

The first mention of the bagua in Feng Shui precedes its mention in the I-Ching. It is closely associated with the astral charts known as the Hetu and Luoshu, in which the arrangement of trigrams is linked by astronomical events of the 6th millennium BCE, and with the Turtle calendar from the time of Emperor Yao, dating to 2300 BCE.

FU XI AND THE BA GUA

Chinese myth recalls that the sage emperor Fu Xi created the 'ba gua' through observation of the world as seen in the pattern of markings on the back of a mythical Dragon Horse that emerged from the Yellow River. These eight markings became the trigrams of the I-Ching, which symbolize the natural world as heaven, earth, fire, water, lake, mountain, wind and thunder.

Fu Xi laid the trigrams out as an eight-sided map that became the bagua motif, similar to the shape of a turtle shell. Each side of the eight-sided map corresponds to the compass directions, the seasons, and the eight areas of life experience: career and journey, knowledge and self-awareness, helpful people and travel, family and health, children and creativity, wealth and prosperity, fame and reputation, and relationships and marriage.

As a diagram, the bagua is a miniature representation of the universe. In ancient China, map-makers placed north at the bottom and south at the top, east on the right and west on the left, because this is a map looking outward at the universe, which supposes that you are lying down, facing the sky with your feet in the north, head in the south, west to the left, and east to the right.

An earth terrain map supposes that you are lying face down, facing the earth, so that east is on the left. However, if east were on the left of the bagua, it could be interpreted as looking inward into universal energies within one's self. Those bagua that have north at the top and south at the bottom are solely used by Westerners for convenience.

Each of the trigrams has a specific meaning, ranging from Qian, which consists of three unbroken lines symbolizing Yang, heaven and father, to Kun, with three broken lines symbolizing Yin, earth and mother. The eight trigrams arranged in the bagua motif are, conceptually, a template or ruler within Daoist cosmology to track change.

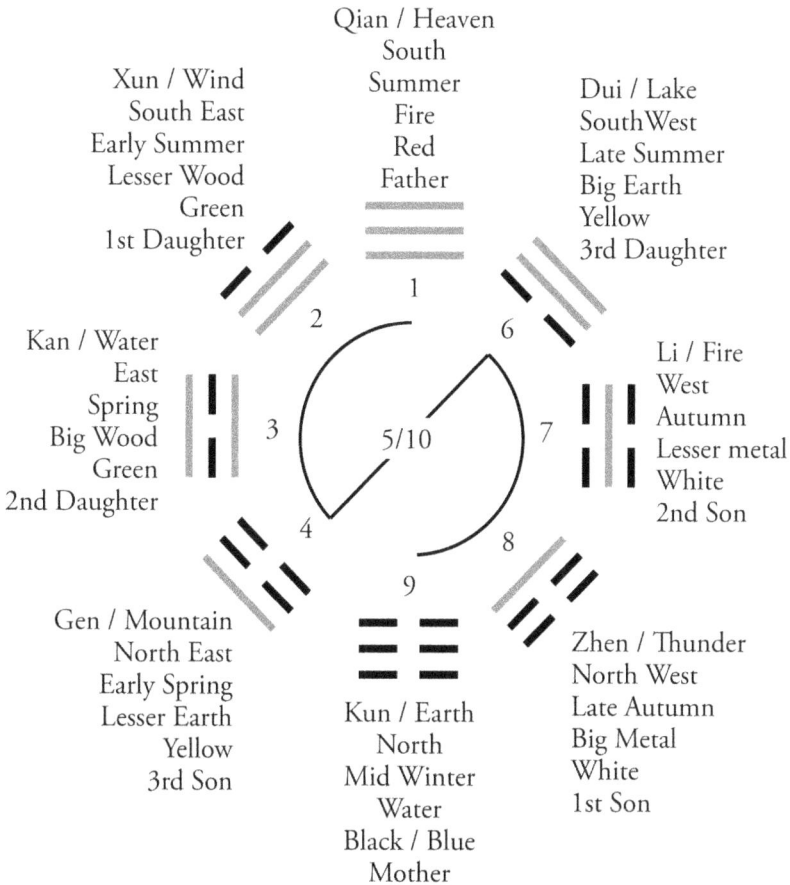

Qian / Heaven
South
Summer
Fire
Red
Father

Xun / Wind
South East
Early Summer
Lesser Wood
Green
1st Daughter

Dui / Lake
SouthWest
Late Summer
Big Earth
Yellow
3rd Daughter

Kan / Water
East
Spring
Big Wood
Green
2nd Daughter

Li / Fire
West
Autumn
Lesser metal
White
2nd Son

5/10

Gen / Mountain
North East
Early Spring
Lesser Earth
Yellow
3rd Son

Zhen / Thunder
North West
Late Autumn
Big Metal
White
1st Son

Kun / Earth
North
Mid Winter
Water
Black / Blue
Mother

Xiantiantu - Pre-celestial Ba Gua
(Primordial / Early Heaven / Fu Xi sequence)
Hetu or Yellow River chart number arrangement.
Traditional / Form School - Abodes of the Dead (yin)

There are two versions of the bagua. Firstly, the Xiantiantu or pre-celestial sequence used in exorcism and burials; it is also prominent in various inner martial arts styles. Secondly, the Houtaintu or post-celestial sequence used for divination. In Feng Shui, the Houtaintu is regarded as the pattern for determining the significance and auspicious qualities of special relationships.

XIANTIANTU – PRE-CELESTIAL / FU XI

In the Xiantiantu bagua, the trigram Qian/heaven is at the top or high point, and the trigram Kun/earth is at the bottom or lower point. The trigrams are situated opposite their contrary to form pairs, both in balance and harmony. The adjustment of trigrams is symmetrical by forming exact contrary pairs.

This pre-celestial arrangement represents the perfect balance of yin and yang, picturing the conditions of a perfect world – a static model of the universe before change, in its primordial, ideal state, symbolizing the perfect, ideal force in a universe where there is no movement, no evolution and time does not exist.

The Xiantiantu is used for positioning and siting Yin Houses or Homes of the Dead – burial sites. In Daoist sorcery, it was used for talismans, rituals, temples and exorcism of malign spirits or forces, and is found on charms and the costumes and equipment of exorcists.

HOUTIANTU – POST-CELESTIAL / MANIFEST / KING WEN

If the Xiantiantu describes a static universe before change, the Houtaintu describes the patterns of environmental changes. Ken/water is placed downwards, with Li/fire at the top. Zhen/thunder is in the east, and Dui/lake in the west.

The post-celestial arrangement represents the manifest universe of change in its natural state. It tells us about movement and the cyclical nature of the universe, such as birth, growth, sickness and extinction. It is the sequence employed by the Luopan compass used in Feng Shui to analyze the movement of chi that attracts us.

King Wen of Zhou (1200 BCE) was inspired to create the post-celestial sequence by the pattern of dots on the shell of a mythical Dragon Turtle that emerged from the Luo River. The pattern was given the name Luoshu, meaning the Luo River Chart. This pattern of dots formed a 3x3 magic square known as the Luoshu Square.

The Houtiantu is mainly used for divination rather than exorcism. It is employed in astrology, medicine, acupuncture, architecture, and in Feng Shui analysis for Yang Houses, Homes of the Living, residential sites, where it is used to site homes and businesses.

Ken / Water
South
Summer
Fire
Red
2nd Daughter

Dui / Lake
South East
Early Summer
Lesser Wood
Green
3rd Daughter

Kun / Earth
South West
Late Summer
Big Earth
Yellow
Mother

9

4

2

Zhen / Thunder
East
Spring
Big Wood
Green
1st Son

3

5

7

Xun / Wind
West
Mid Autumn
Lesser
White Metal
1st Daughter

8

6

1

Gen / Mountain
North East
Autumn
Lesser Earth
Yellow
3rd Son

Li / Fire
North
Mid Winter
Water
2nd Son

Qian / Heaven
North West
Late Autumn
Big
White Metal
Father

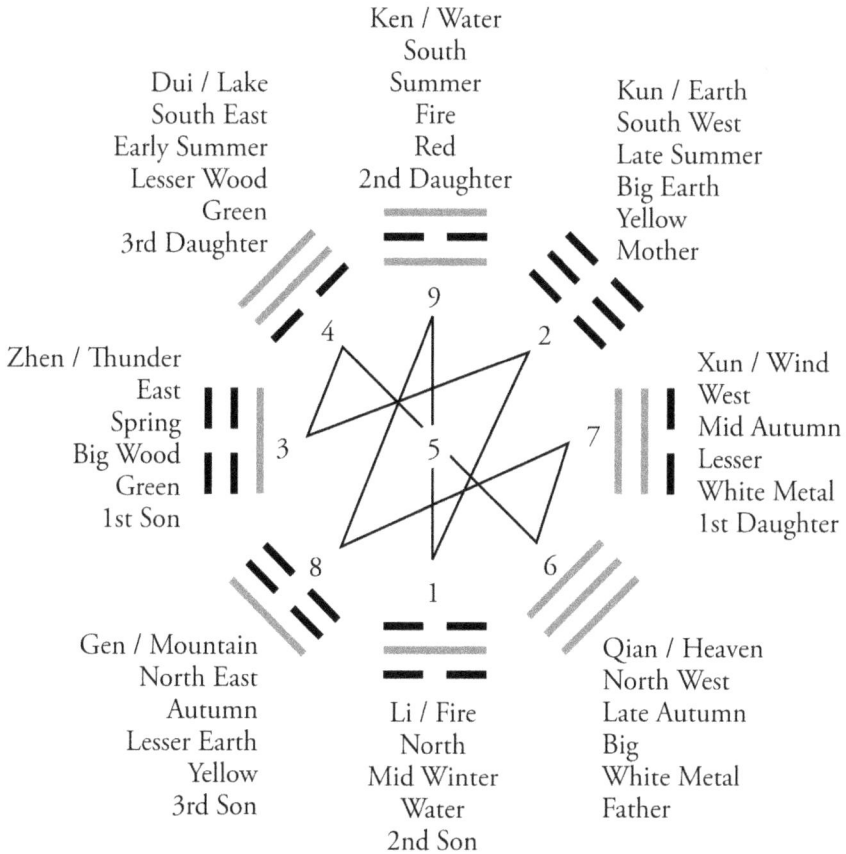

Houtaintu - Post-celestial Ba Gua
(Modified /Late Heaven /Manifest/ King Wen sequence)
Luoshu or Luo River map number arrangement
Compass School - Abodes of the Living (yang)

TRIGRAM ARRANGEMENTS

The arrangement of the trigrams arises from the numbers traditionally assigned to Wu Xing or Five Phases theory, in which the five elements were ordered in various ways in order to portray different types of relationships.

Five Phase theory associates each of the sequential numbers from 1 to 10 with a particular phase or element. The numbering of the phases is taken from the cosmological order; the evolutionary order in which the elements were supposed to have come into being – water, fire, wood, metal, earth. They are assigned to the numbers 1 through 5, and then over again to the numbers 6 through 10 – water 1-6, fire 2-7, wood 3-8, metal 4-9, earth 5-10. Each pair of adjacent numbers differs by 5. The first number is called the Production number, and the second number is called the Completion number.

However, the five elements are arranged in different orders in each bagua sequence. The pre-celestial bagua follows the Mutual Production order, in which each element gives rise to the next one. Together, they form a cycle of gradually increasing yang, followed by gradually increasing yin. This cycle resembles the annual order of the seasons and the daily cycle of day and night. The order is: water 1-6 north, fire 2-7 south, wood 3-8 east, metal 4-9 west, earth 5-10 center. Its Wu Xing generative flows counterclockwise – water feeds wood, wood brings fire, metal brings water, fire brings earth.

In the post-celestial sequence, the positions of numbers, if read counter-clockwise, corresponds to the Mutual Conquest sequence of the five elements. The numbers that refer to the same element or phase appear adjacent to each other: metal 4-9 south overcomes wood 3-8 east, wood overcomes earth 5 center, earth overcomes water 1-6 north, water overcomes fire 2-7 west, fire overcomes metal. Destructive flows clockwise – water quenches fire, fire melts metal, metal chops wood, wood draws water.

FAMILY MEMBERS

The trigrams are based on the universal principle of there being two absolute opposites. This is a reference to two major trigrams, Qian/heaven with three unbroken yang lines, and Kun/earth with three broken yin lines. Yang lines ascend towards heaven. Yin lines descend towards earth. The great yang trigram Qian is always at the top of the bagua. The great yin trigram Kun is always at the bottom of the bagua.

The mixing of these two great energies creates the six mixed, inner trigrams that contain all the energies in between the great parental yang father and the great parental yin mother.

Water 1/6

Fire 2/7

2   1   6

7   Earth 5/10   3

4   9   8

Metal 4/9   Wood 3/8

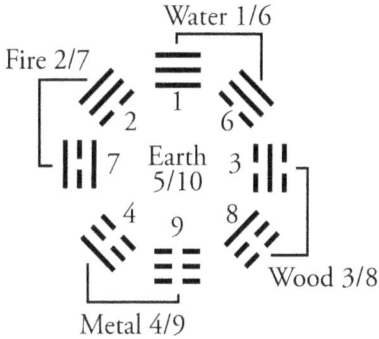

Pre-celestial
Mutal production sequence

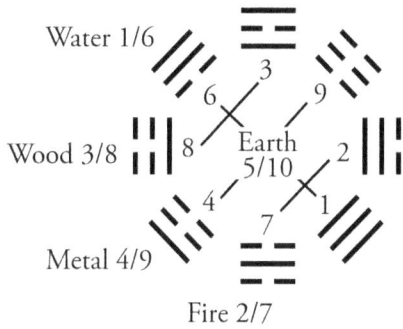

Water 1/6

6   3   9

Wood 3/8   8   Earth 5/10   2

4   7   1

Metal 4/9

Fire 2/7

Post-celestial
Destructive conquest sequence

Ba Gua and the Wu Xing - Five Phases or Elements

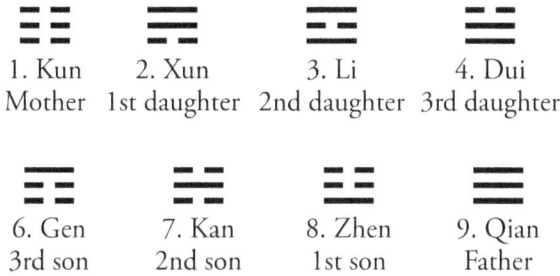

1. Kun   2. Xun   3. Li   4. Dui
Mother   1st daughter   2nd daughter   3rd daughter

6. Gen   7. Kan   8. Zhen   9. Qian
3rd son   2nd son   1st son   Father

Polarity of family relationships in the trigrams of the I-Ching

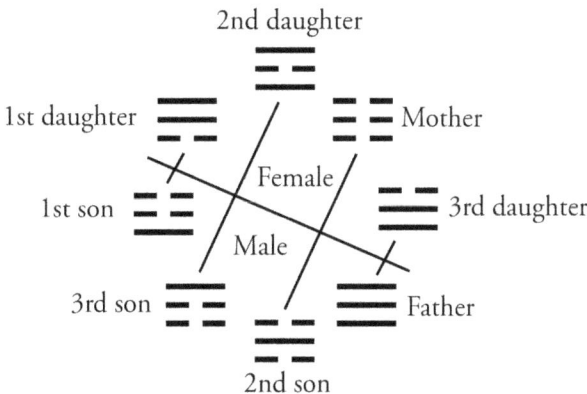

2nd daughter

1st daughter   Mother

Female

1st son   3rd daughter

Male

3rd son   Father

2nd son

Bilateral symmetry of the family sequence in the Post-celestial Ba Gua

These inner trigrams have different combinations of both parents, so that there is female within the male, and male within the female. They indicate two male, two female and two neutral (child) trigrams – two of each because there are two parents.

This occurs because the Luoshu numbers match the Hetu numbers in their assignments to do with family roles in the trigrams. If the Luoshu numbers are applied to the Hetu numbers, they provide a sequence in which the yang lines are associated with males and the yin with females – making Qian and Kun into father and mother, respectively.

They represent a family consisting of father, mother, three sons and three daughters – not in the mythical sense in which the Greek gods peopled Olympus, but in what might be called an abstract sense; that is, they represent not objective entities but functions.

The sons represent the principle of movement in its various stages – beginning of movement, danger in movement, rest and completion in movement. The daughters represent devotion in its various stages – gentle penetration, clarity, adaptability, and joyous tranquillity. The ancient Chinese used this gender chart to predict and select a baby.

WESTERN BAGUA

The bagua is most familiar to Westerners from their interaction with Feng Shui, Kung Fu, Qigong, and the I-Ching – the most popular Chinese divination system used in the West.

Feng Shui became popular in the West thanks to the Bagua of the Eight Aspirations. In this system, each trigram corresponds to an aspect of life, which, in its turn, corresponds to one of the cardinal directions. This made it possible to simplify Feng Shui and bring it within the reach of everyone. The Western bagua focuses more heavily on the power of intention than the traditional forms of Feng Shui.

In ancient China, map-makers placed north at the bottom, south at the top, east on the right, and west on the left because this is a map looking outward at the universe, which supposes that you are lying down, facing the sky with your feet in the north, head in the south, west to the left, and east to the right. An earth terrain map supposes that you are lying face down, facing the earth, so that east is on the left. However, if east were on the left of the bagua, it could be interpreted as looking inward into universal energies within one's self. Bagua that have north at the top and south at the bottom are solely used by Westerners for convenience.

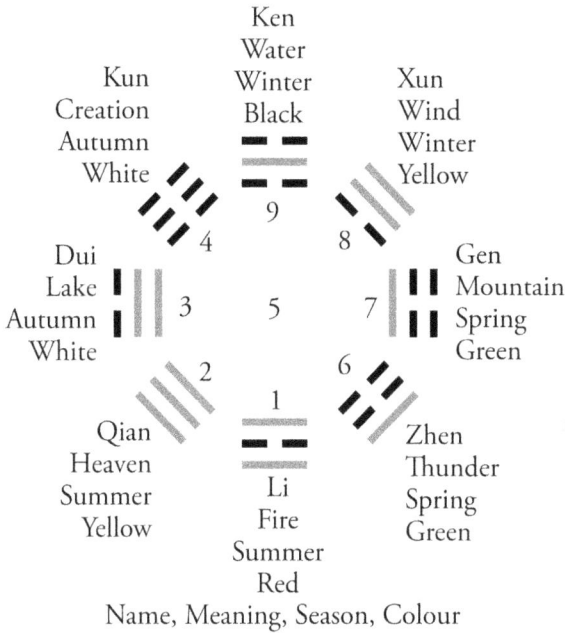

Kun
Creation
Autumn
White

Ken
Water
Winter
Black

Xun
Wind
Winter
Yellow

Dui
Lake
Autumn
White

Gen
Mountain
Spring
Green

Qian
Heaven
Summer
Yellow

Zhen
Thunder
Spring
Green

Li
Fire
Summer
Red

Name, Meaning, Season, Colour

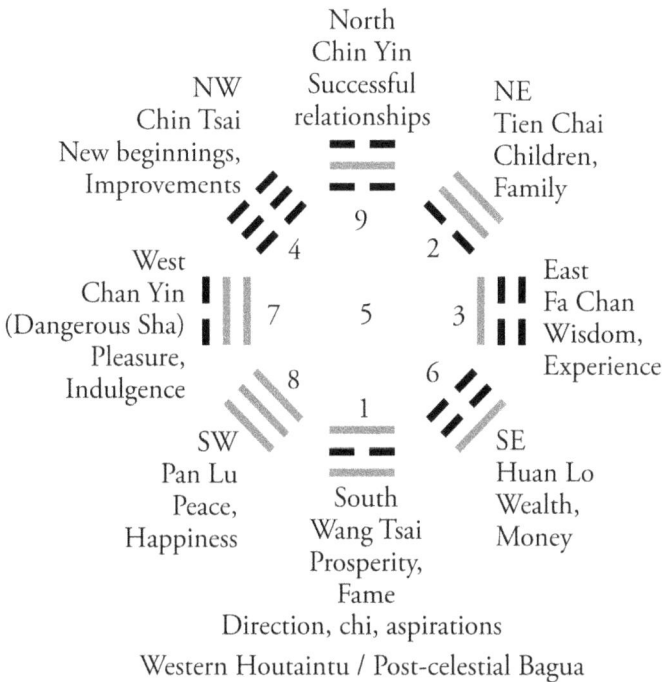

NW
Chin Tsai
New beginnings,
Improvements

North
Chin Yin
Successful
relationships

NE
Tien Chai
Children,
Family

West
Chan Yin
(Dangerous Sha)
Pleasure,
Indulgence

East
Fa Chan
Wisdom,
Experience

SW
Pan Lu
Peace,
Happiness

South
Wang Tsai
Prosperity,
Fame

SE
Huan Lo
Wealth,
Money

Direction, chi, aspirations

Western Houtaintu / Post-celestial Bagua

1. Qian / Chien
HEAVEN / AETHER
head
strong
creative
white/grey/silver
Circle
Father
HEAD
HORSE
BENEFACTORS
Helpful people
Blessings / Travel
Bottom Right Palace
NORTHWEST

2. Xun / Son
WIND / WOOD
penetrating
gentle
purple/blue/red-brown
Rectangular
Column
1st daughter
HIP
FOWL
WEALTH
abundance
Prosperity
Top Left Palace
SOUTHEAST

3. Ken
WATER
abysmal
dangerous
aquarium / ponds
black/blue
Undulating free forms
2nd son
EAR
PIG
CAREER
Path in life
Communications
Bottom Middle Palace
NORTH

4. Gen / Kun
MOUNTAIN
resting / stand
keeping still
completion
blue/black/greens
Square
3rd son
HAND
DOG / WOLF
KNOWLEDGE
Wisdom
Skills
Bottom Left Palace
NORTHEAST

5. Dui / Tui
METAL
pleasure / tranquil
complete / devotion
swamp / marsh
white/grey/silver
Circle
3rd daughter
MOUTH
SHEEP
CHILDREN
Creativty
Future
Middle Right Palace
WEST

6. Li
FIRE
light-giving
dependence
clinging / adorable
red/purple/orange
Triangle
2nd Daughter
EYE
PHEASANT
FAME
Reputation
Public Relations
Top Middle Palace
SOUTH

☳

7. Zhen / Chen

WOOD

initiative

movement

green

Rectangular

Column

1st son

FOOT

DRAGON

FAMILY

Foundation

Physical Health / Past

Middle Left Palace

EAST

☷

8. Kun

EARTH

receptive

devoted

yeilding

pink/red/beige/white

Rectangle

Mother

BELLY ORGANS

COW

MARRIAGE

Relationships

Love

Top Right Palace

SOUTHWEST

Correspondences begin with the trigram's Luoshu number assignment, followed by its name, element, 3 virtues, colour, family member, body part, animal, 3 aspirations, Loushu square position and cardinal direction.

Expanded Feng Shui correspondencess for the eight trigrams of the Houtiantu ot Manifest Bagau

Kan
Water

Dui
Lake

Kun
Earth

3

6

9

Zhen
under

8

5/10

2

Xun
Wind

4

1

7

Gen
Mountain

Qian
Heaven

Li
Fire

Houtiantu / post-celestial bagua
Houses of the Living analysis

Hetu and Luoshu River Charts

In Feng Shui, the Hetu and Luoshu River Charts are two ancient celestial diagrams that form the foundation for understanding the relationship between numbers 1 to 9, yin-yang, the five elements, and the eight compass directions. They are believed to have originated in antiquity, inspired by patterns observed on the backs of mythical creatures that emerged from water. Both diagrams are powerful tools, offering insights into the fundamental principles that govern the flow of energy and the relationships between different aspects of the environment.

Employed by Daoists and Confucianists, these core cosmological diagrams are foundational to Feng Shui principles. They help practitioners to understand how different elements interact and work with each other, which is crucial for optimizing the energy flow in a space. They are often used in conjunction with each other to create a more comprehensive understanding of the interplay of energy, space and time.

Both diagrams are formed of black and white dots arranged in specific patterns that represent the numbers 1 to 9. The white dots represent yang, and the black dots represent yin and correspond with the five elements.

The arrangement of dots and numbers is linked to the trigrams and compass directions, allowing for a deeper understanding of special arrangements and their impact on the environment. Certain number combinations are considered auspicious or inauspicious and are used to guide decisions in Feng Shui practices, such as choosing locations for buildings or arranging furniture.

HETU – YELLOW RIVER CHART

The term 'Hetu' is short for 'Huang He Tu', which translates as 'Yellow River Chart'. Legend has it that the sage king Fu Xi created the eight trigrams after seeing the pattern on the back of a mythical Dragon Horse that emerged from the Yellow River or Huang He. After recording the pattern, he paired each trigram with its opposite and arranged them in an octagonal sequence, known by various names including the Fu Xi sequence, pre-celestial or early heaven bagua.

Because the Hetu sequence forms a cross and the pre-celestial sequence is circular or square, there are various ways the trigrams could be assigned. The inner numbers 1-4 could map the cardinal points, and the outer numbers could correspond to the corners, or it could be the absolute opposite.

Fu Xi

Dragon Horse

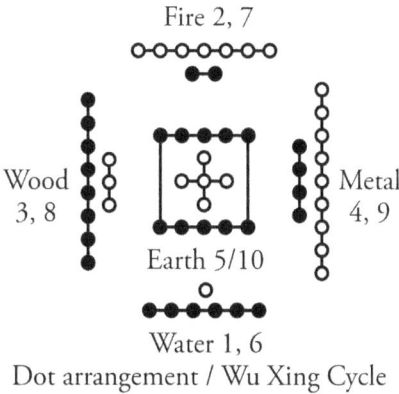

Dot arrangement / Wu Xing Cycle

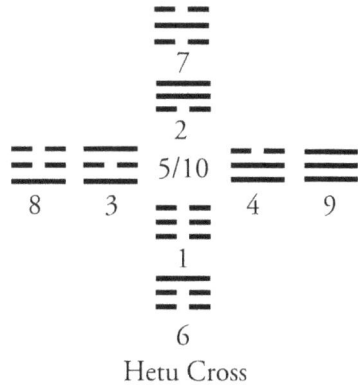

Hetu Cross

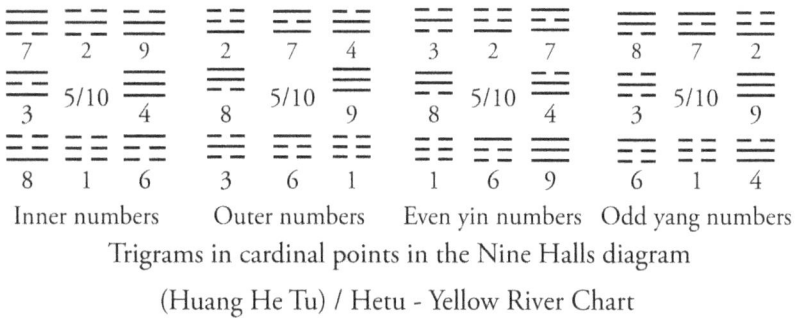

Inner numbers   Outer numbers   Even yin numbers   Odd yang numbers

Trigrams in cardinal points in the Nine Halls diagram

(Huang He Tu) / Hetu - Yellow River Chart

While the white dots representing odd numbers could correspond to the cardinal points, the black dots representing the even numbers could correspond to the corners, or vice versa.

Although Fu Xi is thought to have lived circa 2600 BCE, it has been suggested that it may have been the Song scholars, Chen Toun or Shao Yong, who first attributed the Hetu to Fu Xi, circa 1000 CE. The Hetu was referred to in documents of the late Zhou period (777–221 BCE), and compared with the trigrams during the Han dynasty (202 BCE–220 CE), but the earliest surviving illustration comes from the 10th century CE.

LUOSHU – LUO RIVER CHART

The term 'Luoshu' translates as 'Luo River Map/Chart'. It is a form of mathematical magic square, a numerical chart in which patterns of white dots are odd numbers and the black dots are even numbers.

Yu the Great (2200–2100 BCE), founder of the Xia dynasty, was sitting by the banks of the River Luo when a Dragon Turtle emerged from the water. The pattern of dots inscribed on its shell in a 3x3 grid became known as the Luoshu or Luo River Chart.

When King Wen of Zhou was in prison during the Shang dynasty (1152–1056 BCE), he modified Fu Xi's trigram arrangement according to the Luoshu chart. The new arrangement became known as the King Wen sequence, the post-celestial or Manifest Bagua.

The earliest surviving mention of the Luoshu appeared during the Warring States (5th-3rd century BCE). Zhuang Zi (360–286 BCE) mentioned The Nine Luo in the Great Commentary of the I-Ching.

Initially, it appears that this pattern was kept secret, referred to indirectly by other names, such as the Nine Halls or Nine Palaces diagram. Zhen Luan finally revealed the numbers and their positions in the 6th century, and Zheng Xuan published a drawing of them in the 10th century.

The Luoshu number sequence represents the manifest universe of change in its natural state. It tells us about movement and the cyclical nature of the universe, such as birth, growth, sickness and extinction.

LUOSHU SQUARE – NINE HALLS / PALACES DIAGRAM

The Luoshu number sequence was converted into a magic square using a 3x3 grid. Mathematically, there are eight versions of the 3x3 square, the Luoshu version being exactly similar to the square of Saturn and its sigil in Western occultism.

King Wen with the post-celestial Bagua

Dragon Turtle

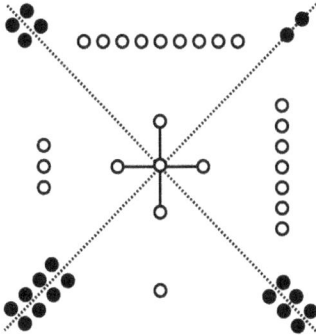

Luoshu dot arrangement

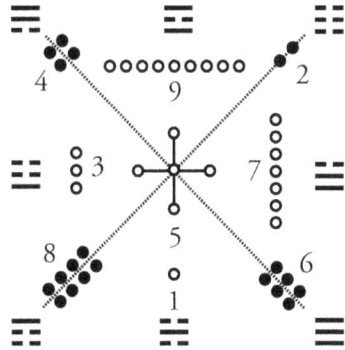

Trigram assignments

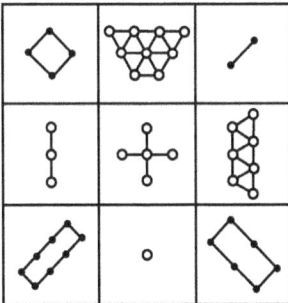

Magic number square

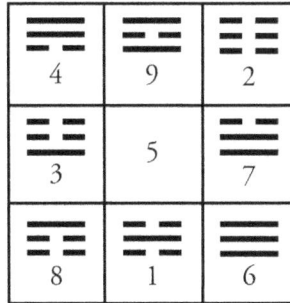

Luoshu square / Nine Halls

(Luo Shu Tu) / Luoshu - Luo River Chart

The first known magic squares are from China, circa 2000 BCE. Records of the Luoshu chart date back to 650 BCE, but don't refer to the square until 570 CE. The Luoshu square became an important model for time and space and served as a basis for city planning, tomb design and temple design, used to designate spaces of political and religious importance.

Numerically, the odd and even numbers alternate on the periphery of the Luoshu pattern. Four even, yang numbers, 2, 4, 6, 8, are in the corners or the four ordinal points. The five odd, yin numbers, 1, 3, 7, 9, are in the cardinal points and form a cross with 5 in the center cell. The rows, columns and diagonals add up to 15. 15 is the number of days in each of the 24 cycles of the Chinese solar year. Since 5 is the center cell, the sum of any two other cells is 10, and opposite corners add up to 10 – the number of the Hetu.

The sequence of Luosho numbers is such that the elements control each other in the Ko cycle in a pendular motion across the center, and generate each other in the Sheng cycle. It has a more practical application to the strategically important earth chi.

The position of the numbers when read counter-clockwise corresponds to the Mutual Conquest sequence of the five elements. Metal 4/9 overcomes wood 3/8. Wood overcomes earth 5/10. Earth overcomes water 1/6. Water overcomes fire 2/7, and fire overcomes metal.

HETU AND LUOSHU CONNECTIONS

The two charts also contain principles that involve number sequences that can be associated and interconnected with one another. Pairs of the Hetu numbers can be found in the Luoshu. The number sequence of the Hetu forms a cross of pairs of numbers. These same pairings of numbers are also found within the Luoshu square. Such an affinity allows the interconnection of chi energies between both number sequences.

When the trigrams in the Hetu sequence are paired with their decimal value, they form a 'sigil/signature' when joined in a continuous line. When the sigil is flipped and rotated 45 degrees, it replicates the sigil found on the Luoshu square when all the numbers are joined in sequence by a continuous line. The Loushu sigil is formed by the lines that trace the flow of chi from yin to yang throughout the square and, therefore, throughout the universe. In the West, this sigil, formed on a 3x3 magic square, is known as the Sigil of Saturn.

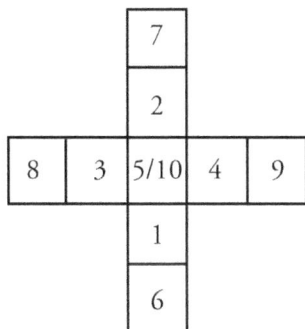

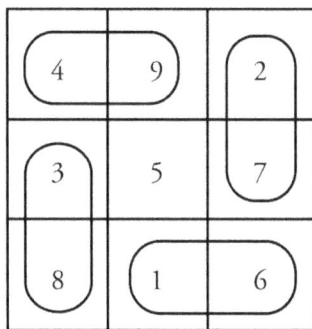

Hetu cross   Hetu pairings in the Luoshu

Hetu number pairs in the Luoshu square

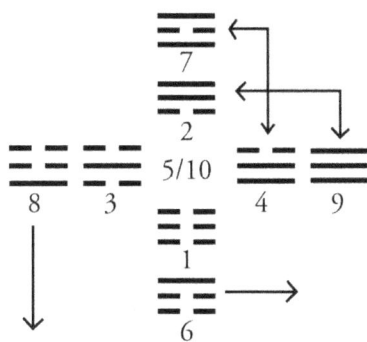

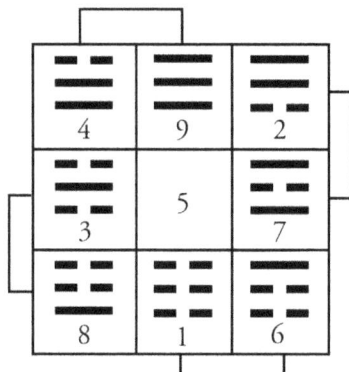

Hetu cross conversion to the Luoshu square

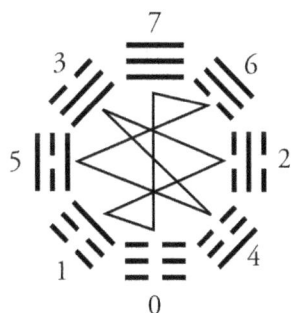

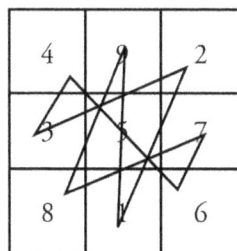

decimal sigil of   flipped and   Luoshu sigil
the Hetu   rotated 45 degrees   (Sigil of Saturn)

Relation between the Hetu and Luoshu sigils

Luopan – Feng Shui Compass

Another important Feng Shui tool is the Feng Shui compass or Luopan. Before the compass, people had to rely on landmarks, constellations or other visual means to help them navigate and steer themselves in the right direction – not only in which direction to go physically, but also in which direction to go spiritually or intuitively.

The oldest precursor of the magnetic compass in China is the Zhinan Zhen or 'south-pointing compass needle', invented in the 4th century BCE. The original magnetic compass developed for Feng Shui, it featured the 'two cords and four hooks' diagram, direction markings and a magnetized spoon in the center.

Another early precursor of the Luopan, unearthed from tombs that date between 276–209 BCE, is the Shi or Shipan, meaning 'astrolabe', a cosmic or divination board, also sometimes called a Liu Ren astrolabe. These astrolabes consist of a lacquered, two-sided board with astronomical sightings. Along with divination for Da Liu Ren, the boards were commonly used to chart the motion of Tai Yi through the Nine Palaces. The markings are virtually unchanged from the Shipan to the first magnetic compass or Luopan.

The Luopan is an image of the cosmos based on turtle shells used in divination. At its most basic level, it serves as a means to assign proper positions in time and space, to accurately determine the direction of buildings or space to create a detailed map. It is a complex tool because of its intricate details and the complexity they involve.

The Compass School schematic of the earth plate, heaven plate and grid lines is part of the 'two-cords and four-hooks' geometric diagram in use since the Warring States period. The wooden base, known as the earth plate, is square in shape so it can be easily aligned against structures and buildings. The earth plate is generally red in colour to act as a strong protection, keeping negative energy away from the Luopan.

The magnetic center represents the center of the universe and is known as the heaven pool or heaven pond. It is where chi begins, where yin and yang ebb and swell, flowing with each other, and where 'rest' and 'action' interact in all aspects of the universe.

The magnetic compass is set into a metal plate known as the heaven plate or heavenly dial that is surrounded by a series of concentric rings, ranging from 3 to 40 or more. Each ring has a specific meaning and orientation purpose, inscribed with the characters for the stems and branches, zodiac signs, the glyphs representing celestial numerals, the eight trigrams and the 64 hexagrams.

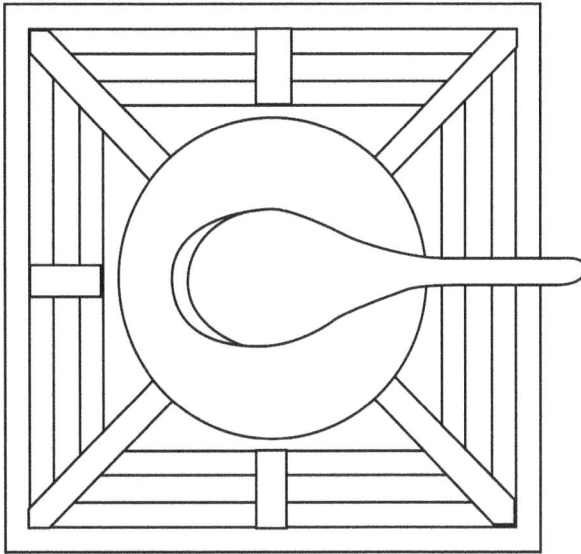

South-pointing magnetic spoon compass

Lunar / Solar Astrolabe
Stems - inner Branches - middle
Elements - outer and center

Although there are many types of Loupan, common types include the San He, San Yuan and Zong He Luopan. Each of these has several common rings, including the trigram arrangements and the 24 directions.

SAN HE LUOPAN – THREE HARMONIES / COMBINATIONS

Said to be used in the Tang dynasty, the San He or Three Harmonies Luopan contains three basic 24 direction rings. Each ring relates to a different method and formula. Sometimes referred to as the Form School, it focuses on the harmonious relationship between landforms, water and the building's orientation, particularly in relation to mountains and rivers.

SAN YUAN LUOPAN – THREE CYCLES

The San Yuan Luopan, also known as the Jiang Pan or Yi Pan because of the presence of the hexagrams of the I-Ching, incorporates many families used in San Yuan or Three Cycles. It focuses on the cyclical nature of time and its influence on energy flow.

It utilizes the concept of three cycles or San Yaun, each spanning 60 years, to make a 180-year period, and further divides these 60-year periods into three periods of 20 years each. It focuses on the time-related aspects, analyzing the influence of periods and cycles.

The techniques grouped under the name Flying Star are an example of popular San Yuan methods. Another is Dragon Gate Eight Formations using water formulae to identify and create areas with good Feng Shui. Xuan Kong Da Gua is an intricate form using the 64 hexagrams to evaluate directions in greater detail.

The San Yuan Luopan is used to determine the facing direction of a building and calculate the distribution of energy in different sectors. It analyzes the Flying Star combinations for each period to understand the energy flow and identify areas that are auspicious or inauspicious.

ZONG HE – HARMONIZE / INTEGRATE

The Zong He Luopan is a specialized compass used by the Three Cycles system and the Three Harmonies systems. It contains the 3x24 direction rings of the San He and the 64 hexagrams ring of the San Yuan for analyzing the internal and external environment.

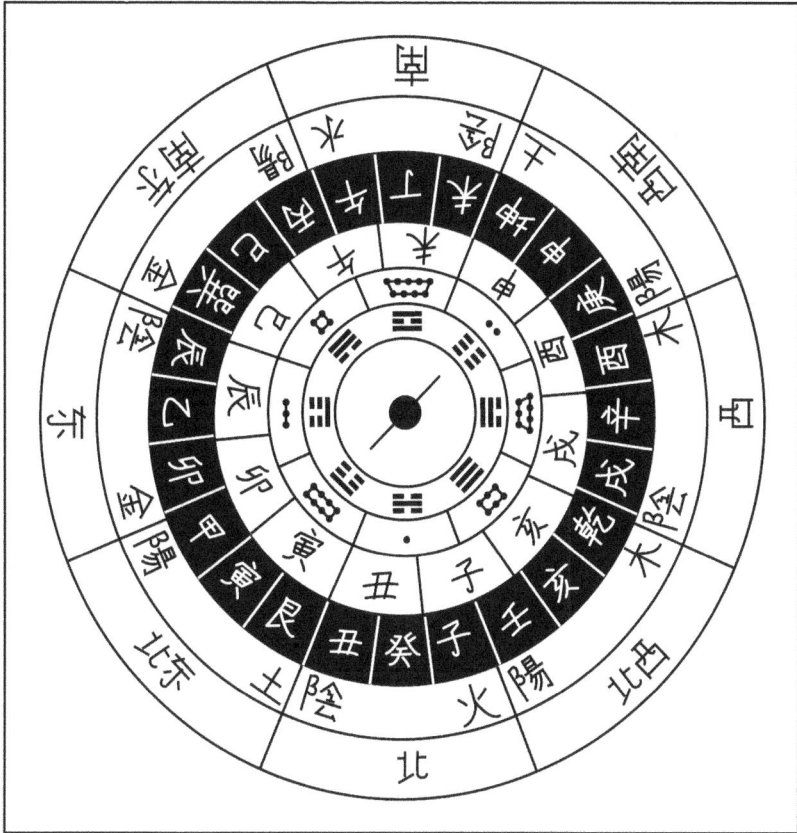

Earth Plate / Pan (square)
Heaven Plate / Pan (circle)

Outer Ring Inwards

1. compass points

2. yin - yang / elements

3. 24 mountains (4 Trigrams names)

Eight Heavenly Stems, (12 Earthly Branches)

4. Zodiac animals (12 Earthly Branches)

5. Celestial Numerals

6. Trigrams (Post-celestial sequence)

7. Compass needle

Compass School - basic rings of a San Yuan Luopan

Feng Shui Schools

Based on the observation of heavenly time and earthly space, Feng Shui has founded many schools in the East and in the West. The Traditional School or classical Feng Shui dates back to Neolithic times and was used in agriculture, burials and buildings. The Form School developed out of the Traditional School in the 9th century CE. It was originally concerned with the location and orientation of tombs and temples, before progressing to the consideration of homes and other buildings without the use of a compass in any way.

The Compass School is a more recent Feng Shui technique based on the eight cardinal directions, each said to have unique chi. Analysis is based on the eight compass sectors and the trigrams of the bagua. It involves numerical calculations based upon the direction in which a building faces, which is determined using a Feng Shui compass or Luopan.

Today, Feng Shui experts combine both the Form and Compass systems, looking first at the undulations of the surrounding countryside and consulting the compass to note the alignment of the surrounding mountains and rivers of the site under consideration.

Modern or Intuitive Feng Shui is the Western adaptation of some levels of traditional Feng Shui. Instead of Chinese culturally specific symbols, cures more appropriate to Western lifestyles and tastes are being used. In the West, Feng Shui practices mainly focus on the bagua, with contemporary uses for architects and geologists, as well as landscape ecologists, environmental scientists and landscape architects.

Western schools included Eight Aspirations, the Pyramid School and the Black Hat Sect or Tantric Buddhist Feng Shui, invented in the USA in the mid-1980s, a combination of Tibetan Buddhism, Daoism and classical Feng Shui.

TRADITIONAL / CLASSICAL FENG SHUI

Still more popular in the East than the West, traditional or classical Feng Shui dates back thousands of years to Neolithic times. It was used to analyze the environment for the siting and orientation of tombs and agriculture, before being used to plan the layouts of temples, palaces and cities.

It is based on science and the interaction of heaven and earth; the principles of classical Feng Shui are founded on the interaction of the five elements and the balance of yin and yang energies.

The practice was first documented around 860 BCE, before the two great flourishings of Feng Shui during the Zhou dynasty (770–221 BCE), with another great flowering during the Han dynasty (206 BCE–220 CE). In the 19th century,

Yang Yo-sing compiled the first manual of Feng Shui, systematically describing the characteristics of scenic formation. This book became the standard text for the Form School of Feng Shui.

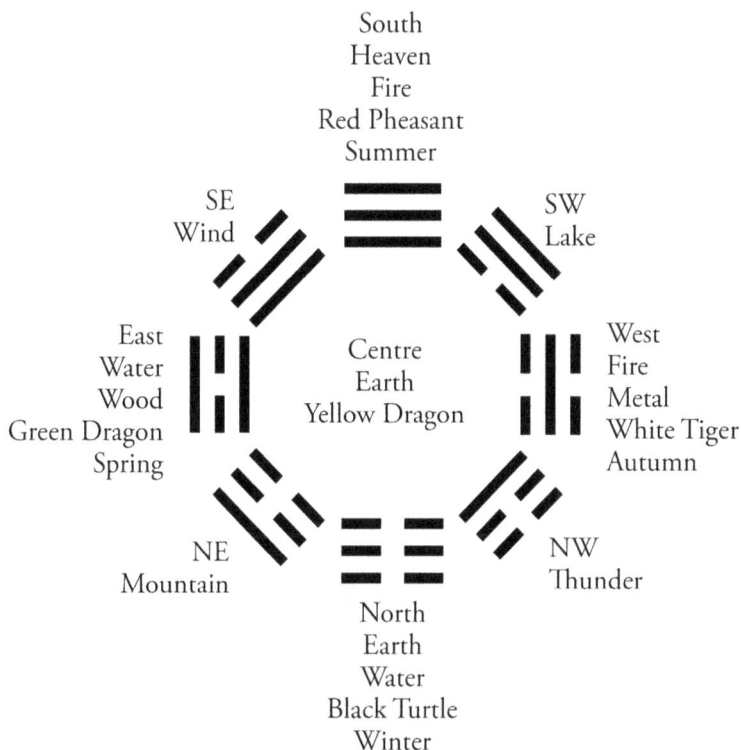

South
Heaven
Fire
Red Pheasant
Summer

SE
Wind

SW
Lake

East
Water
Wood
Green Dragon
Spring

Centre
Earth
Yellow Dragon

West
Fire
Metal
White Tiger
Autumn

NE
Mountain

NW
Thunder

North
Earth
Water
Black Turtle
Winter

Pre-celestial Ba Guu -Traditional and Form schools

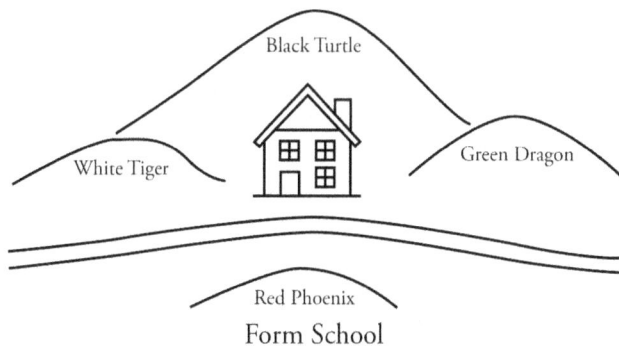

Black Turtle

White Tiger

Green Dragon

Red Phoenix

Form School

SAN HE – FORM SCHOOL

The oldest documented form of traditional Feng Shui, San He or Form School, also Landscape School, is based on the actual landscape of the countryside and the symbolism of natural shapes found in the landscape. It does not use the compass directions in any way.

It was originally concerned with the placement and orientation of tombs for the dead; later its principles were transferred to buildings for the living. It examines the 'form' of physical objects and shapes in the natural and built environment, along with transformational elements, the flow of chi and the manifestations of yin and yang. Form School emphasizes the importance of selecting an auspicious site that has dragons' energy or dragons' breath.

Various natural formations were symbolic of animal shapes and their energies, represented by the Si Xiang, the 4 Symbols or the 4 Auspicious Beasts – four mythological totemic creatures appearing among the Chinese constellations along the ecliptic that are viewed as the Guardians of the Four Directions.

The direction of south corresponds to summer, warmth and vitality; its symbolic animal is the Red Phoenix, representing beauty and goodness. From the north comes winter, cold, snow and darkness, symbolized by the Black Turtle, representing long life and endurance. Located on the left, east corresponds to spring, blue seas and new growth; its symbolic animal is the Green or Azure Dragon, representing majesty and magnificence. West, on the right, corresponds to autumn and snowy mountains, symbolized by the White Tiger, representing bravery and strength. The Yellow Dragon or Snake – yellow symbolizing the earth element – corresponds to the Middle Kingdom or center.

The Form School concept of careful examination of land formations – mountains, hills, valleys and water formations – relies on intuition and examining the shapes and symbolism in one's environment without referring to the compass directions for Feng Shui analysis.

SAN YUAN – COMPASS SCHOOL

The Compass School came around 100 years after the Form School, during the Song dynasty (888-961 CE), when scholars living in the flat plains of the north composed their own answer to the Form School symbolism of the points of a compass.

They called it Compass School analysis, and it uses science and mathematics to determine the best possible direction of chi or energy. A Feng Shui compass called a Luopan is used to determine the direction of the home and where the eight sources of chi are placed.

There are auspicious and inauspicious directions of chi that impact on each of the Eight Mansions. This helps to orient the bagua map onto where the energies are in the house, dividing a site into the eight compass points associated to the five elements and a life aspiration.

Birth dates are sometimes taken into account in certain calculations that help identify the relationship between individual people and the energy patterns of the environment. This has enabled the Compass School to employ various astrological tools such as Ba Zhai or Eight Mansions, Xuan Kong or Flying Star, Nine Star Ki, and Si Zhu or Four Pillars.

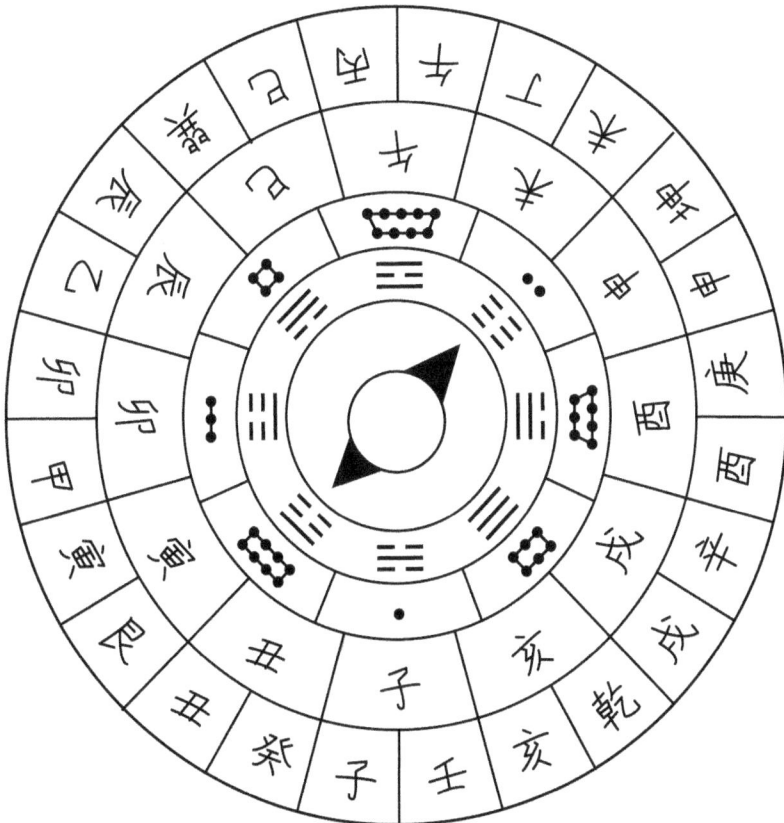

Compass School (Luopan)
Center out - compass needle, trigrams, celestial numerals.
12 Earthly Branches (zodiac). 24 Mountains

Intuitive / Western Schools

A contemporary, Western interpretation of Feng Shui has gained popularity, particularly in the USA, since the 1960s. This modern or Western approach is based on the psychology of how to achieve goals through a targeted focus on the different aspects of life, as well as classical Feng Shui principles.

The Modern or Intuitive School combines a Western approach to Feng Shui with intuition and readings of energy. Practitioners follow the Western approach in form, but their intuition plays a big part in their recommendations.

In the West, modern Feng Shui methods are based on the layout of space, such as a house or business, and the arrangement of furnishings and decorative objects to maximize the flow of chi within the space.

Schools of Western Feng Shui include the Intuitive School, the Life Aspiration School, the Pyramid School, and the Black Hat Sect or Western Feng Shui.

The Life Aspiration School is based on the principle that each of life's aspirations has a colour, element, and direction associated with it. The bagua is used to determine each direction and its associated aspirations – family and health, wealth, marriage, children, benefactors, career, fame, knowledge.

The Pyramid School is the most personalized type; it seeks to marry Eastern and Western Feng Shui in form, but intuition plays a big role in the recommendations made. The Black Hat Sect, also known as Western Feng Shui, is a mixture of oriental beliefs and is thought of as being 'New Age'.

INTUITIVE SCHOOL

Intuitive is the Western adaptation of some levels of traditional Feng Shui, albeit a simplified, modern version that introduces the cultural symbols that are more familiar in the West. In China, red is considered auspicious for money; in the West, being 'in the red' means loss of money, while green mostly represents money.

It also makes it very easy to use the bagua map in relation to your home by aligning the map to the front entrance of a structure without having to use a compass. It is also referred to as 'inner-self', as you are developing a faith and habit of referring to your own intuition.

EIGHT LIFE ASPIRATIONS SCHOOL

The Eight Life Aspirations style of Feng Shui is a simple system which co-ordinates each of the eight cardinal points of the compass with a specific aspiration or station, such as physical and emotional life, family, wealth, fame, career, etc., which come from the bagua's government of the Eight Aspirations.

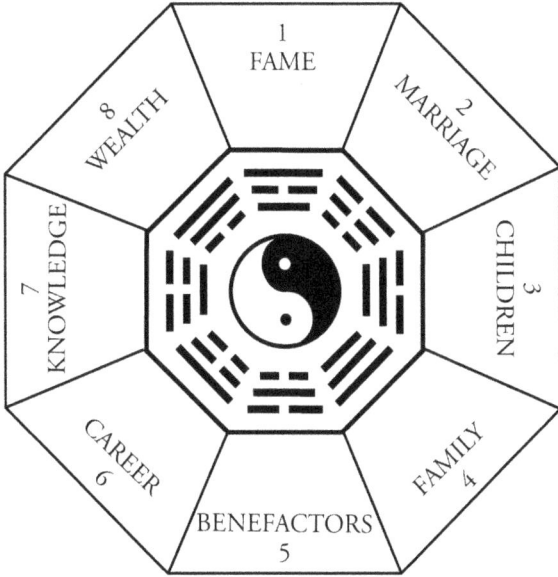

Eight Life Aspirations School

Black Hat Sect colour assignments

Aspirational Feng Shui is based on the principle that each of life's eight aspirations has a colour, element, and direction associated with it. The bagua is used to determine each direction and its associated aspirations – family and health, wealth, marriage, children, benefactors, career, fame, knowledge. Life Aspirations is not otherwise a geomantic system.

PYRAMID SCHOOL

Not TO be confused with the pyramid-based Vastu Shastra or Vedic geomancy, the Western Pyramid School is the most personalized type. It seeks to marry Eastern and Western Feng Shui in form, but intuition plays a big role in the recommendations made.

It is a contemporary adaptation of Chinese Feng Shui, integrating psychology, cultural anthropology, physics, and other environmental considerations to assess how an individual experiences their environment.

Several aspects distinguish it from other schools. Firstly, an underlying premise is that an individual's current symptoms, issues and personality expressions take precedence over their birthdate. For that reason, much emphasis is placed on the development and utilization of diagnostic tools like the bagua map.

There are two forms of bagua map that can be laid over a floor plan to find the proper alignment of the front door. The Compass School entails using a compass to discover which direction your front door is facing. From the compass coordinates, the floor plan is placed in alignment with the corresponding direction of the bagua map. In the Western version, the superimposed bagua and floor plan is aligned with the front door at the bottom of the bagua map.

BLACK HAT SECT

Professor Lin Yun from Berkeley College, USA, invented the Black Hat Sect, also known as Western Feng Shui, in the mid-1980s. It incorporates a mixture of many beliefs and practices, including Tibetan Tantric Buddhism, Daoism, Form School, interior design, psychology, colour therapy, intuition and common sense. The Black Hat Sect is also known as 'New Age' Feng Shui, and since compass directions of Flying Stars are not taken into consideration, it is considered the least accurate kind of Feng Shui.

PROSPERITY

PRIMARY BUSINESS
RELATIONSHIPS

FAME &
REPUTATION

Finance, cash flow, abundance. WOOD	Public relations, reputation, building FIRE	Partnerships & contracts, HR. EARTH
Business structure, leadership, new projects WOOD	Unity, health of the business EARTH	Marketing, creative & production, project completion METAL
Training & development, business library EARTH	Mission statement, communications, reception area WATER	Business networks, client & vendor relations METAL

GROWTH
TEAMWORK, NEW BEGINNINGS

PRODUCTIVITY
CREATIVE EXPRESSION

KNOWLEDGE &
SKILL-BUILDING

CAREER
BUSINESS JOURNRY

TRAVEL &
HELPFUL PEOPLE

ENTRANCE SECTOR

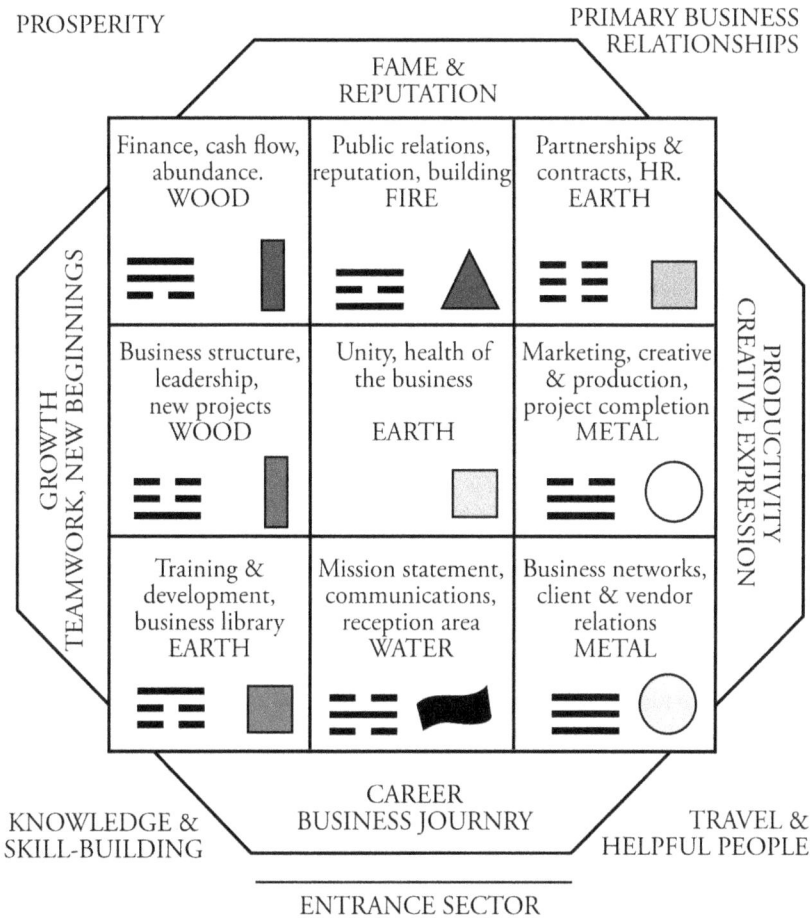

Ba Gua Map - Feng Shui Office

Ming – Life

In Chinese metaphysics, 'ming', meaning 'life', is the Chinese art of destiny or fate, often understood as astrology by Westerners. It is based on traditional astronomy and the lunar-solar calendar, flourishing during the Han dynasty (202 BCE–220 CE). It uses the principles of yin-yang, five elements and the stem and branch system for the time calculation of the year, month, day and hour. These concepts are not readily found or featured in Indian or Western astrology.

The Chinese astrological system has developed independently from the Western system since at least the 5th century BCE. It is believed to have been passed down from Sumerian and Babylonian (Chaldean) cultures to the Chinese almost 5,000 years ago, while the system of 28 Mansions is very similar, although not identical, to the Indian Nakshatra system.

The main difference between Chinese systems and Indian and Western astrology is that the Chinese use the Chinese calendar based on a system of rotating characters known as the Gan Zi or Heavenly Stems and the Earthly Branches, whereas in Indian and Western systems, the methods of astrology and horoscopes rely on the movement of the planets.

PLANETS

According to Chinese astrology, a person's destiny can be determined by the positions of the major planets at that person's birth, along with the positions of the sun, moon, comets, and the person's time of birth and zodiac sign. The system of zodiac signs was built from observations of the orbit of Jupiter or the Year Star to divide the celestial circle into twelve sections of twelve years.

The original system of Chinese astrology was based on the five major planets in our solar system – Mercury, Venus, Mars, Jupiter and Saturn – known as 'Five Houses' or 'Five Planets' astrology. The Sun and Moon were added later to make 'Seven Stars' and provided the foundations for what is known as the 28 Lunar Mansions.

This method proved an extremely accurate horoscope for society as a whole but was unsuitable for individuals, so two new systems of astrology were developed, one based on the solar calendar, called Ba Zhi or Eight Mansions, and the other based on the lunar calendar, known as Zi Wei Dou Shu or Purple Star astrology.

To the Chinese, planets do not hold as much importance as the stars, and they are named with the five elements. Mars and fire, Jupiter and wood, Venus and metal, Mercury and water, Saturn and earth. The appearance of the colour and shape of the planets was used in astrology to predict important events – e.g., if Saturn appears red, calamity is at hand.

XING – STARS

The Chinese word for star is 'xing'. Its glyph is derived from a more complicated character of three twinkling stars, drawn as three sun signs. The general term for asterisms is 'xing gun' or 'group of stars'. The modern Chinese term for constellation is 'xing zuo'. The older term of 'xing guam' is used only in describing constellations of the traditional system. The 'zuo' glyph means 'public official' and formed the English translation of 'official' for Chinese stars, but historically, it is a variant glyph of 'gong', meaning 'temple palace' in the pictogram of a large city.

星　日　月

Xing	Tanyang	Yueliang
Planet / Star	Sun	Moon
(determinative)	Yang	Yin
	3-legged Crow	White Hare

木　火　土

Mu Xing	Huo Xing	Tu Xing
(Wood Star)	(Fire Star)	(Earth Star)
Jupiter	Mars	Saturn
benevolence	radicalism	Chi
fortune	violence	Buffalo
Wild Boar	Donkey	

金　水

Jin Xing	Shui Xing
(Metal Star)	(Water Star)
Venus	Mercury
Female Immortal	Female Magistrate

7 Luminaries / Planets and their correspondences

SHEN SHA – SYMBOLIC STARS

When Chinese astrology refers to stars, it doesn't necessarily mean the stars of the sky; it often refers to mathematical points in the heavens or to the numbers 1–9 that correspond to the elements and trigrams. In Chinese astrology, there are more than 180 Shen Sha or symbolic stars, representing the different relations of the specific positions and interactions of the Heavenly Stems and the Earthly Branches.

The term 'symbolic stars' is sometimes translated as 'gods and devils', but in fact, the symbolic stars do not relate to ghosts or celestial beings – in this case, 'Shen' means the 'beneficial influence', and 'Sha' means the 'baneful influence' of the cyclical signs of the Heavenly Stems and the Earthly Branches.

The calculation of symbolic stars is logically connected to the theory of yin-yang, five elements, 10 Cords, Na Yin or melodic elements theory, 12 energy states, etc. The symbolic stars are like the 'leaves' of the Heavenly Stems and the Earthly Branches in the big tree of Chinese astrology and metaphysics and can provide very specific information in the horoscope analysis. The symbolic stars are used in many methods of Chinese astrology and metaphysics, such as Zi Wei Dou Shu, Da Liu Ren and Feng Shui.

NINE EMPERORS

To the ancient Chinese, the most important stars were Beiji, the North Pole Star (Polaris), and those that form the constellation of Beidou (the Big Dipper). Together with other close-by asterisms, they form the center of the vault of the starry sky of the northern hemisphere or Tian (heaven). The Big Dipper, as the mother of nine stars, is in charge of the production and life of heaven, earth and all things.

These nine stars are formed from the seven stars of the Big Dipper and the two attendant stars either side of the center star of the Dipper's handle. They are known as the 9 God Emperors of the Dao Body and the 9 Stellar Sovereigns of the Big Dipper. Their names are Heavenly Emperor, Purple Subtly, Lusty Wolf, Giant Crate, Store of Wealth, Civil Chief, Pure and Chaste, Military Chief, and Troop Destroyer. These nine stars are the numinous root of the nine heavens. The nine palaces of yin and yang refer to the nine stars and their doors, five sacred mountains and the four holy rivers that correspond with the nine stars as their Abyss and Mansion.

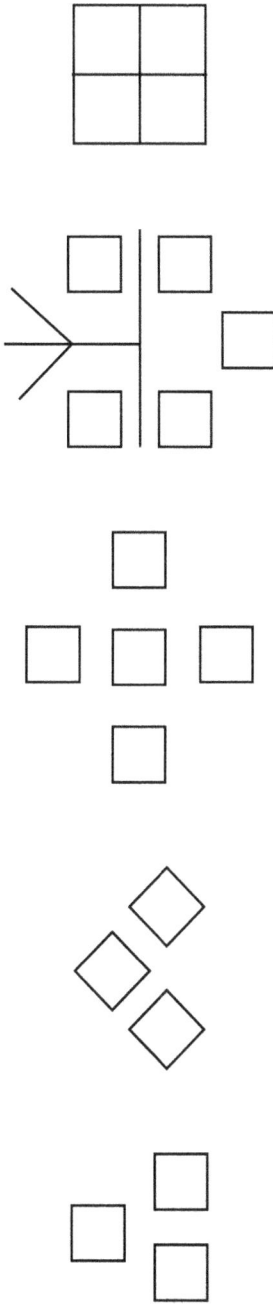

star / constellation / god / ancestor (Shangdi)
Xing / Star - Shang dynasty glyph variants

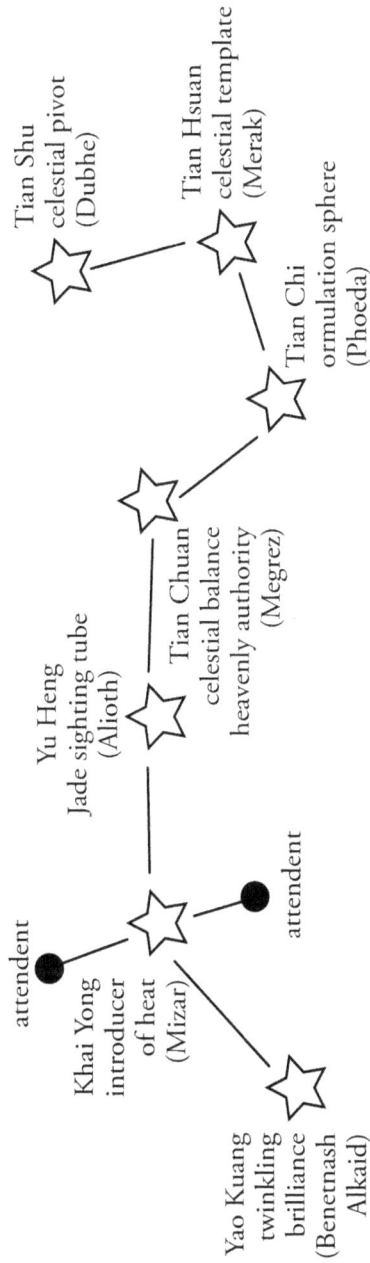

Tian Shu
celestial pivot
(Dubhe)

Tian Hsuan
celestial template
(Merak)

Tian Chi
ormulation sphere
(Phoeda)

Tian Chuan
celestial balance
heavenly authority
(Megrez)

Yu Heng
Jade sighting tube
(Alioth)

attendent

attendent

Khai Yong
introducer
of heat
(Mizar)

Yao Kuang
twinkling
brilliance
(Benetnash
Alkaid)

9 Emperors - Northern/Big Dipper constellation

Si Xiang and the 28 Xiu

The Chinese developed a system of 283 constellations, with identities based on natural objects, rather than deities or historical figures, as the ancient Greeks did. Constellations are placed in Mansions or Houses, and the brightest star is called the Emperor Star, the fainter stars are the Princes.

Traditional Chinese cosmology is mainly based on the position, relationships and movement of the sun, moon, the five major planets of the solar system, and the 28 constellations in the sky. This system was established during the Warring States period (330–221 BCE) and was specifically used for the purpose of observing and monitoring the impact of climate change on agriculture and reflecting and forecasting celestial influences on politics and warfare.

The first recorded Chinese vision of the sky was found on Oracle bones inscribed around 4000 BCE, with images of the Big Dipper, the Green Dragon and White Tiger. Chinese astronomers divided the sky of the northern hemisphere into five regions or Palaces called Gong, each associated with a symbolic animal and a colour.

The rest of the sky contains the equatorial constellations grouped into the four directions. In addition, Chinese astronomers identified 28 segments in the sky, known as the Xiu or Lunar Mansions. The Chinese constellations are grouped into four directions and also fall within one of the 28 lunar Mansions.

SI XIANG – 4 CELESTIAL ANIMALS

Since ancient times, the Si Xiang or 4 Celestial Animals, also called the 4 Symbols, 4 Gods, 4 Guardians and 4 Auspicious Beasts, are four mythological creatures appearing among the Chinese constellations along the ecliptic and are viewed as the Guardians of the Four Directions.

Unrelated to the twelve animals of the zodiac, they represent the four quarters of the sky, equated with the four compass directions and a middle region. The middle region was the most important, as it housed, among its stars, the celestial image of the emperor, surrounded by his family and civil and military officials. This part of the sky has constellations such as 'Prince', 'Concubine' and 'Throne', and it is a reflection of life on earth.

These mythical creatures have been syncretized into the Wu Xing system as follows: Azure Dragon, east, wood – Red Phoenix, south, fire – White Tiger, west, metal – Black Turtle, north, water. The fifth principle is Yellow Dragon, center, earth.

| Black Turtle (Black Warrior) North Winter Black Water | Azure Dragon (Green Dragon) East Spring Green Wood | Red Phoenix (Red Pheasant) South Summer Red Fire | White Tiger (Unicorn) West Autumn White Metal |

Si Xiang - 4 Symbols / Auspicious Beasts

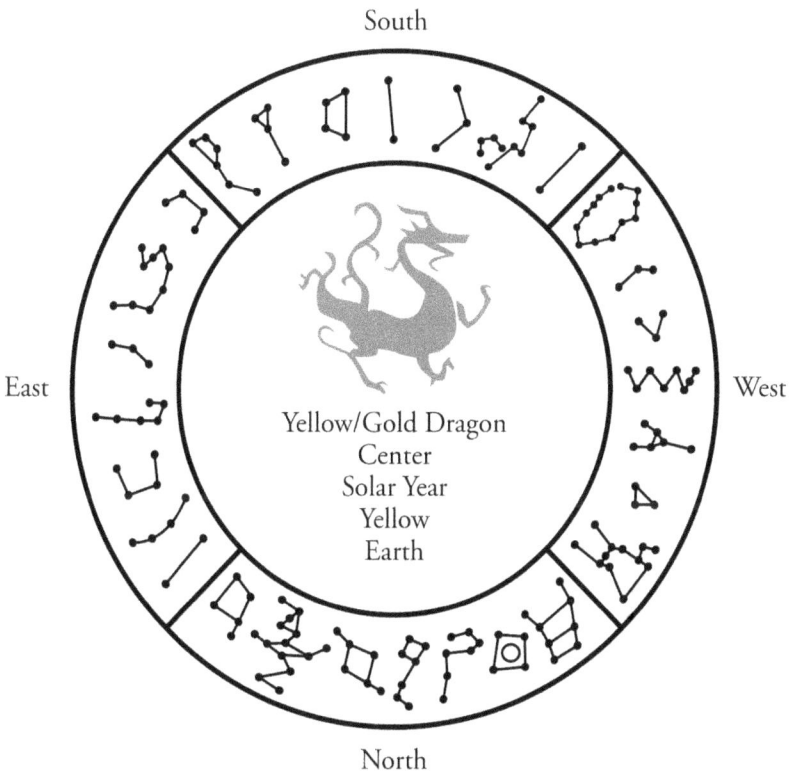

Yellow/Gold Dragon
Center
Solar Year
Yellow
Earth

28 Xiu - Constellations / Lunar Mansions

Before the four animals, there were only three: the Red Bird, the Green Dragon and the White Unicorn. In the Tang dynasty, 4, 5, 12, 24 and 36 animals of the Chinese zodiac were in use, but the earliest showed only three. Because of astrological significance, the White Tiger replaced the Unicorn, and the Phoenix gave way to the unidentifiable Red Bird, sometimes a Pheasant. The Turtle was a later but not the last addition, as many texts refer to the northern constellation not as the Turtle, but as the Black Warrior.

In some versions, the Turtle, coiled by a Snake, giving more meaning to the image, symbolizes the Black Warrior. The Snake as the Dragon represents chi, the primordial power of the universe, and the constellation of Draco at the northern ecliptic pole. The Turtle represents the cosmos, with its shell as the dome of the sky and its plastron (underbelly) as the squared earth. At the same time, they represent two of the four constellations that perfectly enclose in a square the northern ecliptic pole centered in Draco.

28 XIU – CONSTELLATIONS, LUNAR LODGES, MANSIONS

The 28 constellations predate the 255 star groups of 300 BCE. They were vertical strips of sky that acted as markers for following the nightly progression of the moon as it orbits the earth every month, like a zodiac, thereby providing the basis for a lunar calendar.

The 28 lunar lodges or Mansions (xiu – to stay the night) are the same series of 28 constellations, encircling the sky in the vicinity of the celestial equator. They define the celestial coordinates of other star groups as well as specifying the locations of the sun, moon and other planets. They appear on the Feng Shui compass or Luopan as one of its outer rings.

Regarded as having great astrological importance, each constellation is associated with an animal and a particular day of the lunar cycle. It is believed that when the moon moves through these constellations on their designated days, fortunes relating to auspicious and inauspicious activities for that day should be observed.

For Chinese astro-political divination, they have various linked meanings and associations; the first is with the 28 Generals. In Imperial China, the Emperor made sacrifices at the Temple of Heaven to the 28 constellations, as they were the abode of the gods. They became known as the 28 Generals, after the names of the constellations were conferred on various noblemen who perished in battle, slain by Guang Wudi of the Eastern Han dynasty, making them into gods and deities. The 28 Generals are summoned by Daoist priests to descend in order to control and subdue demons.

Jiao	Kang	Di	Fang	Xin	Wei	Ji	Dou
Horn	Neck	root	Room	Heart	Tail	Winnow	Southern
earth	sky	badger	Hare	fox	tiger	basket	Dipper
dragon	dragon	Earth	Sun	Moon	Fire	leopard	unicorn
Wood	Metal	East	East	East	East	Water	Wood
East	East					East	South

Nai	Nu	Xu	Wei	Shi	Bi	Kui
Ox	Girl	Emptiness	Rooftop	Camp	Wall	Legs
Metal	Bat	Rat	Swallow	Bear	Porcupine	wolf
South	Earth	Sun	Moon	Fire	Water	Wood
	South	South	South	South	South	West

Lou	Wei	Mao	Bi	Zi	Shen	Jing
Bond	Stomach	Hairy	Net	Turtle	3 Stars	Well Prop
dog	Pheasant	Head	raven	Beak	Ape	Tapir
Metal	Earth	cockerel	Moon	Monkey	Water	Wood
West	West	Sun	West	Fire	West	North
		West		West		

Gui	Liu	Xing	Zhang	Yi	Zhen
Ghost	Willow	Star	Extended	Wings	Chariot
sheep	deer	Horse	Net	snake	worm
Metal	Earth	Sun	Deer	Fire	Water
North	North	North	Moon	North	North
			North		

28 Xiu and their correspondences

12 Mansions, 12 Sections and 24 Palaces

In order to mark the passage of time and the seasons, Chinese astronomers primarily used the orientation of the Big Dipper constellation relative to Beiji or the North Star (Polaris) in the early evening. They used the Big Dipper's rotational path to mark the cyclical progression of the year and the seasons within it. The Chinese have a cyclical concept of time; just as night follows day, so would the energies of yin and yang alter in a predictable manner on a yearly basis.

In China, mystical concepts of time are mainly linked to the measurements of the movement of the sun along the celestial equator or ecliptic. Ancient Chinese astronomers achieved this by dividing the sky into various sections – 12 Houses, 12 Sections and 24 Solar Terms – to measure the time on a yearly, monthly, daily and hourly basis. These time-measuring systems revolve around the measurements derived from observing the movements of celestial bodies throughout the year, including the sun, moon, Jupiter and the constellations of the northern hemisphere.

12 MANSIONS / HOUSES – 12 MONTHS

The 12 Mansions of the Yellow Path refers to the path along which the sun seems to move. Each year has 12 lunar and solar months, making it the ideal reasonthat the Yellow Path is divided into 12 sections. The ancient Chinese determined the seasons through the pointing of the direction of the handle of the Big Dipper. During winter, the handle points downwards, north, at early evening. In the spring, the handle points east at early evening, and so on. Accordingly, they divided the horizon into 12 sections and gave them names for linking to the directions to which the handle of the Big Dipper points over 12 months. Together, they are referred to as the 12 Earthly Branches and are arranged clockwise when applied to the 12 Houses of the Yellow Path.

The ancient Chinese determined the coordination of the sun on the shortest and longest days of the year. They determined the equatorial coordinates of the sun through the observations of the constellations in the southern sky at midnight, when the sun is on the opposite side to the constellation which crossed the meridian.

Through observation, ancient astronomers found that the sun and the planets seem to move in an anti-clockwise direction along the zodiac. Because the 12 Branches were arranged in a clockwise direction, astronomers set up the 12 Ci system for measuring the location of the sun and the planets along the celestial equator or ecliptic.

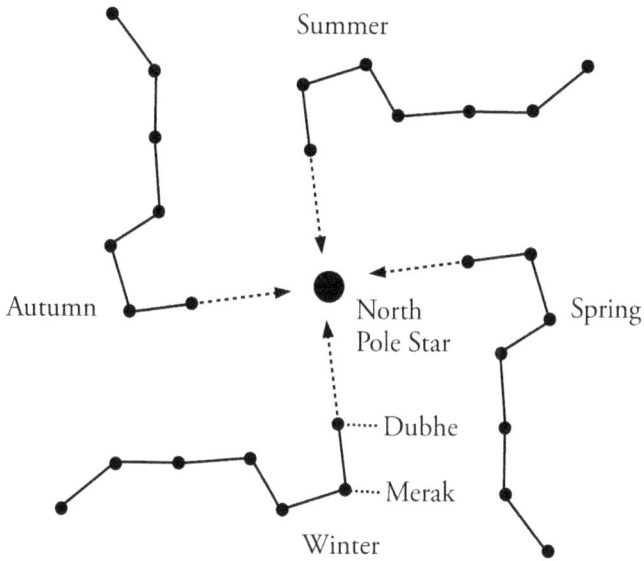

Summer

Autumn

North
Pole Star

Spring

Dubhe

Merak

Winter

Tianman - Pivot of Heaven (North Pole Star and the Big Dipper)

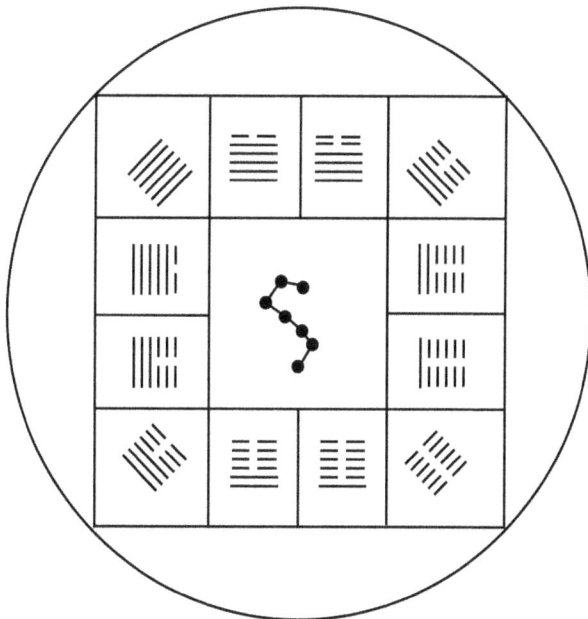

12 Soverign Hexagrams in the 12 Mansions surrounding the Big Dipper

12 CI – 12 SECTIONS

12 Ci means 12 sections on the celestial equator. The sun, moon and planets apparently move through time in seasonal order. Originally, the 12 Ci were divided in order to delineate the movement of Jupiter through its 12-year orbit, with a leap year every 144 years. Each of the 12 Ci has its own name, and Jupiter moves through one Ci each year. In the early stages, the 12 Ci were bound to the 28 Xiu. 8 of the 12 Ci contain 2 Xiu, and 4 of them contain 3 Xiu.

During the Warring States period, they became separated from the 28 Xiu, being measured according to the position of the sun against the background of stars. The main role of the 12 Ci in astrology was that Jupiter's position in the 12 Ci had astrological meaning, especially concerning drought, floods and harvest – on the other hand, the 12 Ci were combined with the 28 Xiu in the field allocation system.

24 SOLAR TERMS

As early as the Shang dynasty (2000 BCE), the Chinese had already established four major solar terms – the spring and autumn equinoxes and the summer and winter solstices. During the Zhou dynasty, the eight solar terms were established, with the start of spring – spring equinox, start of summer – summer solstice, start of autumn – autumn equinox, and start of winter – winter solstice.

The 24 solar terms were established in the year 104 BCE, during the Han dynasty. Based on the sun's position in the 12 Houses throughout the year and practical needs of agriculture in ancient China, the date of each of the 24 solar terms is basically fixed. They formed an important kind of calendar in China, indicating the different periods of seasons, the changes of weather, some natural phenomena, and more, guiding farmers' agricultural production generally. Common people also follow the calendar to watch out for weather changes and a healthy life.

The 24 solar terms can be divided into three groups of varying terms. The first group has eight terms, including the four start dates that mark the beginnings of each of the four seasons, while the equinoxes and solstices reflect the height of changes of the sun from the astronomy aspect.

The second group embodies natural phenomena of twelve terms, including Insects Awakening, Pure Brightness, Grain Full and Grain in Ear. The remaining 12 terms form the third group that reflect climate changes, Slight Heat, Great Heat, End of Heat, Lesser Cold, Great Cold, tell the temperature changes. Rain Water, Grain Rain, Light Snow and Heavy Snow reflect the precipitous levels. White Dew, Cold Dew and Frost Descent reflect the dropping process and degrees of temperature.

Insects Spring Clear and
The Awaken Equinox Bright Grain
Rains Rain
Spring 0
Begins 330 Summer
Begins
30
Great Grain
Cold 300 Buds
Slight 60
Cold Grain in
Ear
Winter 270
Equinox Summer
90 Solstice
Heavy Slight
Snow 240 Heat
Light 120 Great
Snow 210 Heat
Winter Autumn
Begins 150 Begins
180
Hoar-Frost Stopping
Falls Cold Autumn White the Heat
Dews Equinox Dews

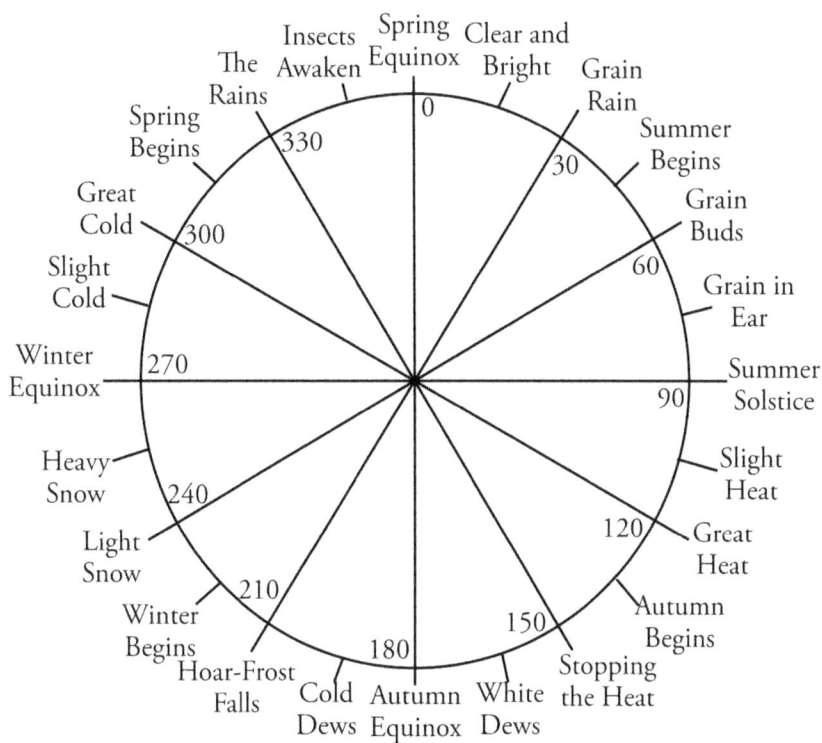

12 Ci and the 24 Solar terms

Calendar and Zodiac

In the Chinese tradition, calendars, almanacs and zodiacs are closely related to complex mystical concepts of time, similar to and as common as they are in the West; only cultural differences separate them.

A calendar is any system by which time is divided into days, weeks, months and years. An almanac is a book or table listing astronomical, astrological, agricultural and nautical data, alongside other events of the year such as holidays, and sometimes historical and statistical information.

A zodiac is a set of signs assigned to various time periods in a calendar. In the West, the zodiac identifies a 12-month astrological cycle within a solar year. In China, the zodiac identifies each year of a 12-year cycle within a 60-year celestial system. It has variants employed in Korea, Vietnam and Japan.

LAOLI – TRADITIONAL CHINESE CALENDAR

Officially, modern China uses the Yangli calendar, their name for the Western Gregorian calendar. The name for the traditional Chinese calendar is Laoli. Because the Chinese also call the Laoli the New Year calendar or Nongli, it is often referred to as the Juili or old calendar.

Most Chinese people still refer to their traditional calendar and almanacs for holidays like the New Year and the Lantern Festival, as well as auspicious dates for weddings, funerals, moving house or starting a business.

The traditional Chinese calendar is lunar-solar, meaning that it is a composite of two calendars. The first is a lunar calendar with the months linked to the phases of the moon, used as a ritual or religious calendar. The second is a solar calendar based on the position of the sun along the ecliptic during the earth's orbit, used in agriculture.

The lunar calendar is based on the moon's cycle equalling one lunar month, with each month starting on the day of the new moon. To make 12 months, each month has 30 days in odd (yang) months and 29 days in even (yin) months, making a 355-day year. Every 30 years there are 11 leap years with 355 days per year, making New Year possible in any of the four seasons.

The solar calendar is based on the position of the sun along the ecliptic during the earth's orbit of 365 days per solar year. It is divided into 12 months of varying lengths between 28 and 31 days, with a leap year of 366 days every 4 years.

The solar calendar marks the hours, days and minutes it takes for the earth to complete an entire circle (orbit) around the sun. Each 24-hour day was divided into 12 intervals, each two hours long.

鼠　牛　虎　兔

1. Zi / Rat　　2. Chou / Ox　　3. Yin / Tiger　　4. Mao / Rabbit

龍　蛇　馬　羊

5. Chen / Dragon　6. Si / Snake　　7. Wu / Horse　　8. Wei / Sheep

猴　雞　狗　豬

9. Shen / Monkey　10. You / Rooster　11. Xu / Dog　12. Hai / Pig

12 Chinese zodiac animals (standard characters)

12 Chinese zodiac animals (anti-clockwise)

The day began with midnight, which lasted from 11pm till 1am, and each of these 12 double hours was named according to the Earthly Branches, who were the 12 animals of the zodiac. Days were arranged in blocks of 10 and corresponded to the 10 Heavenly Stems.

The lunar New Year begins on the first or second new moon after the winter solstice. The solar New Year usually begins on the 3rd or 4th of February, traditionally the first day of spring (Li Chun). This date is used to calculate a person's astrological or divinatory birth chart.

HUANG DAO – YELLOW PATH ZODIAC

During the Chou dynasty, another phase was added to the lunar-solar calendar, a classification system based on the lunar calendar known as the Chinese zodiac or 'Huang Dao', meaning 'Yellow Path', a reference to the sun travelling along the ecliptic with the 12 months of the year along the yellow path.

Like the stem and branch system, the zodiac animals were created principally to count calendar years, before the hours of the day, and later, to a lesser extent, the days and months of the year. To count the years, it assigns an animal and its attributes to each year in its repeating 12-year cycle that corresponds to the 12-year orbital period of the planet Jupiter.

The origin of the 12 animals is in the Tang dynasty (circa 600 CE) at the earliest, but in the earlier Han dynasty, 12 animals were used to simplify the calendar for common use, by replacing the obscure 12 Earthy Branches.

Traditional time division was mostly related to the number 12. One Ji equals 12 years, 1 year has 12 months, and one 24-hour day has 12 double hours or Shi Chen. The day, being a microcosm of the year, is also divided into twelfths.

Each two-hour division of the day is named after a zodiac animal which is believed to embody the state of the balance of yin and yang at that moment. In the traditional Chinese lunar-solar calendar, each animal is linked to the lunar months of a solar year by the 24 solar terms.

Because there are 12 full moons in one year, the zodiac was associated with astrology. Magical texts of the Han dynasty don't just refer to 12 animals but to 36, each of the 12 animals being accompanied by two others of a related species. 28 of these have survived as the accompanying animals for the spirits of the 28 constellations.

As a set of popular symbols, the animal signs did not have any great significance, but there were various folktales linked to their origin that show the 12 animals were different from today's. The same zodiac animals are used in many cultures neighbouring China.

Solar Calendar
Center - sun. Inner - 12 branches. Middle - Hexagrams. Outer - Zodiac

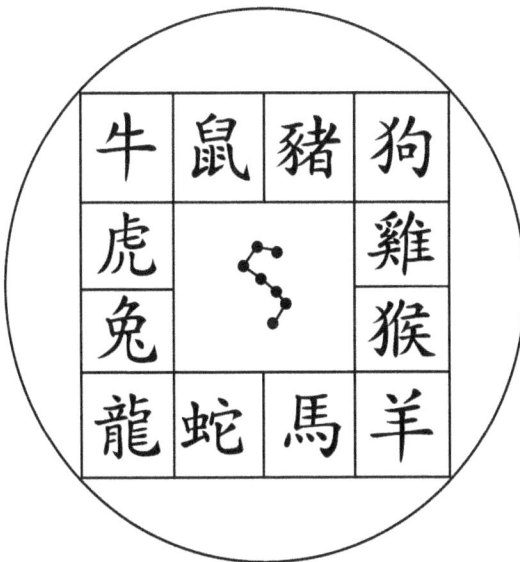

12 Chinese zodiac animals in the 12 Houses
(cycle of 12 years within a 60 year cycle)

Zi Wei Dou Shu – Purple Star Astrology

The Chinese nobility studying the doctrines of fate developed Zi Wei Dou Shu or 'Calculating the Purple Star' during the Han dynasty from Daoist inner alchemy. Older than the 4 Pillars system, they share the same origins. It is counted as first among the 'Five Great Divine Arts', being called 'the number-one divine art in the world'.

Unlike Western astrology, Purple Star doesn't look at the position of the earth around the sun; instead, it observes the position of the stars to formulate a chart to analyze a person's entire existence.

Today, Purple Star astrology is a combination of two older systems that revolves around the North Star and 108 major and minor stars, analyzing their strengths and how they interact within life's 12 palaces.

The Purple Star future chart is composed of 12 palaces containing the 12 aspirations of life: self, siblings, spouse, children, wealth, health, travel, friends, career, property, spiritual, and parent palaces. Additionally, there is a Body palace, which, when combined with stems in each palace, reveals various destinies.

Purple Star numerology determines the position of the 12 palaces based on a person's year, month, day and birth hour to create a horoscope, combining the combinations of stars in each palace to connect with hexagrams, yin-yang, astronomy, geography and fortune-telling to predict a person's life fortune.

These stars are graded according to brightness; the brighter the star, the more influence it has in a region or palace. The North Pole Star is called Zi Wei – the Emperor Star or Purple Star – the most prominent star in the sky. It is used to coordinate or chart the day, as it is approximately aligned with the earth's axis of rotation. Dou refers to the Big Dipper constellation that points to the North Star. Shu means calculations.

The Shi or cosmic board of Purple Star is made up of 12 destiny palaces or courts. There are three sections based on the common idea that a person's life and destiny are dependent on three factors – 1. heaven as predetermined destiny and luck; 2. earth as environment and nurture; 3. man as nature, thought and changeability.

The heaven chart is the natal chart used to predict the events and nature of the questioner's day and hour of birth. The earth chart is the decade chart used to predict the events and nature of a specific decade in the questioner's life. The man chart is the year chart used to predict the events and nature of a specific year in the questioner's life. There is also a separate small period chart used to predict events in a smaller time frame.

Creating a Purple Star chart requires the exact date, time and place of birth to determine the Four Pillars of Destiny as a time frame for the chart based on the year, month, day and hour of birth.

The 108 stars are distributed across the 12 palaces based on the 4 Pillars. Each star has unique attributes and influences different areas of life. Each of the 12 palaces represents a specific domain. The interactions between the stars and their positions in the palaces provide deeper insights.

There are 14 major stars, 6 of which are favourable stars, and the remaining 8 are challenging stars. In addition, there are also 6 lucky stars and 6 unfavourable stars. Each star's power is based on its palace position. It isn't a static system; it tracks how destiny unfolds through time.

Purple Star is a destiny study, not a personality study as in Western astrology. It focuses on telling the questioner about predetermined fate and luck, as well as about that of decades, years and other time frames to help build a successful and prosperous life.

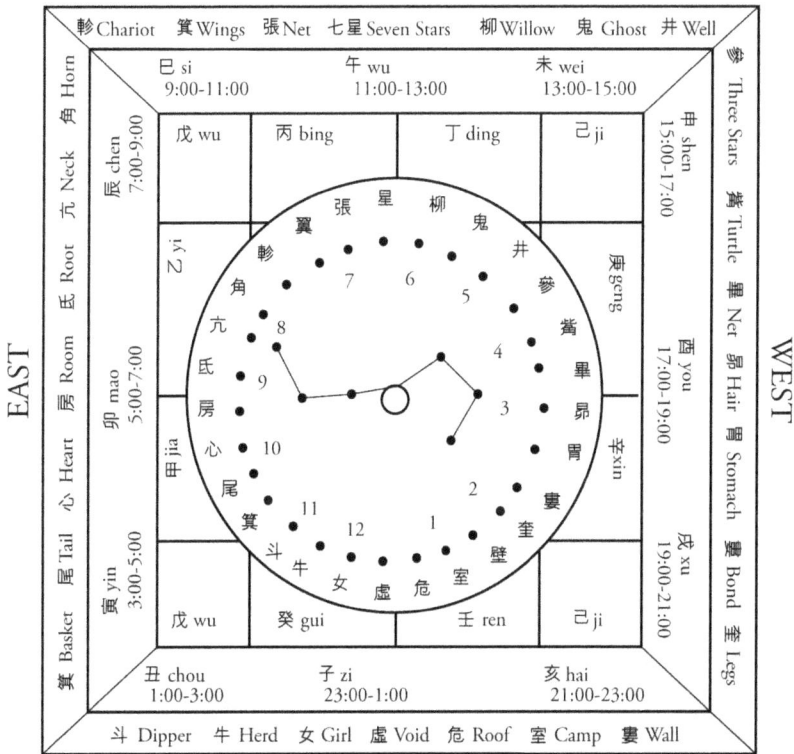

Zi Wei Dou Shu / Purple Star cosmic board

Feng Shui Astrology

The Feng Shui Compass School utilizes various systems of astrology to analyze compatible aspects between people and buildings. They are Ba Zhai or Eight Mansions, Xuan Kong or Flying Star, Nine Star Ki, and Si Zhu or Four Pillars, three of which employ the Luoshu Square to find auspicious and inauspicious directions when applied to the bagua map.

Most commonly and simply, the zodiac sign of the year that the house was built and the zodiac sign of the head of the household are compared for auspicious and inauspicious aspects.

MING GAU – KUA / DESTINY NUMBER

Some schools, like Ba Zhai, Flying Star and Nine Star Ki, begin an astrological reading by finding the subject's or object's destiny number, its Ming Gua or Kua number, calculated from birthdate and gender identity, which are assessed together to correspond with a Kua number, which determines the auspicious and inauspicious directions.

This is done by adding the last two digits of the birth year together until left with a single digit; e.g., 2017 = 8. Males then subtract this number from 10; e.g., 10 – 8 = 2, this is the Kua number. Females add their single-digit number to 5; e.g., 2017 = 8 + 5 = 13 = 4, this is the Kua number.

Once the Kua number has been found, it is used to find other birth numbers from specialist charts based on the 60-year cycle or on correspondences with the elements, directions and trigrams. In Feng Shui, the Kua number can be used to decide whether a house or office is going to be auspicious, based on the direction of the front entrance.

BA ZHAI – 8 MANSIONS / DIRECTIONS

One of the most crucial methods of the Compass School is based on the concept that each of the eight compass directions holds a different type of chi. Factors including astrology and numerology are added around this central premise.

The 8 trigrams of the I-Ching are correlated to each of the directions. The eight trigrams, along with their particular direction, also correspond to a Kua number, between 1 and 9. They are also associated with a particular element that carries a particular form of chi. This system is given the name 8 Mansions or Ba Zhai in Chinese metaphysics.

Eight Mansions Feng Shui is a personalized system that categorizes individuals and their homes into East and West groups, based on their birth year and gender. It identifies auspicious and inauspicious directions for each person and their living spaces, aiming to harmonize the flow of chi for improved well-being, influencing areas like work, sleep and activity locations.

4	9	2
South East	South	South West
Wood	Fire	Earth
Light Green	Red	Pink
3	5	7
East	Center	West
Wood	Earth	Metal
Dark Green	Yellow	Black
8	1	6
North East	North	North West
Earth	Water	Metal
White	Blue	Grey

Ming Gau/ Kua Number Magic Square

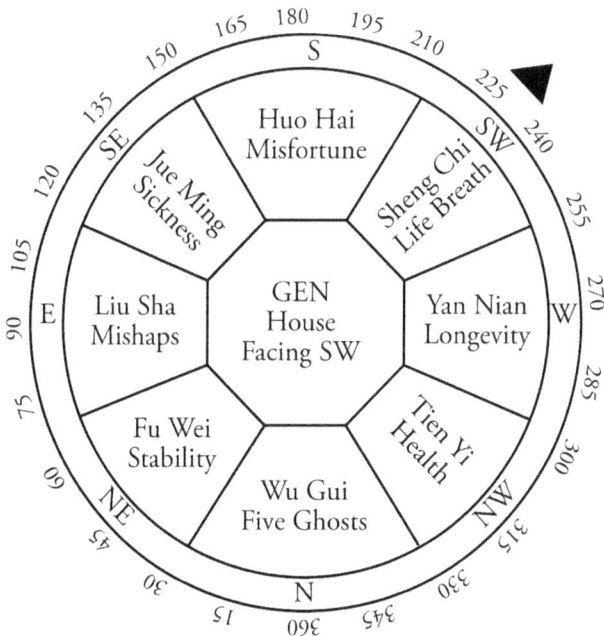

Ba Zhai / 8 Mansions Kua Destinty Chart

The 8 Mansions formula is comprised of 4 cardinal directions (N, S, E, W) and the 4 sub-cardinal or quaternary directions (NW, SW, NE, SE). This formula enables the suggestion of favourable and unfavourable directions of an individual.

By positioning oneself and living spaces according to these directions, one can potentially enhance one's health, wealth, career, relationships, and overall well-being, according to Feng Shui. While 8 Mansions focuses on individual and special orientations, it can be combined with other Feng Shui schools such as Flying Star for a more comprehensive approach.

If a person is unable to tap into their auspicious direction, the principle of Na Jia is used to suggest alternative positive directions to harness the positive effects of chi. Na Jia means to adopt the Heavenly Stems for positive effects in one's life. The four annual afflictions, Tai Sui – Grand Duke Jupiter, Wu Wong – Five Yellow, Sui Po – Year Breaker, and San Sha – 3 Killings, cannot affect the Heavenly Stems. Therefore, they bring positive chi and stability for a longer period of time.

The 8 Mansions formula is one of the most fundamental formulas of classical Feng Shui, as a Feng Shui audit is impossible without the application of the 8 Mansions formula. The system focuses on the Kua number of an individual, the 24 Mountains, and the location of a property.

ER SHI SI SHAN – 24 MOUNTAINS

The 8 Mansions are further divided into 24 sub-directions known as Er Shi Si Shan or 24 Mountains. They consist of the four sub-cardinal directions, represented by their trigram names, Kun, Chien, Xun, Kan; coincidentally, they are the even numbers, 8, 6, 2, 4, in the Luoshu square, plus the 12 Earthly Branches and 8 of the 10 Heavenly Stems. The remaining two Heavenly Stems are appointed to the earth element and situated in the center of the compass.

When displayed on a Luopan, the 24 Mountains are often marked by abbreviations such as N1, N2, N3, SW1, SW2, SW3, etc., displayed in one of its rings around the center compass. Each of the 8 Mansions is 45 degrees and is further divided into 3 x 15 degree segments, so 8 x 3 = 24. The sub-directions of the 360 degree circle are the basis for the 8 Mansions, the Flying Star and the Water Dragon formulas.

丙　午　丁　未　坤　申

3. Stem　VII. Branch　4. Stem　VIII. Branch　Trigram　IX. Branch
Ping　　　Wu　　　　Ting　　　Wei　　　　　Kun　　　Shen
　　　　South　　　　　　　　　　　　　SouthWest

庚　酉　辛　戌　乾　亥

7. Stem　X. Branch　8. Stem　XI. Branch　Trigram　XII. Branch
Keng　　Yu　　　　Hsin　　Xu　　　　　Chien　　Hai
　　　　West　　　　　　　　　　　　　NorthWest

戊　己

5. Stem　6. Stem
Wu　　　Chi
　　Center

壬　子　癸　丑　艮　寅

9. Stem　I. Branch　10. Stem　II. Branch　Trigram　III. Branch
Jen　　　Zi　　　　Kuei　　　Chou　　　Ken　　　Yin
　　　　North　　　　　　　　　　　　NorthEast

甲　卯　乙　辰　巽　巳

1. Stem　IV. Branch　2. Stem　V. Branch　Trigram　VI. Branch
Chia　　Mao　　　i　　　　Chen　　　Xun　　　Si
　　　East　　　　　　　　　　　　　SouthEast

24 Directions / 24 Mountains

XUAN KONG – FLYING STAR SCHOOL

In the Eastern world, Xuan Kong or Flying Star is a classical form of Feng Shui practiced outside of China across Southeast Asia. It is considered to be the highest form of Feng Shui, the mother system that consists of the Flying Star Feng Shui techniques. It has the same foundations as other traditional schools, following the principles of yin and yang, the five elements interchange, energies of the eight areas, directions, trigrams, and the dynamic movement of stars of the Luoshu square. It is different from other Feng Shui schools, as it takes into consideration a time factor to create a chart of the present energies.

Popularized in the Qing dynasty by Grandmaster Shen Zu Ren, Flying Star Feng Shui uses time, space and objects to create an astrological chart to analyze positive auras and negative auras of a building. These include wealth, mental and physical states, success, relationships with external parties, and the health of the inhabitant. It can be used for both yin and yang structures.

Flying Star divides time into periods of 20 years, with nine periods creating a complete cycle of 180 years. For example, until 2024, we were in period 8 with its predominant characteristics defined by the earth Feng Shui element and the energies of the NE direction.

Time is calculated using a table that gives the chi number for the year of the building. Space is calculated using a Loupan or compass to determine the precise direction of a structure or item. The most important ring on the Luopan is the 24 Mountain ring, in which each direction is subdivided into three sections. Using yin and yang, the facing side of a building is determined by the side of the building that receives the most yang chi. The positioning of objects such as a mountain, a skyscraper or water determines good or bad chi.

A Flying Star chart can be done on an annual, monthly, daily or hourly basis, and it shows the movement of both positive and negative energies in any given space. Creating a Flying Star chart requires three numbers, beginning with the Kua or year number, to find the month and day number using specialized charts. These numbers represent time, space and objects to create an astrological chart to analyze positive auras and negative auras of a building.

On the chart, the Ming Gau, Kua or year number becomes the base star. The base star is positioned in the central palace of a chart. To the right of the base star is the facing star, and opposite, on the left, is the sitting star. The sitting star is always opposite the facing palace. The sitting star is the number of the sitting palace.

Mountain/Sitting Water/Facing
SE   Star   S   Star   SW

3 6 7	7 1 3	5 8 5
4 7 6	2 5 8	9 3 1
8 2 2	6 9 4	1 4 9

E   ...   W

Period, Base, Fire, Star

NE   N   NW

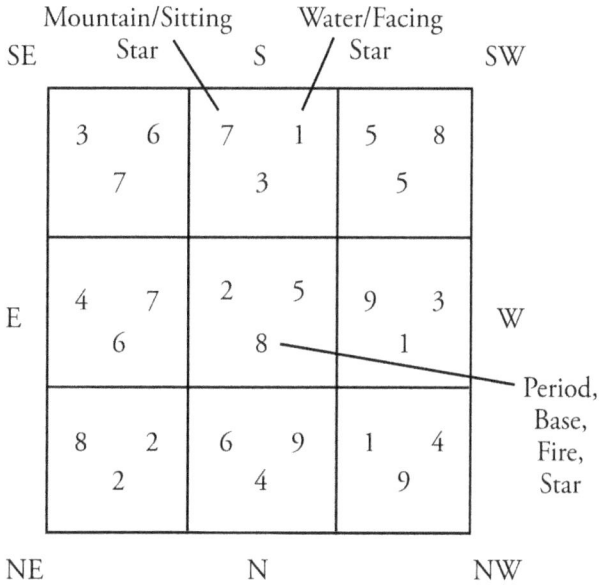

Chart for period 8

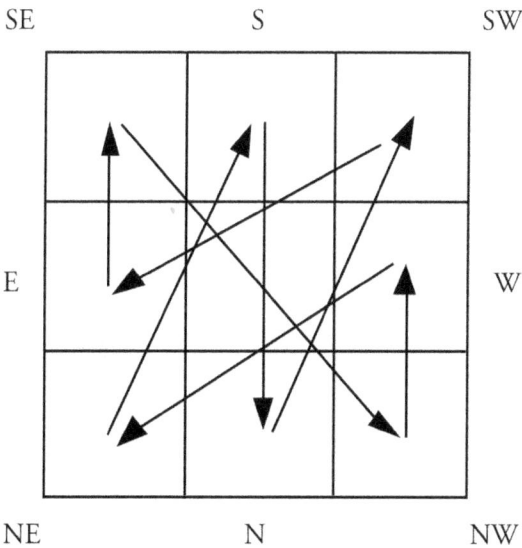

SE   S   SW

E   W

NE   N   NW

Movement around the Luoshu square from NW

Xuan Kong - Flying Star School

JIU GONG FEI XING – NINE PALACE FLYING STAR SCHOOL

In the Luoshu, the Flying Stars are the numbers 1–9, arranged on the Luoshu square. In the Luoshu, every number represents one of the trigrams of the I-Ching, which in turn corresponds to an element, cardinal direction, season, hour, colour, family member, organ, ailment, and many others. The numbers always move to the lower right (west), lower left (east), upper center (south), lower center (north), upper right (southwest), upper left (southeast), and back to the center, following the direction flow formed by the Luoshu sigil. This creates Nine Palace Flying Stars or Jiu Gong Fei Xing, whereby palaces are the nine sectors overlaid onto the layout of the heavens in astrology, or a home or premises in Feng Shui.

A Flying Star chart consists of three numbers in each palace of the Luosho square. They are called the base star, facing star and sitting star. Constructing a Flying Star chart requires the date that the building was occupied by the owners and the facing wall of the building. Creating a Flying Star chart always begins with the base star. The date of the building determines the number that occupies the base star portion of the central palace. Base stars always fly in the Luoshu path. Once all the base stars are distributed among the nine palaces, the facing star in the Luoshu is determined by the facing direction of the building. This number is the facing star. The sitting star is always opposite the facing palace. The sitting star is the number of the sitting palace.

To the Chinese, these nine stars reflect the astronomical importance of the North Star and the seven stars and one satellite that form the Big Dipper constellation. In their flying sequence, they move around the sections of the Luoshu square, starting from the center and moving northwest. These sections are called palaces; in each palace there is a mountain or sitting star, water or facing star, and a fire or base star, each represented by a number and a colour. The way the stars interact with each other has a positive or negative effect.

The nine stars and the aspects they signify are as follows: Star 1 – success, wealth. Star 2 – sickness, separation, miscarriage. Star 3 – lawsuits, misfortune. Star 4 – romance, academic achievement. Star 5 – sickness, death, casualties, lawsuits. Star 6 – wealth, achievement, travel, authority. Star 7 – robbery, fun, imprisonment. Star 8 – fame, wealth, happiness. Star 9 – luck, celebration. The stars 1, 4, 6, 9, are good stars – and 2, 3, 5, 7, are bad stars, although this can change depending on whether they appear as timely or untimely.

Southeast	South	Southwest
Illness 2 Mishap	Destruction 7 Loss	Happiness 9 Lasting wealth
Victory 1 Achievment	Quarrels 3 Hostility	Fatality 5 Disaster
Luck 6 Windfall	Wealth 8 Prosperity	Progress 4 Relationship
Northeast	North	Northwest

East ... West

Nine Palace Flying Star chart for 2024

Southeast	South	Southwest
Victory 1 Achievment	Luck 6 Windfall	Wealth 8 Prosperity
Happiness 9 Lasting wealth	Illness 2 Mishap	Progress 4 Relationship
Fatality 5 Disaster	Destruction 7 Loss	Quarrels 3 Hostility
Northeast	North	Northwest

East ... West

Nine Palace Flying Star chart for 2025

Of the two following forms of astrology, one uses stars and is a modern Japanese adaptation of traditional Chinese methods. The other uses pillars and is neither a school of Feng Shui nor a system of astrology.

JIUGONG MINGLI / JUIXING MINGLI – 9 STAR KI (QI/CHI)

Both Chinese names translate as 'Nine Palace Star Destiny Numerology' or 'Nine Star Destiny Numerology', known in the West as '9 Star Ki'. It is a popular form of Japanese astrology, sometimes referred to as Feng Shui astrology, as it is often used alongside Feng Shui principles. It is an adjustment or consolidation made in 1924 by Shinjiro Sonoda to traditional Chinese divination and geomancy methods such as Flying Star, the Ming Gua number from Eight Mansions, and the combination of the Luoshu Square with the Post-celestial Bagua.

It derives its name from the idea that there are thought to be nine-year and nine-month cycles of ki/qi/chi on earth, which are related to the solar and seasonal cycles, that have common effects across the planet on people's mental and physical development and experiences throughout their lives.

In traditional Feng Shui astrology, it is used to analyze and harmonize energy flows, based on time, date and location, to predict actions like planting crops or making journeys, and to understand how individuals and environments interact.

This makes it possible to determine the most auspicious times, especially for particular activities, using star-based numerology to understand personality, relationships and life paths, while its use in Feng Shui focuses on how energy flows through the environment.

As a system of I-Ching prediction, it uses the idea of nine stars to represent the numbers 1-9, making it particularly useful within Feng Shui, as the nine energies are the same as those used by the 8 trigrams.

Astrologically, the system is based on the concept that nine elemental or key stars, each with its own unique characteristics, are the nine variations of the elements (four yin and yang elements, the yin earth element stands alone) and how they are positioned within the Luoshu square at given times. They have the most influence, in that each direction combines with the chi of the earth and the heavens at the time of birth to create a different chi or energy for each person.

One's fortune is divined by calculating a three-number 'ki' from one's date of birth. First, the Honmei star or 'True Feeling Star' – the principal adulthood or year number describing one's most mature mind/heart/karma or spirit type. The year number provides insight onto your outer nature and relates to how people see you.

Second, the Getsumei star or 'Month-Life Star' – the character, childhood or month number, describing one's physical connection to the earth; namely one's more primitive or physical features. The month number is your emotional or child nature. The day number is your inner adult nature.

Getsumei - month star
Number / Element

Honmei - year star
Zodiac sign

南

午
九
巳
辰
四
未
二
申

東 東
卯
三
五
七
酉
西

寅
八
一
丑
子
六
戌
亥

Keisha
diretion

北

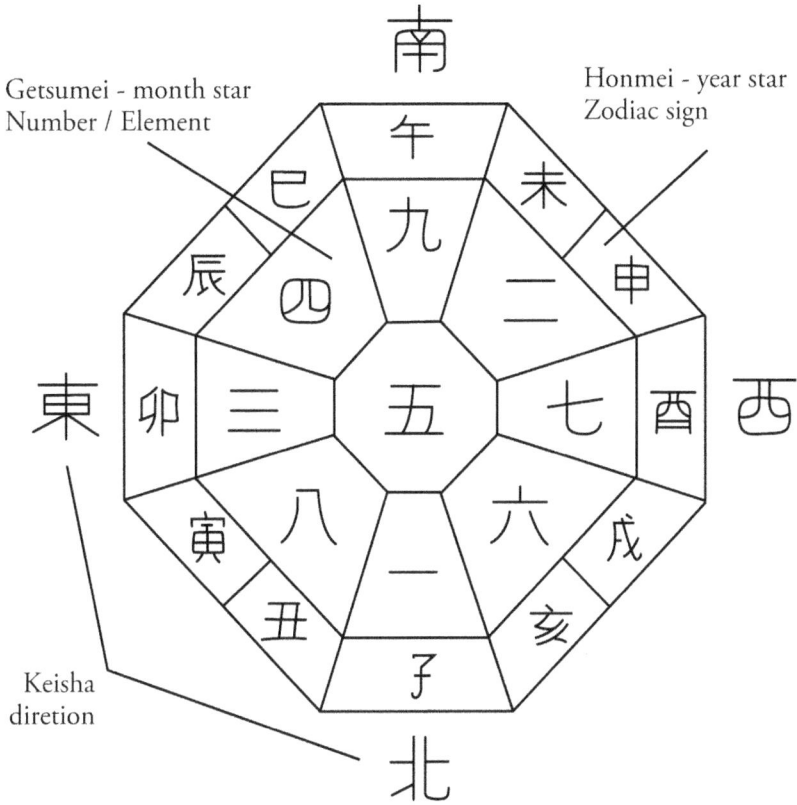

9 Star Ki - Kotan Jyoi Ben cosmic board

These numbers are used to reveal personality traits, strengths, weaknesses and potential life paths that provide insight into compatibility with others. Feng Shui principles are then applied to the living and working environment to enhance the flow of positive energy based on individual Nine Star Ki profiles. The Nine Star Ki stars are numbers that represent those cycles.

SI ZHU – FOUR PILLARS / BA ZI – 8 CHARACTERS

Si Zhu or Four Pillars is also known as Ba Zi or 8 Characters. It is an astrological system that analyzes a person's fate based on their birth year, month, day and hour. These are the Four Pillars, their full title being Zi Pen Si Zhu – Four Pillars or Emperors of Destiny. Each of the pillars is ascribed two characters, one stem and one branch, making 8 in all, giving it the name of Ba Zi or 8 Characters.

Ba Zi utilizes 8 characters from the system of 10 Heavenly Stems and 12 Earthly Branches, each associated with one of the five elements, to create a unique astrological profile. This profile is then interpreted to understand a person's personality, potential and life path.

By analyzing the relationships between the elements and the various pillars, one can gain insights into a person's strengths, weaknesses, relationships, career prospects and overall destiny. This system can also identify periods of good and bad luck, potential opportunities and challenges.

Individually, the year pillar represents the characteristics shared with those people born in the same year. This pillar comprises the elemental energy of the year's stem and the typical manifestation of its branch or the year's zodiac sign.

The month pillar represents a person's archetypical inner qualities, especially those that indicate a deeper, wiser, older self that becomes more apparent over the years. The day pillar is generally the most significant; it indicates one's everyday personality, the socialized version of oneself.

The hour pillar represents the natural, spontaneous, untutored self that expresses itself through play and creative activity, indicating how the private self reacts to stress, or times of crisis, as well as when fully relaxed or in the company of children.

By analyzing the relationships between the characters and the pillars, one can gain insights into a person's strengths, weaknesses, relationships, career prospects and overall destiny. This system can also identify periods of good and bad luck, potential opportunities and challenges.

Schools like Four Pillars, which is not a Feng Shui school of astrology, do not require a Ming Gau or Kua number; they utilize the Gan Zi number system of the 10 Heavenly Stems and the 12 Earthly Branches, based on the sexagenary cycle and the year, month, day and hour of birth, zodiac sign and five elements, which are calculated to determine house and personality compatibility. Four Pillars is not astrology, but it is used like it's a personal astrology.

時 HOUR	日 DAY	月 MONTH	年 YEAR	
丁	壬	丙	丁	Heavenly Stems
Ting Yin Fire	Jen Yang Water	Ping Yang Fire	Ting Yin Fire	
未	戌	午	巳	Earthly Branches
Wei Goat Yin Earth	Xu Dog Yang Earth	XWu Horse Yang Fire	Si Snake Yin Fire	
丁 己 乙	丁 戊 辛	丁 己	庚 丙 戊	Hidden Stems

Ba Zi - 8 Characters (Gan Zi - Stem and Branch)
placed on the Zi Pen Si Zhu - Four Pillars of Destiny.

Pu – Prediction (Divination)

The Chinese word 'Pu' translates as 'prediction', as in divination, and includes astrology. It features practices like osteomancy – the cracking of shells and bones; plastromancy – casting yarrow stalks; astrocalendics – weather divination, especially clouds and vapours; oneiromancy – dream interpretation; and physiognomy – facial features. The mysticism of the I-Ching and its hexagrams feature prominently in this art.

The term 'Pu' actually refers to the archaic process of using tortoise shells or yarrow stalks to seek answers from the gods or spirits. Shells and bones inscribed with signs are heated until cracks appear, and their patterns are then interpreted. Individual yarrow stalks are used in a specific counting process to generate a hexagram, which can be interpreted; coins can also be used for this I-Ching method.

Pu processes involve contacting deities or spirits through a series of questions and observations to solve doubts and make decisions in matters of state, agriculture and health.

There are other divination systems other than the I-Ching, some of which cross over into astrology and Feng Shui. Feng Shui deals with the arrangement of space and harmony and can be seen as a form of divination, as a way to influence one's fortune.

Popular prediction studies in this art include Da Liu Ren, Qi Men Dun Jia and Tai Yi Shen Shu, collectively known as San Shi, the 3 styles or 3 rites. All three draw divination from cosmic boards, relying on numerical analysis to reveal one's path and future. Two other numerological divination systems are Plum Blossom and Iron Plate.

DIVINATION TOOLS

Pu actually refers to the archaic process of using divination tools, such as tortoise shells, yarrow stalks, coins, divination boards and wooden blocks or 'moon blocks' called 'Poe', to seek answers from the gods or spirits. The process involved contacting deities or spirits through a series of questions and observations.

A well-known method is osteomancy, in which shells and bones are inscribed with signs before being heated until cracks appear and their patterns interpreted. The practice called Kua Chun, meaning 'drawing straws', represents plastromancy as divination, using yarrow sticks, coins or wooden blocks (Poe). Cleromancy, meaning 'random selection', is divination using dice and other such devices. The I-Ching employs two main methods of cleromancy in which either fifty yarrow stalks or three coins are used in a specific counting process to generate a hexagram, which would then be interpreted.

Other methods include Jouben, meaning 'moon blocks' or 'Poe'; Fuji, meaning 'planchette writing' or 'spirit writing'; and Omikuyi, which is a Japanese word meaning 'sacred lot', random fortunes written on strips of paper in Buddhist and Shinto temples. Also Tung Shing, the Yellow or Imperial Calendar, solar-based divination and almanac.

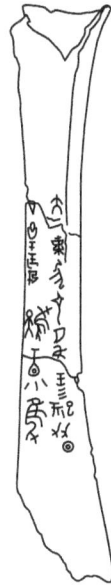

Animal Bone

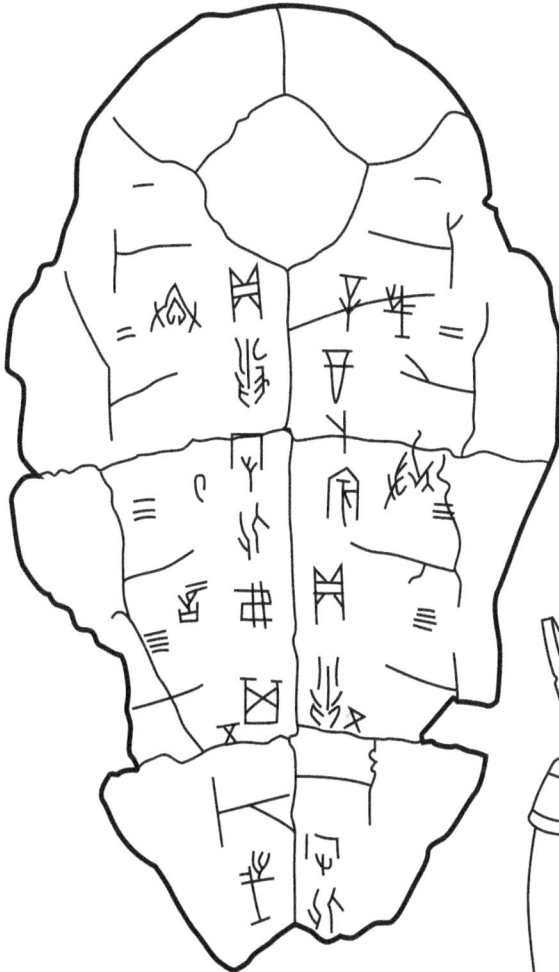

Turtle Shell

Divination Sticks

Divination Tools

SHI / LIUREN - ASTROLABE / COSMIC / DIVINATION BOARD

A Chinese cosmic board, known as a Shi or a Liuren astrolabe, is a divination tool used particularly during the Han dynasty in cosmology and Feng Shui. Such boards are typically lacquered and feature astronomical sightlines, used for divination and charting the movement of celestial bodies – notably the North Pole star and the Big Dipper. For the ancient Chinese, heaven radiated out from the axis formed by a linkage between the North Pole Star and the Big Dipper.

In ancient China, Shi served as the basis for a wide range of beliefs and practices in astrology and religion, used to determine the most auspicious orientation for burials, tomb layouts and furnishings. They were formed from a static, square earth plate and a rotating dome or disc, representing heaven.

The design of cosmic boards is based on the 'Liubo' gaming board, which is based on a diagram known as 'Ding', the 'squared northern culmen'. This heavenly square became the inspiration for many magic squares, including sundials, cosmic boards, diviner's boards, gaming boards (Liubo), the Hetu and Luoshu squares, and the Luopan or Feng Shui compass, as well as TLV mirrors – all representations of the Supreme God as Ding, the squared northern culmen.

Cosmic boards and Liuren astrolabes from the Six Dynasties period (222–589 CE) onwards have consisted of a Heavenly Plate placed over an Earth Plate. On the square Earth Plate are three groups of inscriptions. The outer band has 36 animals – the 12 zodiac animals associated with the Earthly Branches, plus the 28 animals associated with the Xiu or Lunar Mansions. The disc-shaped Heaven Plate is divided diagonally into four sections that allocate 9 animals, 7 xi and 5 stem and branch to a section.

Complex astronomical calculations and astrological triangulations are obtained by rotating the mobile disc around the square base to obtain adjustments corresponding to specific moments of the day, month and year, which would all play a part in this divination process. A diviner examined current sky phenomena to set the board and adjust their position in relation to the board.

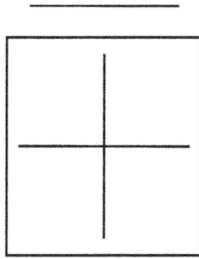

Ding / Di (God Above)

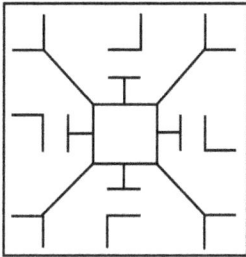

Squared Northern Culmen (Heaven)   Liubo gaming board

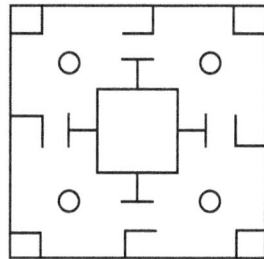

Graphic origin of the Cosmic Board

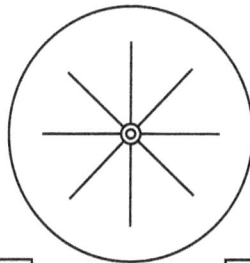

Heaven Plate

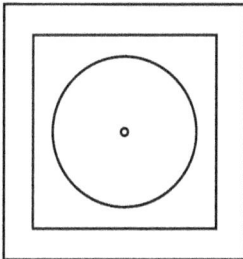

Earth Plate   Earth Plate
(front)   (back)

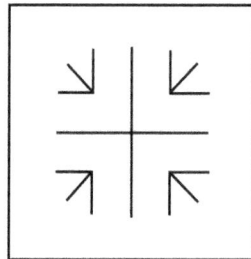

Han dynasty cosmic board design

San Shi – Three Styles / Rites

San Shi is a unique form of Chinese divination that covers the three levels incorporating Da Liu Ren, relating to events to the person – Qi Men Dun Jia relating to events to the locality and regional environment with timings, and Tai Yi Shen Su relating to macroscopic events to the country or continent.

DA LIU REN – BIG 6 WATER TECHNIQUE

Da Liu Ren is a form of Chinese calendrical astrology. It stands out unequivocally as the highest level of divination studies. It is used to seek divine answers and guidance on all levels of life, even in military applications. This system is heavily influenced by the accuracy of celestial observations triggered by events in the mortal world. It is frequently used to predict outcomes of certain events based on the observation of good or bad omens. This is similar to the Plum Blossom technique used with the I-Ching – while Ba Zi with its eight characters, and Zi Pen Si Zhu with its Four Pillars of Destiny, are a simplified derivatives of Da Liu Ren.

The name Da Liu Ren translates literally as 'Big 6 Water Technique', because the 'Heavenly Star' Ren, indicating Yang water, appears 6 times in the 60-year cycle. These 6 Ren, each with a different branch, indicate an entire movement in the sexagesimal cycle, during which something may appear, rise to maturity and then decline and disappear. Thus, the 6 Ren indicate the life cycle of phenomena.

Divination in Da Liu Ren is determined by the relational types of the elements and yin-yang between and among the 3 Transmissions, 4 Classes, 12 Generals and the Heaven and Earth Plates. Its cosmic board is modeled after the concept of atomic nucleus in ancient nuclear physics. That is to say that the atomic nucleus contains 720 particles, or 1440 subatomic particles per atom.

This enables the board to contain 1440 possible arrangements in all of the permutations for the 60-day cycle, with 12 double hours per day, and with the day and evening aristocratic arrangements. The close matching between the actual nuclear structure of the Da Liu Ren divination mechanism of the cosmic board in all its permutations allows for extremely accurate mathematical prediction.

The main diviner's board consists of a stationary square Earth board and a circular rotating Heaven board centered on the 24 fortnightly periods and Tai Sui dating. The main board itself is drawn with a 16-square grid, with the outer 12 squares taking on characteristics and the four inner squares being empty.

A Da Liu Ren cosmic board is an array with the 3 Transmissions on top, the 4 Classes, their Heaven and Earth pan portions, the 12 Generals, and the Heaven pan superimposed above the Earth pan. Vacancies are noted in the right margin, along with the date and Ju number. The fixed, unmoving Earth pan marks the positions of the 12 Branches; the Heaven plate spirits rotate around the Earth pan.

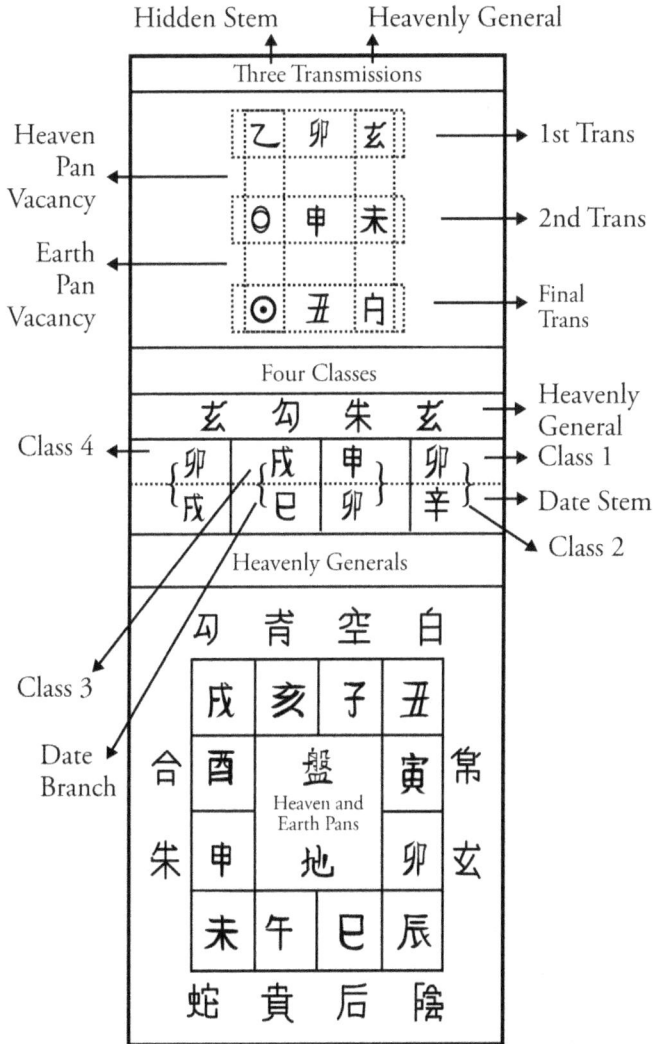

Da Liu Ren cosmic board

QI MEN DUN JIA – MYSTERIOUS GATES ESCAPING TECHNIQUE

This technique was originally devised to help form military strategy and tactics. It was used during the Warring States period at the Battle of the Red Cliffs and by the Ming Emperors to secure their empire. Over the centuries, it grew in popularity and expanded to include a number of other types of divination, including medical divination, matchmaking, childbirth, travel and personal fortune. Today it includes contemporary applications, most notably for business and finance.

Qi Men Dun Jia is based on astrological observations and consists of various aspects of metaphysics, including the doctrines of yin-yang, the 5 elements, 8 trigrams, 10 Heavenly Stems and 12 Earthly Branches, as well as the 24 solar terms that are the 24 points of the lunisolar calendar. Flying Star Feng Shui is a derivative of Qi Men Dun Jia.

The Qi Men Dun Jia cosmic board consists of a 3 x 3 magic square of nine palaces, which includes a Heaven plate and an Earth plate, a spirit plate, 8 gates and a Star plate. The various symbols rotate around the palaces with each double hour of the day, making a total of 1080 different configurations of the Qi Men Dun Jia cosmic board. These situations are recycled four times per year and are divided by the yin and yang halves of the year.

TAI YI SHEN SHU – GREAT YI MIRACULOUS CALCULATION

Tai Yi Shen Shu is used to predict macroscopic events like wars or the meaning of a supernova. Its methodology is quite similar to the others, with a rotary Heaven plate and a fixed Earth plate.

While the art makes use of the 8 trigrams and 64 hexagrams as a foundation, analysis is conducted from the Tai Yi cosmic board and the array of symbols thereon, with special reference to the proportion of symbols in specific places. Important symbols include the Calculator, the Scholar and Tai Yi.

A number of spirits rotate around the 16 palaces of the Tai Yi cosmic board. Each cosmic board contains a number of counts or numbers; the Host count and the Guest count taking primary importance over the Fixed count. A rendering of the portion of the symbols and counts of '1 Yang Dun' array for Tai Yi divination. The entire series consists of '22 Yang Dun' and '72 Yin Dun' arrays for Tai Yi.

One form of Tai Yi Shen Shu has been popularized over the centuries to predict personal fortunes. Genghis Khan, Emperor of China in the Yuan dynasty, used Tai Yi to gauge his chances of invading Japan, which indicated that he would be unsuccessful that year.

己 蓬 **3** Ji Shower 壬 惊 虎 Ren Fear Tiger	庚 心 **8** Geng Heart 乙 开 合 Yi Open Combo	丙 仟 **1** Bing Trust 丁 休 阴 Ding Rest Moon
丁 英 **2** Ding Grace 癸 死 武 Gui Death Tortoise	辛 芮 **4** Xin Tie 辛 Xin	戊 辅 **6** Wu Ad 己 生 蛇 Ji Grow Snake
乙 禽 **7** Yi Beast 戊 景 地 Wu Scene Earth	壬 柱 **9** Ren Column 丙 杜 天 Bing Stop Sky	癸 冲 **5** Gui Dash 庚 伤 符 Geng Hurt Chief

Qi Men Dun Jia cosmic board

Tai Yi Shen Shu cosmic boards

I-Ching – Book of Changes

The I-Ching or Book of Changes is an ancient Chinese text comprised of two books: the Book of Oracles, a divination system using line symbols called 'gua' (divinatory symbols), and the Book of Wisdom that reveals the underlying principles of yin-yang. This combination mixed movement with action and posed the question "What am I to do?" As a result of this, the I-Ching was lifted above the level of an ordinary book of divination to become a book of wisdom.

The originator of the I-Ching is said to be the legendary sage king Fu Xi, one of the three Sovereign Emperors who ruled the world after the Flood, circa 2600 BCE. According to tradition, the Ba Gua or 8 Trigrams were revealed to him in the markings on the back of a mythical Dragon Horse (sometimes said to be a turtle) that emerged from the Haung He or Yellow River. The markings are known as the 'Hetu' and his arrangement of the trigrams is called the Xiantiantu or pre-celestial bagua.

By the 9th century BCE or earlier, this system is known to have been used throughout all levels of Chinese society. It precedes the compilation of the I-Ching during the Zhou dynasty of the 2nd century BCE.

In the 7th century BCE, China produced two of its greatest philosophers – Confucius, the founder of Confucianism, and Lao Tzu, the founder of Daoism and author of the Tao Te Ching or the I-Ching. This system, along with others, is thought to have been in its current form by the 3rd century BCE.

During the 2nd century BCE, it is said that King Wen, founder of the Zhou dynasty, reformed the arrangement of the trigrams in the Fu Xi bagua to create the King Wen sequence or Houtiantu, the post-celestial bagua. In the same century, Lao Tzu's original text, as it was revered and practiced, was re-written by Zhou Dunyi. As the oldest Chinese philosophical text, the divination text called the Changes of Zhou or Zhou Yi became the core of the I-Ching.

In 136 BCE, Emperor Wu of Han named the Zhou Yi as 'first among the classics', dubbing it the 'Classic of Changes' or I-Ching. Emperor Wu's placement of the Zhou Yi among the Five Classics was informed by a broad span of cultural influences that included Confucianism, Daoism, Legalism, yin-yang commentary, and Wu Xing physical theory.

While the Zhou Yi does not contain any cosmological analogies, the I-Ching was read as a microcosm of the universe that offers complex, symbolic correspondences. The official text was literally set in stone, as one of the Xiping Stone Classics.

The canonical I-Ching became the standard text for over 2000 years, until alternative versions of the Zhou Yi and related texts were discovered in the 20th century. In the canonical I-Ching, the hexagrams are arranged in an order dubbed the King Wen sequence that generally pairs hexagrams with their upside-down equivalent, although in eight cases, hexagrams are paired with their inversion.

After the Chinese communist revolution in 1911, the I-Ching was no longer a part of mainstream Chinese political philosophy but maintained its cultural influence as China's most ancient text. Chinese writers offered parallels between the I-Ching and subjects like linear algebra and logic in computer science.

Translated into Western languages many times, the earliest complete Western copy of the I-Ching was a Latin translation by the Jesuit missionary Jean-Baptiste Regis in the 1730s, published in Germany in the 1830s. The text gained significant acknowledgment during the counter-culture revolution of the 1960s with the translation of the 1923 German version by Richard Wilhelm, later translated into English by Cary F. Baynes, with a foreword by Carl Jung. Later publications in 1986 and 1996 incorporate many of the new discoveries of the 20th century, attempting to reconstruct the Zhou period readings.

HEXAGRAMS

The basic unit of the I-Ching is the hexagram or 'gua', meaning 'divinatory symbol' – a figure composed of six stacked horizontal lines, each line is either broken (yin) or unbroken (yang). Along with numbers and simple statements, hexagrams were used as oracles.

In antiquity, oracles were in use everywhere; the oldest among them confined themselves to the answers Yes and No. This type of oracular pronouncement is likewise the basis of the I-Ching. Yes was represented by a simple unbroken line (yang), and No was represented by a broken line (yin).

However, the need for greater differentiation seems to have been felt at an early date, and the single lines were combined in pairs, creating 4 two-line signs (bigrams). To each of these combinations a third line was added. In this way, the eight trigrams came into being. The trigrams were then paired with themselves and each other to form the 64 hexagrams.

Upper Trigram → / Lower Trigram ↓	Qian creative	Zhen	Kan	Gen	Kun	Xun	Li	Dui
Qian creative	1. Chien creative	34. Ta Chuang power of the great	5. Hsu nourishment	26. Ta Ch'u taming power of the great	11. Tau peace	9. Hsao Chu taming power of the small	14. Ta Yi possession in great measure	43. Kuai btrakthrough resoluteness
Zhen arousing	25. Wu Wang innocence the unexpected	51. Chen arousing, shock; thunder	3. Chun initial difficulty	27.1 providing nourishment	24. Fu return turning point	42.1 increase	21. Shih Ho biting through	17. Sui following
Kan abysmal	6. Sung conflict	40. Hsieh deliverance	29. K'an the abysmal water	4. Ming youthful folly	6. Shig the army	59. Huan dispersion dissolution	64. Wei Chi before completion	47. K'on oppression exhausttion
Gen keeping still	33. Tun retreat	62. Hsiao Kuo preproderance of the small	39. Chien obstruction	52. Ken keeping still mountain	15. Ch'ien modesty	53. Chien devolpment progress	56. Lu wanderer	30. Hsien influence wooing

45. Ts'ui gathering together

28. Ta Kao preponderance of the great

49. Ko molting revolution

58. Tui joyous lake

35. Chun progress

50. Ting the couldron

30. Li the clinging fire

38. K'uei opposition

20. Kaun contemplation view

57. Sun gentle wind

37. Chia Jen the family the clan

61. Chung Fu inner truth

2. Kun receptive

46. Sheng pushing upward

36. Ming I darkening of the mind

19. Lau approach

23. Po splitting apart

18. Ku decay

22. Pi grace

41. Sun decrease

8. Pi union

48. Ching the well

63. Chi Chi after completion

60. Chieh limitation

16. Yu enthusiasm

51. Heng duration

55. Feng abundance fullness

54. Kuei Mei marrying maiden

12. P'i stagnation standstill

44. Kou coming to meet

13. T'uang Jen fellowship with men

10. Lu conduct

Kun receptive

Xun gentle

Li clinging

Dui joyous

Formation, names and correspondences of the Hexagrams of the I-Ching

I-Ching Divination

In the I-Ching, yin and yang are converted into 'yao' or 'lines'; the yin-yang formula produced two-line forms – broken lines representing 'yin' and unbroken lines representing 'yang'. These two unigram forms were paired to form bigrams, and a third line was added to form the trigrams.

The trigrams were conceived as images of all that happened in heaven and on earth. At the same time, they were held to be in a state of continual transition, one changing into another – just as transition from one phenomenon to another is continually taking place in the physical world – the fundamental concept of the I-Ching.

In order to achieve even greater multiplicity, to specify a dynamic change, the process of change, the eight trigrams were enlarged to 64 hexagrams by the interaction of each trigram with itself and with the inverse of the remaining seven, to obtain a total of 64 signs.

I-CHING DIVINATION

The ancient method for I-Ching divination included the laboured process of sorting 50 yarrow stalks thrown in a bunch to gain a reading. The more modern method involves the tossing of three individual coins of the same or similar weight and size, with identifiable heads and tails.

The coins are briefly shaken in the hand and then tossed onto a flat surface. In each case the process is done six times, with each outcome producing one line of the hexagram. The hexagram is assembled from the ground up, the bottom line being considered the first line in the text interpretations.

Assigning a numerical value to heads and tails, and then adding the total, determines the line recorded. 3 heads adds up to 9, a circle marks an unbroken changing line. 3 tails adds up to 6, a cross marks a broken changing line. 2 heads and 1 tail (3+3+2) equal 8, and mark a broken unchanging line. 1 head and 2 tails (3+2+2) equal 7, and mark an unbroken, unchanging line.

The six coin-tosses form the 'present hexagram'. Any lines that are 'changing lines' must be changed into their opposite – unbroken lines into broken lines, and vice versa, to produce the 'future hexagram'.

CHANGING LINES

Each of these 64 hexagrams consists of six lines, either positive (yang) or negative (yin). Each line is thought of as capable of change, and whenever a line changes there is a change also of the situation represented by the given hexagram.

Yin   Yang

Unigram

WU CHI

Bigram   Trigram   Hexagram

Tayi (world embryo)

Gau / Divinatory symbols

Beginning of Tai Chi

Winter   Spring   Summer
Old Yang   Young Yang   Old Yang

TAIJI (movement)

Autumn   Winter
Young Yin   Old Yin

Bigrams as the 4 seasons

YIN   YANG

Kun   Chen / Zhen

Tian
Di

Kan   Li

TAI CHI (harmony)

Ken / Gen   Tui / Dui

Xun / Sun   Chien / Qian

Taijitu
(Supreme Ultimate)

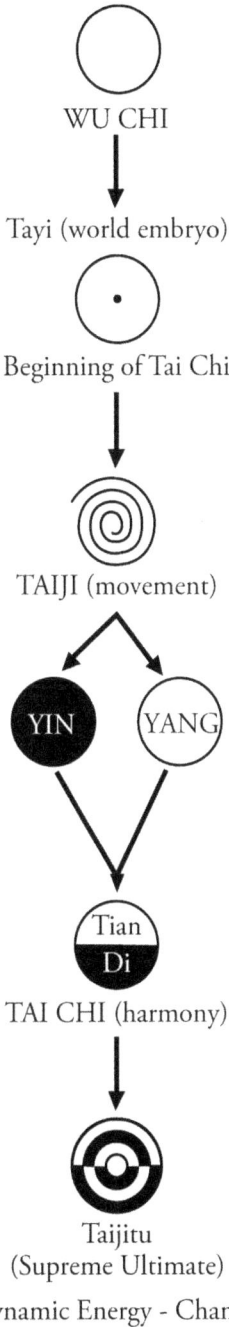

Dynamic Energy - Change.

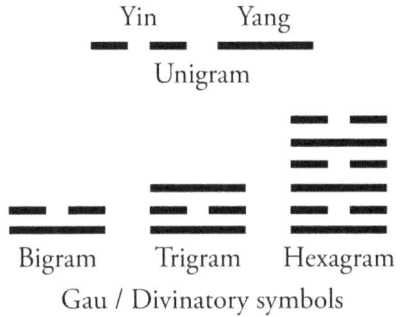

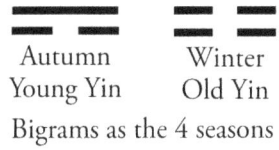

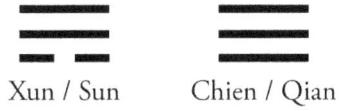

Eight Trigrams - Ba Gau

Each hexagram is also made up of two trigrams. The first, primary or lower trigram shows the inner aspect (person), whereas the second or upper hexagram pictures the outer aspects of the current, ongoing change. Hence, the inner aspect (person) is combined with the outer aspect (a situation). These represent a process of change happening at the present moment.

E.g., Kun – the receptive, earth – represents the nature of earth, strong in devotion; among the seasons it stands for late autumn, when all the forces of life are at rest. If the lowest line changes, we have the hexagram Fu, return, thunder, representing the movement of that which stirs anew from within the earth at the turn of the solstice; it symbolizes the return of light.

As in the example shown, all the lines of the hexagram do not necessarily change; it depends entirely on the character of a given line. A line whose nature is positive (yang), with an increasing dynamism, turns into its opposite, a negative line (yin), whereas a positive line of lesser strength remains unchanged (yang). The same principle holds for negative lines (yin).

Positive lines that move are designated by the number 9, and negative lines that move by the number 8, while non-moving lines, which serve only as structural matter in the hexagram, without an intrinsic meaning of their own, are represented by the number 7.

Thus, when the text reads, "Nine at the beginning means...", then this is the equivalent of saying, "When the positive line in the first place is represented by the number 9, it has this meaning...". If, on the other hand, the number 7 represents the line, then it is disregarded in interpreting the oracle.

The same principle holds for lines represented by the numbers 6 and 8, respectively. The five upper lines are not taken into account; only the 6 at the beginning has any meaning, and its transformation into its opposite, the situation Kun – the receptive, becomes Fu – return.

In this way, we have a series of situations symbolically expressed by lines, and through the movement of these, the structures can change one into another. On the other hand, such change does not necessarily occur, for when a hexagram is made up of lines represented by the numbers 7 and 8 only, there is no movement within it, and only its aspect as a whole is taken into consideration.

Each line begins with a word indicating the line number, base, 2, 3, 4, 5, and either the number 6 for a broken line, or the number 9 for an unbroken line. Following the line number, the line statements may make oracular or prognostic statements.

self   opposite   reverse   other

Trigram combinations creating hexagrams

heaven/spirit — 6th line / 5th line — upper trigram

human/soul — 4th line / 3rd line

earth/body — 2nd line / 1st line — lower trigram

Construction of a hexagram

heads   tails

$2 + 2 + 2 = 6$ ▬ X ▬ Changing Yin

$2 + 2 + 3 = 7$ ▬▬▬ Static Yang

$2 + 3 + 3 = 8$ ▬ ▬ Static Yin

$3 + 3 + 3 = 9$ ▬▬▬ Changing Yang
0

present   future

Static Yin 8 ▬ ▬ — —

Static Yin 8 ▬ ▬ — —

Changing Yang 9 ▬▬▬ 0 → — —

Static Yin 8 ▬ ▬ — —

Changing Yin 6 ▬ ▬ X → ▬▬▬

Static Yang 7 ▬▬▬ ▬▬▬

51. Chen   changing to   19. Lin

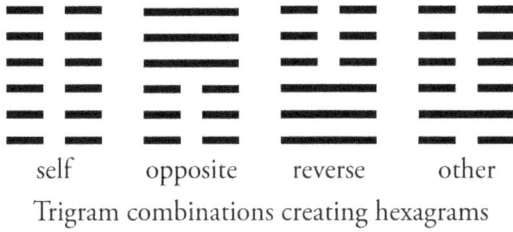

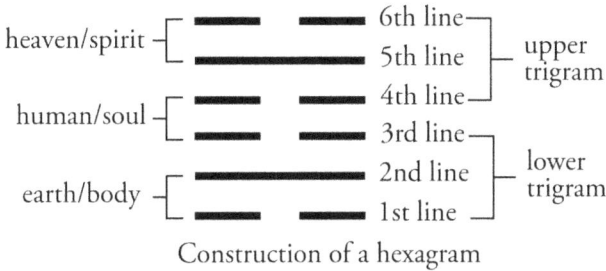

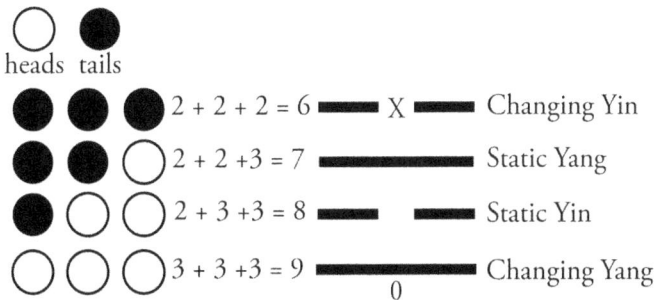

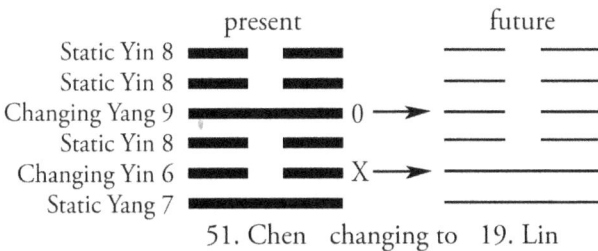

Changing lines forming hexagrams

Primary Hexagrams

Composed of six stacked, broken or unbroken horizontal lines, hexagrams consist of two primary trigrams – the upper and lower trigrams, composed of three lines each. The lower trigram is supposed to show the ongoing changes, whereas the upper trigram will picture the outer aspect of the current, ongoing change. Hence, an inner aspect (a person) is combined with the outer aspect (a situation).

Some hexagrams have a nuclear trigram complex, consisting of the middle four lines, made from the upper and lower primary trigrams. In such cases, the middle two of these four lines overlap each other, allowing the merger of the two middle lines to form one middle line, revealing a 'nuclear' trigram.

4 TIMELESS OR ETERNAL HEXAGRAMS

The two most important hexagrams of the I-Ching are Qian/heaven – the creative, and Kun/earth – the receptive, representing the origin of all things by combining the fundamental forces of yin-yang.

As the trigrams for heaven and earth, father and mother, and husband and wife, they represent the 'out breath' and 'in breath', merging together into a stage of supreme peace. They are the elemental yang and yin that, when included with Kan/water and Li/fire, form the 4 Timeless or Eternal Hexagrams which form the bedrock of the entire system.

Chinese philosopher Lui I Ming formulated that there are four qualities that apply to every situation we find ourselves in; they are represented by the 4 Timeless or Eternal Hexagrams. These four hexagrams stand apart from the remaining 60. They represent the Original Spirit and are out of time.

The other 60 represent the firing times of the firing process or the illumination of the mind. The 'firing process' is an alchemical process called the 'Elixir of Life' or the 'Pill of Immortality', achieved by burning away false yin to reach a state of pure yang.

When the celestial yang is overcome by the mundane yin, reality is obscured. This is like heaven mixing with earth; the middle line of heaven enters into the palace of earth, so that the trigram of earth is filled (middle yin line becomes yang) to become the trigram for water.

When the mundane yin takes possession of the celestial yang, intellectual knowledge and emotions gradually develop. This is like earth mixing with heaven; the middle yin line of earth goes into the palace of heaven, so the trigram of heaven is emptied (middle yang line becomes yin) and becomes fire.

 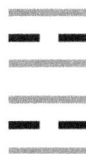

hexagram 30. Li	primary Li/Li	nuclear K'an

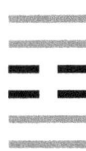 

hexagram 61. Chung Fu	primary Sun/Tua	nuclear Li

Primary and Nuclear trigrams of a hexagram

Qian Heaven	Kun Earth	Kan Water	Kun Earth	Qian Heaven	Li Fire

Heaven and Earth create Water and Fire

   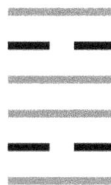

1. Qian Heaven	2. Kun Earth	29. K'an Water	30. Li Fire

4 Timeless or Eternal hexagrams

Yin and yang are no longer pure, and the breath is lost. To return to pure yin and yang energy, one needs to reverse the process in oneself. When one reverses the process, the trigrams of fire and water are seen as the medicine, and heaven and earth are the crucible and the furnace. They are the method or the tools to return to pure yang.

12 SOVEREIGN HEXAGRAMS

Primary hexagrams, such as the 12 Sovereign Hexagrams, signify astronomical reality, used to track planet earth on its orbit around the sun. Sharing the same symbolism, they are matched with the 12 months of the year and the 12 double hours of the day. They also play an important role in the alchemical process of the Elixir of Life.

The 12 Sovereign hexagrams show the waxing and waning of yang energy, which is the essence of the I-Ching. Waxing of yang energy means increasing yang energy until one reaches pure yang, truly unified energy, the presence of Original Spirit or Original Self.

The first 6 hexagrams are about sustaining the firing process, sustaining one's inward gaze with a pure heart and a quiet mind, without letting mundane yin energy interrupt. The sixth hexagram, 24 Return, symbolizes the return of yang energy. This refers to creation, the creation of yang.

"The firing process with its advance and withdrawal, extraction and additives, increasing and decreasing, concentrates a year into a month, a month into a day, a day into an hour, and an hour into a breath." –Li Dao Chun, Book of Balance and Harmony (12th century CE).

12 Sovereign hexagrams of the solar calender and their phases/elements

Fixed seasonal order and 24 hour day of the 12 Soveirgn hexagrams

Mei Hua Yi Shu – Plum Blossom Yi Numerology

There are other divination systems that derive their power from their interpretation of the hexagrams of the I-Ching. They use the numbers 1-8 that correlate with the trigrams and hexagrams linked to birthdate to divine events. Wu Xing Yi or Wen Wang Gua is a method based on the Wu Xing or five elements, correlating trigrams to the celestial stems and earthly branches of the Chinese calendar, and then using those elements to interpret the lines of the hexagram and the text of the I-Ching.

TIE BEN SHEN SHU – IRON PLATE SPIRITUAL NUMEROLOGY

Considered as highly as any of the San Shi, Tie Ben Shen Shu is associated with Shao Yong, who is credited as the author of the 12,000 lines used in Tie Ben divination. Chinese legend has it that there are only five people in the world who have mastered the art of Tie Ben, as learning it is very problematic. It utilizes Ba Zi stem and branch, numerology, the 64 hexagrams and the six family relationships. Its emphasis on the specific quarter-hour (fifteen-minute segment) ensures the relatively high degree of accuracy in comparison with other methods.

MEI HUA YI SHU – PLUM BLOSSOM YI NUMEROLOGY

Plum Blossom is a form of I-Ching divination that uses the time and date of a phenomenon to derive a hexagram, without the need for a physical tool like coins or yarrow stalks. It interprets signs from nature, such as a date, facial expressions or unusual events, as omens to understand future events and reveal cosmic harmony.

By observing nature, animals and humans, the numbers 1-8 are assigned on the basis of certain characteristics that correspond to each of the eight trigrams used to form the hexagrams.

There are ten methods by which the hexagrams are derived. The most common is to take the year, month, day and hour as numbers that correlate with the trigrams to form hexagrams. Other methods take a unique hour that describes a unique situation, such as seeing 7 dogs or 7 birds or the number of knocks on a door. Written notes, telephone numbers, the size of clothes or objects, and even eye colour can be converted to numbers to correlate with the trigrams to form hexagrams.

TI AND YONG TRIGRAMS

First you need to know that there are two main types of trigrams in a hexagram. One is Ti and the other is Yong. Ti is translated as the subject trigram, or as the body trigram. In practice, Ti shows the asking party or the party that is affected/ playing a role.

Yong is translated as the function trigram, the object trigram, the fate trigram. In practice, Yong shows what one is asking about. The trigram that remains unchanged, that is, the one that does not have the changing line, is always Ti/the body or subject trigram. The trigram that contains the changing line is Yong/the object/fate/function trigram/the trigram of what is being asked about.

The system was developed during the Song dynasty by the Daoist scholar and mathematician Shao Yong (1011–1077 CE), who became well-known as an adept predictor of future events through the use of mathematics and perception through Plum Blossom numerology.

He developed the system in the year of the Dragon, in the 12th lunar month, on the 17th day of this lunar month, in the hour of the Monkey; Shao was enjoying the plum blossoms and noticed how two sparrows began to fight on one branch. A moment or two later, he saw the two sparrows fall from the plum branch and started contemplating. He knew that when things are at rest, one cannot perform fortune-telling. But when there is sudden activity, there is reason to do fortune-telling. It is really strange how both sparrows fell together with the branch on the ground. There must be some special reason for this, thought Shao.

So, Shao used the date and time method to construct the hexagram. He took the year of the Dragon (number 5), the 12th month (Tiger 1, Rabbit 2, Dragon 3 and Ox 4 = 12), and the 17th day since the start of the Chinese lunar calendar month. Adding 5 + 12 + 17 = 34. We take out eights until there is a remainder or 0. If it is 0 = 8 = earth/Kun. In this case, we subtract 4 eights from 34, and 2 remains = lake/Dui. This is the top trigram.

To get the lower trigram, Shao added the time of divination (Monkey hour = 9, since we start with Rat 1, Ox 2, as with the year). 34 + 9 = 43. We take out 5 eights, and there are 3 left = fire/Li ☲ – the lower trigram. Thus, if one receives a hexagram with lake on top of fire, it shows that this is hexagram 49.

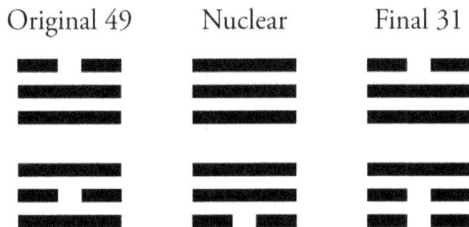

Plum Blossom - Shao Yong's hexagrams

Shan – Mountain

This cryptic-sounding subject is concerned with knowledge and skills that are learned and trained on the mountain. It refers to understanding the laws of nature, the cosmos and the relationship between them. In ancient times, a person needed to go up a mountain to receive such knowledge.

Traditionally, Shan is known as a path of self-improvement, its practitioners sequestering themselves into mountainous regions, immersing themselves in nature and studies in ancient Chinese culture to cultivate the mind. Studies that fall under this art include diet, physical health, martial arts, meditation and self-healing. Sorcery, ritual, talismans and calligraphy also belong to the art of Shan.

Shan transcended mere philosophy in ancient China; it focused on a holistic discipline and way of life revered by experts and scholars alike. Growing beyond physical strength, it includes a range of practices like maintaining dietary habits, meditation, martial arts and calligraphy.

It also encompassed mental strength with an importance on the refinement of character, mental fortitude and fostering a deep connection with cosmic energies. These pursuits were not only for personal well-being; they also formed a foundation upon which the ruling elite could govern with wisdom.

Originating during the Spring-Autumn period (771–476 BCE), Shan embraced lifestyle methods including meditation, breathing techniques, and martial and divine arts. These practices aimed to achieve balance, internal happiness, longevity and a harmonious relationship with nature.

Today, the principles of Shan have seamlessly woven into modern wellness and fitness regimes, practices like Yoga, Tai Chi, Qigong and meditation, centered on achieving mental and physical balance.

QIGONG

Chinese philosophy believes chi (life force, energy flow) to be a vital force forming part of any living entity. Qigong is traditionally viewed as a system of coordinated posture, movement, breathing, awareness and meditation practice to cultivate and balance chi as it interacts between the five elements, yin-yang, and other factors.

It is used for self-healing and self-cultivation that may involve repeating a single, precise set of movements to address specific body or mind aspects to improve physiological and psychological health.

An ancient branch of Traditional Chinese Medicine, Qigong dispenses with things like acupuncture needles, herbal potions, food types and various exercises; instead, it directly connects to the chi of the practitioner with therapeutic intent.

Writing and specifically Qi Calligraphy is a specialized form of Qigong healing and meditation, combining breathing and body movement to create the necessary mental state to achieve perfection in one stroke of the mind, heart and body, akin to that of the swordsman.

Qigong is now practiced worldwide for exercise, healing, meditation, and training for the martial arts. Typically, a Qigong practice involves rhythmic breathing, slow and stylized movement, a mindful state, and visualization of guiding chi.

Stand on Toes
& Bounce 7 Times

Hands Holding
the Sky

Turning
the Head

Seperating Heaven
& Earth

Hold Fist with
Angry Eyes

Bending Back
& Forward

Wiggle Tail &
Swing Head

Open Bow
to Shoot the Hawk

Postures of Tai Chi Chuan

MARTIAL ARTS

Martial arts experts believe that chi can be concentrated in the body, allowing the body to perform almost supernatural feats, such as breaking a concrete block with the side of the hand. Demonstrations of chi in martial arts include the un-raisable body and the unbendable arm. These are not just exercises but tools for rulers to cultivate a balance between strength and wisdom.

Tai Chi is one of hundreds of Qigong forms, specifically a more complex martial art that has evolved into a health-focused practice – rooted sequences of movement focusing the entire body in a flowing form of integrated physical postures, controlled breathing and focused attention to promote physical and mental health through a combination of principles from Qigong. Tai Chi Chuan is a martial art composed of 13 postures thought to date back to 1100 BCE.

In some forms of martial arts, the bagua motif of the eight trigrams has been assigned to teach students how to fight and engage with multiple opponents in all directions of combat, employing a wide variety of techniques and weapons, including joint locks, throws, kicks and strikes with the palm, elbows, fists, and finger tips.

Such martial art styles include Bagua Zhang or Pakua Chang, meaning 'Eight Trigram Palm', based on the philosophies of the I-Ching and the eight trigrams. Aggressive, seemingly linear movements and explosive power from short range characterize Xing Yi Quan. The fighter utilizes tight circles using the six directions of energy – forward, back, left, right, up and down.

Luchen Quan means 'Arhat Fist', named after the holy Buddhist figure. It is the oldest and the representative style of Shaolin Kung Fu and a general name for all the styles of Chinese martial arts. Liu He Be Fa, meaning 'Six Harmonies, Eight Methods', is a unique internal fighting style incorporating elements of Tai Chi Chuan, Bagua Zhang and Xing Yi Quan.

Northern Praying Mantis Kung Fu, combined with Shaolin skills, uses the 'Sticky Hands' technique in its close-range fighting system. It is not related to the Southern Praying Mantis style but is related to the Southern Dragon Kung Fu and Bak Mei.

Southern Dragon Kung Fu is a close-range fighting style of hard and soft techniques rooted in the mythical animal of the Dragon, known for its fluid, flowing movements. Bak Mei Kung Fu, also known as 'White Eyebrow', is an internal-external martial arts style of close-range fighting with powerful hand strikes.

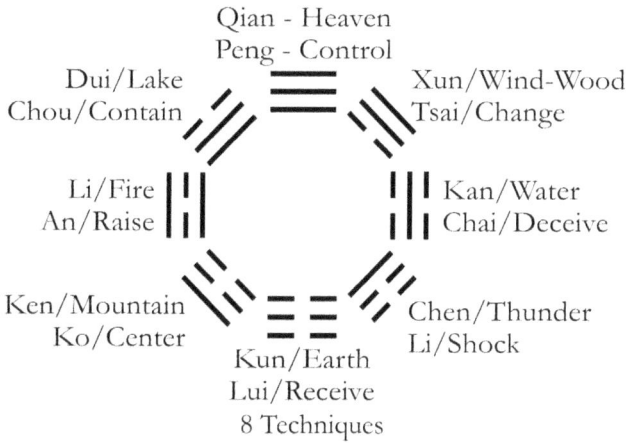

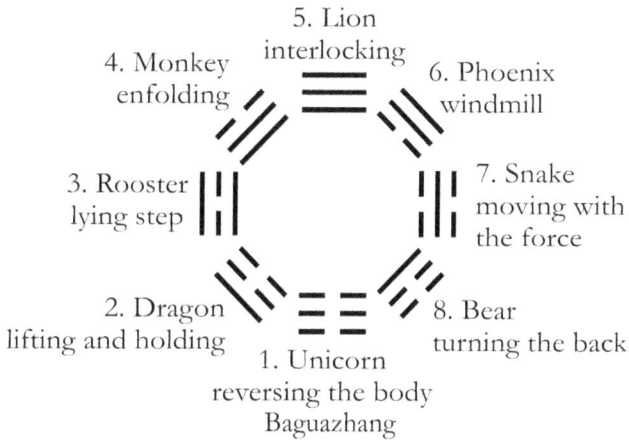

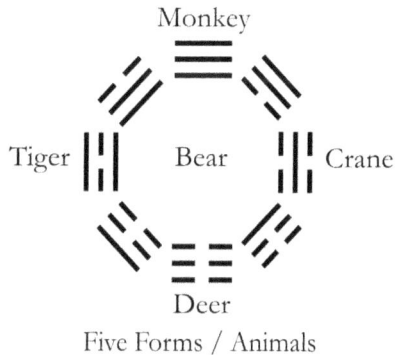

Qian - Heaven
Peng - Control

Dui/Lake
Chou/Contain

Xun/Wind-Wood
Tsai/Change

Li/Fire
An/Raise

Kan/Water
Chai/Deceive

Ken/Mountain
Ko/Center

Chen/Thunder
Li/Shock

Kun/Earth
Lui/Receive

8 Techniques

5. Lion
interlocking

4. Monkey
enfolding

6. Phoenix
windmill

3. Rooster
lying step

7. Snake
moving with
the force

2. Dragon
lifting and holding

8. Bear
turning the back

1. Unicorn
reversing the body

Baguazhang

Fire
Advance

Wood
Look Left

Earth
Center

火

木 → 土

水 ← 金

Water
Retreat

Metal
Gaze Right

Xing Yi Quans

Monkey

Tiger

Bear

Crane

Deer

Five Forms / Animals

Chinese Calligraphy

Calligraphy is an art within Shan, and over the millennia, Chinese characters have been written in various calligraphic styles. Originally a pursuit of the Wu or shaman, writing in China has a long history separate from that of India and the West.

The ancestors of Chinese characters can be traced back to 5000 BCE, derived from the same pictographic source as the trigrams of the I-Ching. Their shared symbolic origins are in the earliest written signs for basic elements such as water, fire and earth.

The calligraphic origins of Chinese characters date back to between 1200 and 1045 BCE, found in an archaic Chinese script called Jiaguwen or Oracle Bone Script – a pictographic script incised into dragon bones and turtle shells for divinatory purposes.

From Oracle Bone Script, Chinese characters developed through a series of changes in form called Seal Scripts, which were carved into stone or bronze between 800 and 100 BCE. The earliest of these, called Jinwen or Bronze Seal Script, first appeared during the Shang dynasty. During the Chou dynasty, Dazhuan or Large-Seal Script was predominant.

In the 3rd century BCE, following a period of political upheaval, the emperor Qin/Chin reunited the Chinese nation. To bond it together, he ordered his scholars to use the Large Seal Script as the model for a simplified script called Small Seal Script or Xiaozhuan. This enabled the standardization of writing for the many different Chinese dialects while suppressing all other variants. It represents the last stage in the development of Old Chinese writing. Today, it is used only on seals or as signatures.

The modern form of today's characters first appeared with the adaptation of 'Small Seal' Script into 'Clerical' Script during the Han dynasty, circa 200 BCE, giving Chinese characters the name by which they are known today – Hanzi or Han characters – the oldest script still in use.

There are four classic Chinese calligraphic styles. The Clerical Script or Lishu, used by official clerks, became popular during the Qin dynasty. In the late Han period, Clerical Script developed into Kaishu or Standard Script. The Caoshu or Cursive Script evolved from Kaishu. The Kaishu style became the dominant character form with the advent of printing technologies during the late Tang and early Song dynasties, whence they became known as Hanzi or Han characters.

These modern forms appeared between 200 BCE and 200 CE – the result of Chin and Han unification. Between 265 and 420 CE, more script reform brought about the Xingshu or Semi-Cursive Script. Xingshu can be written using brush, pencil or ballpoint pen, and because of this, it is taught in schools.

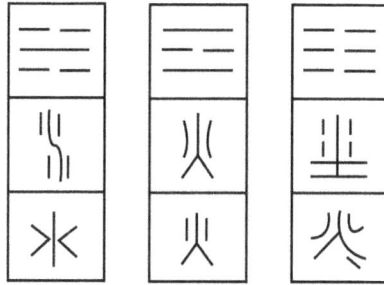

water   fire   earth
Pictogram to Trigram

Jiaguwen   Dazhuan   Xiaozhuan
(oracle bone)   (large seal)   (small seal)

Dao / Tao - development of ancient script styles

Lishu   Kaishu   Caoshu
(clerical)   (standard)   (cursive)

Xingshu   Modern
(running)   (simplified)

Dao / Tao - development of the modern script styles

Today, Chinese-speaking people use two forms of Hanzi. Traditional Hanzi written in Taiwan, Hong Kong, and Macau and by overseas Chinese, and Simplified Hanzi, instituted in 1948 and simplified again in 1977, written in mainland China and Singapore and by the United Nations.

QI CALLIGRAPHY

Within Shan, Qi calligraphy is a specific form of Qigong healing and practice. As a term, 'Qi calligraphy' refers to the art of writing the character Qi/Chi. It is a popular subject, reflecting both the aesthetic beauty of the character and its physical significance in Chinese calligraphy. The aim is to represent the dynamic and vital force in nature with a sense of energy flow, movement and aesthetic appeal.

For centuries, the Chinese have used calligraphy as a tool to ease psychological tension and daily stress. Chinese calligraphy and Qigong are connected through Qi calligraphy – a practice that combines the art and form of Qigong, where the energy or chi, channelled through the calligrapher, is used for healing and recharging. A form of meditation, it is used as a means to enter a special state of consciousness to transform our emotions.

As a form of Qigong, calligraphy is movement of the brush and painting with the breath, using correct posture, breathing and visualization, in which the calligraphy brush is wielded with the same passion as the sword. Swordsmen were often the best calligraphers – both are expressions of the mind that manifest ithemselves in a body movement that tends to seek perfection, achieved by developing calm and inner harmony. The necessary mental state is the same for both arts.

Throughout the centuries, Qi calligraphers have expressed themselves, interpretating the meaning contained within certain auspicious Chinese characters or in the writing of poems, proverbs and quotations from Confucius, Lao Tzu, and other scholars. Amongst the popular calligraphic symbols of this art are Dao, Tai Chi, Yin-Yang, Feng Shui and many others.

Qi calligraphy is also a discipline within Chen or Zen Buddhism (Chinese Buddhism), in which the ideals of Zen are expressed through calligraphy. Exemplifying this is the Enso, a simple circle drawn quickly with a brush, something that takes years of practice. It represents eternity, the perfect meditative state, the 'no thing' or enlightenment, emptiness, freedom and the state of no-mind.

As Buddhism spread outside of India, Chinese Buddhists adopted Daoist traditions. As the Sutras were translated from Sanskrit into Chinese, emphasis switched from the spoken sound to the written letter, because Chinese characters represent meaning, not sound.

Strict adherence to the classical Sanskrit pronunciation of mantras was disregarded, and the letter A, written in the Siddham script, replaced the sound symbol Om as the Seed Syllable Supreme. The written Siddham character 'Amh' is the seed syllable of Mahavairocana, the Great Buddha of Light, and calligraphic meditation on this letter became an important esoteric practice.

Expressions of Qi / Chi

Dao Yin-Yang Tai Chi

Qi Calligraphy

Enso A as OM AMH
(Siddham script) Seed Syllable Supreme

Chan / Zen Buddhist Calligraphy

Auspicious Symbols

Since ancient times, the Chinese have attributed magical powers and influence to written Chinese characters. They believe that they could impact spirits, which were, in turn, believed to be responsible for good and ill fortune. They can be worn as amulets and charms for protection and good luck, making Chinese characters the most commonly used magic symbols in China.

The most popular auspicious characters are used as symbols of good luck. In general, they are believed to possess protective and beneficial powers, warding off evil spirits, attracting good fortune and promoting health and well-being, and are often used as decoration or symbols of well wishes at weddings.

To invoke their desired blessings, they can be written in black or red ink on a white, yellow, green or red surface in any of the traditional calligraphic styles to be used as talismans, or formed from clay, wood or metal to be worn as amulets.

Such symbols were also inscribed on coins, woven into cloth, painted on temple walls or carved into objects such as weapons and bells. An example of this is the Feng Shui Coin, a lucky charm inscribed with auspicious characters to attract beneficial chi and good fortune.

LUCK AND GOOD FORTUNE SYMBOLS

The auspicious character 'Yun' symbolizes 'luck' – that is to say, both good and bad luck. The four auspicious characters of good fortune, Xi, He, Ji, Lu, are to be found at weddings, birthdays and New Year, where they appear on cards, lanterns and banners, written in any of the traditional calligraphic styles.

'Xi' represents happiness. 'He' represents harmonious relationships, especially among family. 'Ji' represents good fortune, and 'Lu' represents prosperity and career advancement.

The characters Fu, Lu, and Shou are associated with the 3 Star Gods, the 4 Blessings and Five-Fold Blessings. These blessings are not merely wishes but are seen as achievable goals. Their symbols are used to inspire and remind individuals to strive for those aspects of a well-lived life. Shuangxi, meaning 'double happiness', and 'Cai', representing wealth, financial abundance and prosperity, are also found among these auspicious symbols.

SANFU / SANXING – 3 STAR GODS (FU, LU AND SHOU)

In the context of Feng Shui, the auspicious characters of Fu, Lu and Shou refer to the 3 Star Gods. Often depicted as three elderly men, they are considered symbolic of good fortune. They are not prayed to but are respected and placed in prominent locations to bring their blessings.

運　和　吉　喜　禄

Yun　　He　　　Ji　　　Xi　　　Lu

Luck　Harmonious　Lucky　Happiness　Prosperity

Auspicious characters for Good Fortune

福　禄　寿　　喜喜

Fu　　Lu　　Shou　　　Shuangxi

Good Fortune　Prosperity　Longevity　Double Happiness

3 Star Gods and Four Blessings

Fu - Blessing, Love

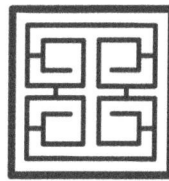 

Lu - Wealth, Prosperity

Shou - Longevity

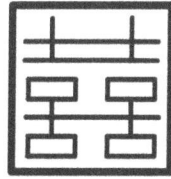 

Shuangxi- Double Happiness

Fu, Lu, Shou, Xi - Four Blessing (square and round Seal script variants)

Xi / Happiness

Cai / Wealth

Representing blessings, good fortune and happiness, Fu is often depicted holding a scroll or child, symbolizing prosperity and family. Standing for wealth, rank and income, Lu is usually depicted wearing an official's hat, signifying career success and high status. Shou is usually depicted holding a peach and a walking stick, symbolizing longevity, long life and good health. Considered as symbols of inner harmony, they are believed to bring unity and good fortune to a household and are placed in homes or offices to bring positive energy.

SIFU – FOUR BLESSINGS (FU, LU, SHOU, SHUANGXI)

The Four Blessings refer to four auspicious characters – Fu represents happiness, joy and good fortune; Lu signifies professional success, career advancement and prosperity; Shou embodies longevity, long life and good health; and 'Shuangxi' or 'double happiness', composed of two 'Xi' characters, represents 'double luck'. These are the four major blessings, the four attributes considered essential for a fulfilling life. They are often represented together as a symbol or a charm to bring good luck and enhance these qualities in those who possess them.

Chinese characters are generally known for their angular forms, but the Four Blessings are commonly written in square and round script variants. Both styles originate from Seal script forms.

WUFU – FIVE-FOLD BLESSINGS

Thought to be over 2000 years old, the concrete forms of good luck are the Five-Fold Blessings – Shou for longevity or long life; Fu for wealth, health and composure; Lu for wealth, prosperity and abundance; Kangming for love of virtue; and Kao Zhong Ming for a peaceful or timely death. The Five-Fold blessings represent the core desires for a fulfilling and prosperous life as depicted in a symbol known as the Wufu or Five-Fold Blessings.

In the Wufu symbol, the auspicious character 'Shou' is placed in the center, surrounded by four bats. Together they represent the Five-Fold Blessings of long life, wealth, health, virtue and a peaceful death. In Chinese, the word 'fu', meaning 'bat', is used as a homophone to infer 'fu', meaning 'blessing'.

The number 5 is an auspicious number in Chinese tradition, closely associated with the five elements which are essential for a good life. As a result, the number 5 appears ubiquitously, as in the Five-Fold Blessings.

Feng Shui Lucky Coin

Wufu - Five-fold Blessings

Fu – Talismans

Fu is the Chinese word for talisman. A talisman is a portable object that is believed to possess magical or religious powers to provide protection, good fortune or healing to its owner. These objects are often inscribed with magic symbols, figures or script to influence events in one's favour or ward off harm. While similar to an amulet, a talisman's function is to bring good luck and positive influence, rather than solely protect against evil.

The magic power of Chinese talismans is derived from the Daoist belief that they were primarily inhabited by spirits; this enabled people to communicate directly with spirits by means of these talismans, without the participation of a medium, as the talismans themselves acted as mediums.

This process originated in ancient beliefs about the power of symbols and their ability to influence the spiritual world. The earliest talismans often incorporated symbols like the Bagua and Taijitu to protect against malevolent forces and attract positive energy, invoking the harmonizing influence of yin-yang and eternal change, the divine order of heaven, earth and mankind, and the workings of the universe through the principle of Wuxing or the five phases.

Daoist philosophy has been called both scientific and mystical at the same time, and this applies equally to the magic art of Daoist talismanic composition. Calligraphers and painters were generally regarded as people able to communicate with spirits, and as a result, the spiritual cult of calligraphy and painting, long venerated by Daoists, became firmly established.

The writing on a Fu is often unreadable to most people – a deliberate style of 'linguistic archaism' or the combination of characters to create a mystical effect. The design can also include non-character symbols like cloud glyphs, and many talismans feature auspicious characters, sometimes written in archaic, magical or talismanic scripts with specific meanings related to luck, prosperity or protection. Some talismans incorporate hidden symbols and puns, using homonyms to convey complex messages and wishes. All the graphic elements must be crafted to align with the talisman's intended purpose.

All in all, Fu represent a sophisticated system of symbolic language that blends script, image and ritual practice to harness spiritual power and achieve specific goals in Daoism.

MAKING, CHARGING AND ACTIVATING FU

The creation of Fu has been a prominent practice in Daoism for over two millennia; the earliest surviving examples date from the Han dynasty, and they emphasize living in harmony with the Dao and channelling spiritual energy.

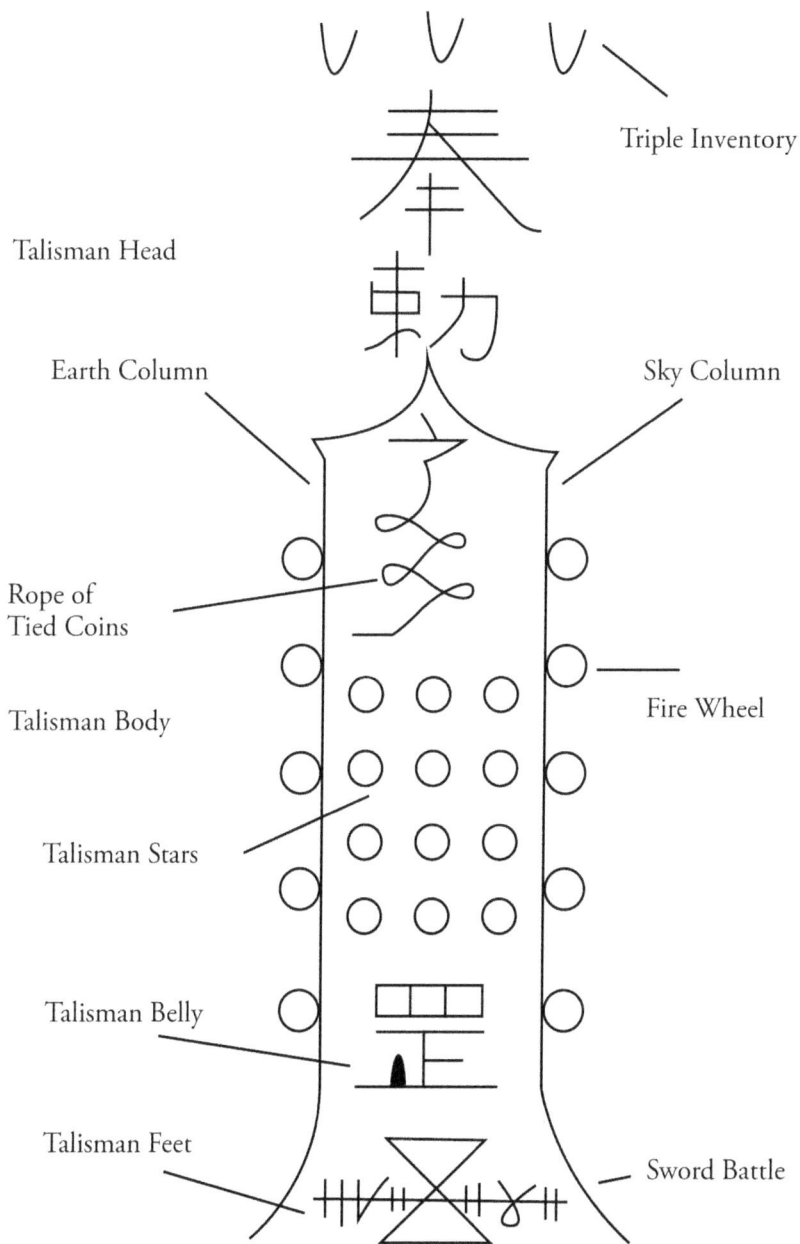

Triple Inventory

Talisman Head

Earth Column

Sky Column

Rope of
Tied Coins

Talisman Body

Fire Wheel

Talisman Stars

Talisman Belly

Talisman Feet

Sword Battle

Common Components of Daoist Talismans

Fu are ideographs – a combination of symbols, drawings and writing that represents a specific intention that are sometimes legible, and sometimes not. They may also include other elements like divinatory diagrams, specific symbols or the names of deities, further customizing their purpose and effectiveness. The ideographs represent a systematic language in which the characters and the symbols form a code to communicate with deities and spirits to facilitate communication between heaven, earth and man.

Making a Fu talisman means learning a specific, often secret, ritual language and a system of glyphs from a qualified practitioner within a specific sect, or from a comprehensive text like the Dao of Craft by Benebel Wen. The process involves designing a talisman using symbolic writing, often a creative or synthesized form of Chinese characters, then ritually charging it with focused energy or chi to achieve a specific metaphysical effect, such as averting misfortune or attracting luck.

Traditionally, the implements needed for creating talismans have included a low, square table to hold all the implements necessary for writing them. On it would be laid out secret talismanic writings, paper of various colours, brushes, red cinnabar ink, black ink and clean water. Five basic colours are traditionally used in paper talismans – since spirits move in all five directions, a suitable colour or combination of colours was needed to control them. Yellow – center, blue – east, red – south, white – west, and black – north.

To charge and activate a Fu, the practitioner must gather chi energy from various environmental sources and channel it in a concentrated form into the talisman; in effect, using the practitioner's force to transmute the properties of that object, the Fu. This is followed with spiritual rituals and incantations, such as verbal spells and symbolic hand gestures called Mudras, and specific timings, such as the waxing or new moon, are often part of the charging process. Materials like consecrated water, oils or crystals may be used to consecrate and empower the Fu. A temple seal can be added, often in red ink, to authenticate the Fu.

Fu can be carried on one's person by an individual, pasted on walls or doorways, or even burnt and mixed with water to be consumed to cure illness. They can be placed in sacred spaces in the environment or burnt and scattered on the wind or water.

Invocation of the Sacred Trinity — (Heaven, Earth, Man, Sun, Moon, Stars, Fulu Shu etc.)

Fu Wen - 'Divine Decree'

Oracle Bone Script 'Victory, Success'

Traditional Ba Gua delineation of the trigram 'Water', for achieving careers goals

I-Ching hexagram 14 for professional advancement

Examples of Talisman Construction

Fulu – Talismanic Script

Fulu literally means 'talismanic script'; it refers to 'asemic' (having no specific speech meaning) Daoist magic symbols and incantations that are often painted or written on talismans.

They are a form of spiritual writing, often used in combination with magic symbols and incantations, used to invoke blessings and channel divine forces to summon, command or communicate with deities or spirits. They are believed to have various powers for protection or exorcism, and are used for various purposes, including healing and invoking spiritual energy in medicine and other practices.

Daoists were primarily concerned with the magic power of calligraphy and considered its effectiveness to lie above all in the line traced by the magicians' feet during dance, a line which represents a vortex, a spiral of magic. The vortex or spiral representing energy in the celestial half of a talisman is believed to symbolize thunder and lightning.

Ascending and descending lines are found in various types of talismanic calligraphy and are a reference to the invisible lines of contact between celestial beings and terrestrial beings below.

Fulu practices developed during the Six dynasties period (3rd-6th centuries CE) and became integrated into broader Daoist practices. Their techniques were passed secretly from priests to their students and differ between sects. They are part of Fulu Daoism, a form of Daoism focused on talismanic ritual, where the power of the written word was transferred to the spiritual realm, giving talismans their perceived efficacy.

In order to protect the talismanic 'mystery', a number of Fulu or talismanic script styles were developed. Fulu deviate from the standard forms of Chinese calligraphy, often incorporating stylized strokes, spirals or other symbolic elements. They are not distinct scripts used in everyday writing but rather a special form of writing used for talismanic purposes, believed to possess inherent magical or supernatural power, used to invoke power, protection, blessings, ward off evil or heal illness.

A feature of talismanic scripts is the irregular, distorted, elongated or exaggerated strokes that create a unique and sometimes unreadable appearance. They are deliberately more exaggerated than standard forms, adding a sense of power and dynamism. Such scripts are specifically designed for talismans, often blending elements of Seal script and other scripts, often mixed with other non-linguistic inscriptions based on magic script characters, figures and formulas that enhance its power and healing. They are sacred writing styles regarded as part of Fulu.

Rounded - Yin

Square - Yang

Rounded - Yin

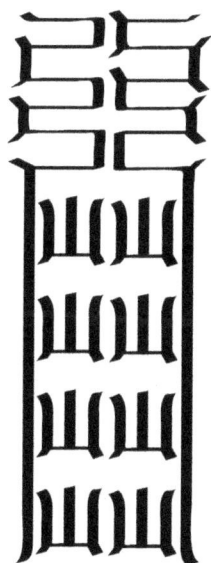

Square - Yang

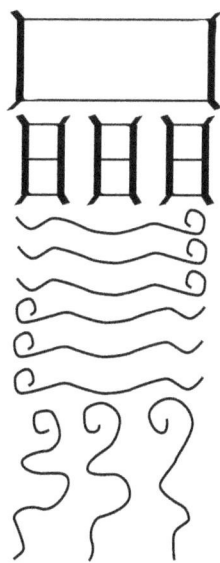

Square and Rounded

Talisman Script Styles

CATEGORIES OF FULU

While the term Fu refers to the talisman itself, the term Fulu often refers to the symbols and scripts themselves; it can also refer to the broader tradition of Daoist practices that utilize these symbols. Priests from different sects or schools may have had their own variations of Fulu, reflecting the diverse approach within Daoism.

Handed down by early Daoist mystics, the unusual graphology of protective charms and spells was received by the mystics from the spirits, having become archaic script forms – that is, those commonly unrecognizable scripts with a graphic composition charged with magical powers. It is common to find elements of Seal script on talismans, as it is considered to be a more ancient and esoteric style.

Talismanic scripts deviate from the standard forms of Chinese calligraphy, often incorporating stylized strokes, spirals or other symbolic elements. They are not distinct scripts used in everyday writing but rather a special form of writing used for talismanic purposes, believed to possess inherent magical or supernatural power, used to invoke power, protection, blessings, ward off evil, or heal illness.

The variety of occult graphic compositions is enormous, ranging from the spontaneity of trance-drawings to the meticulous draughtsmanship of pseudo-scientific diagrams and magic charts. At first, the shaman used curving lines to contact the spirit world. Later, in popular occult art, this took on the opposite function, as they became the one way to outwit evil spirits, who can move only in a straight line.

This helped to generate two main styles of Fulu – the hard, square, male, yang style, to be written under sunlight derived from earth, metal or fire forms; and the soft, rounded, female, yin style based on the swirls of wind and water, to be written under moonlight. Some combine both styles.

Fulu concerning supernatural events and enquiries can be constructed from dots joined by a straight line to represent the arrangement of stars in a constellation. Some talismans are based around the thickness of brush strokes. While not specifically a script style, the Flying White Tiger technique uses a flat brush to create flowing strokes that can be applied to Fulu scripts, adding a sense of ethereal beauty.

True Form talismans are charts; aniconic diagrams organized in a puzzling configuration depicting mountain-inspired paradises, such as grotto-heavens, sacred sites, and Diyu or hells. Daoists believe that True Form talismans have the power to uncover the 'true forms' of the spirits, demons and numerous entities that inhabit the world, as well as places such as mountains. They are used for communication and protection.

| Weather stop rain | Geomantic yin-yang | Medical healing lungs | Supernatural constellation dots |

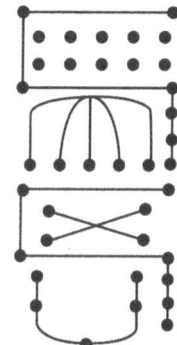

Talisman Types

Subdue great demons
Celestial script

Sheng - Life
protecct the body

Unite man and spirit

Brushed Technique Talismans

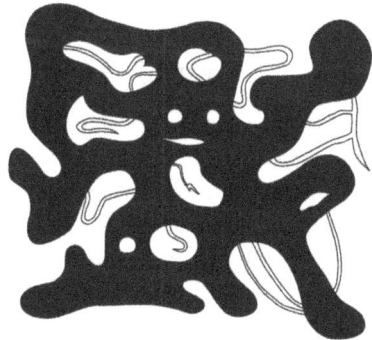

True Form - Talismans of the Sacred Mountains

Magic and Ornamental Scripts

Over the millennia, Chinese scribes have produced many magical and ornamental scripts, the majority of which are descended from the ancient Seal script form, whose antiquity is taken as a measure of its magical power. Because of this, it is used as a foundation for many scripts. Such scripts have been used on weapons, bells, coins, jade, and all manner of other objects.

TIANSHU – HEAVENLY / CELESTIAL SCRIPT

With its origins in the Hetu and Luoshu River charts, the most prominent variant of Fulu or talismanic Seal script is known as Celestial script. It refers to sacred writing and symbols believed to be revealed directly by heaven, often used as powerful talismans and tokens of authority to communicate with celestial beings, connecting earthly affairs to celestial ones.

It can be incorporated into talismans to manipulate spiritual forces or events central to earthy affairs. The understanding and use of celestial scripts are part of the esoteric tradition within Daoism, often requiring deep knowledge and vigorous practice to interpret and utilize effectively.

MAGIC AND ORNAMENTAL SCRIPTS

There are many mystical and symbolic scripts, such as 'lucky mushroom script' (zhying zhuan), 'bell and tripod seal script' (Zhongding Zhuan), 'dripping dew script' (Chuilu Zhuan), and so on.

There are also various jade scripts, like jade chopstick script (Yujin), a kind of Seal script which is round and gentle. Magical jade script does not refer to a specific script but rather to the practice of using magical characters found on jade objects. Jade itself is considered a mystical stone, believed to possess powers of protection, wisdom and longevity.

BIRD/WORM/FISH/INSECT SCRIPT

The bird and worm script (niaochongshu) is a special type of Seal script. It is also called 'niaoshu' or bird script, 'chongshu' or worm script, 'yushu' or fish script, and 'kunchongshu' or insect script, as all the characters are given the shape of birds, worms, fish or insects.

The script first emerged during the Spring-Autumn period (771–476 BCE), becoming popular in the Warring States period (476–221 BCE). Because of its attractive style, Chinese aristocracy used the script on their personal seals and for inscriptions on weapons, bells, and other metal objects.

Counted as one of the eight scripts used in the Qin Empire, it is actually only a decorative calligraphic style, not appropriate for everyday use because it is not very easy to read. The script went into decline after the Qin emperor unified the writing system with the small seal script, but it has been occasionally revived since.

Fulu - Celestial script talismans from the Water Margin

Bells and Tripod Script   War Club script

Lucky Mushroom   Jade Character   Tadpole

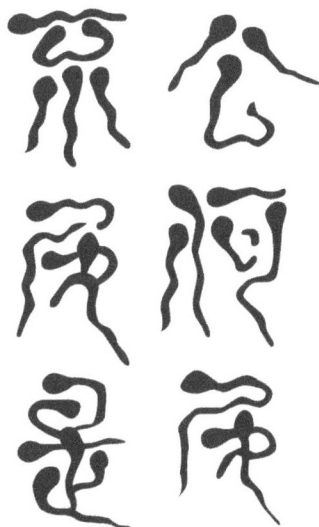

Magical Scripts

KEDOU – TADPOLE SCRIPT

Tadpole script refers to a primitive script from the late Neolithic to the early Bronze Age in ancient China. It first appeared in the late Shang period and was used to write inscriptions and sacrificial texts on bamboo, bronze, pottery, and other works.

The tadpole shape came about because there was no pen and ink, just a bamboo strip and lacquer to write on it. Because the bamboo is greasy and the lacquer is thick, the script was rendered thick at the head and thin at the tail, just like a tadpole.

CLOUD WRITING

In China, clouds (xiang yun) are auspicious symbols representing good fortune and heaven. Cloud formations were associated with the movement of spirits, which were believed to dwell in the mist. These spiritual contacts could be controlled by the magic power of calligraphy, and various cloud motifs serve this purpose. Thus, a variety of superbly linear and vapoury cloud script forms derive their shape and their magical power from cloud formations.

While cloud patterns themselves are not a script, they can be found alongside or incorporated into other forms of Chinese writing, particularly in decorative calligraphy and some talismans.

SQUARE SCRIPTS

The medieval Square script tradition of the Far East produced a style of calligraphy that is no longer used for everyday writing but is still employed in a decorative or talismanic capacity. It is an arrangement of the strokes that make up a Chinese character into a quadratic or geometric formation. Today it is most commonly a form of ornamental script used on amulets, talismans and temple walls. The Nushu or 'woman's script' was derived from Square script.

The first Square script style, called Jiudiez, Nine-Fold Script, Nine Bends or Layered script, was developed in China during the Song dynasty (960–1279 CE). It is a highly stylized form of Chinese calligraphy derived from the small seal script but with tightly convoluted strokes in lateral lines.

From the Nine-Fold script developed the Square seal scripts of Basiba, Phags Pa, Horyig, Tangut and Manchu, written in China, Mongolia and Tibet.

Basiba is a stylized Seal script from the Yuan period (1279–1368 CE). It has a very quadratic appearance and is also called 'Fangtizi', meaning 'square script'. The script is found preserved in monumental inscriptions (stelae), on official seals, badges of rank or identification, paper currency and coins. There is also a Ten-Fold script style inspired by Islamic Square Kufic script forms.

Talismanic Cloud writimg

Ornamental Bird/Worm/Fish/Insect script

Nine-Fold Seal Script · Basiba/ Phags Pa Square Scripts · Ten-Fold Script

Further Reading

PRINT

Blackwell Encyclopedia of Writing by Florian Coulmass – Blackwell Publishing.
Sacred Calligraphy of the East by John Stevens – Shambala.
Tao Magic: The Secret Language of Diagrams and Calligraphy by Laszlo Legeza
– Thames & Hudson.
Chinese Shamanic Cosmic Orbit Qigong by Master Zhingxian Wu – Singing
Dragon.

WEB

ancientscripts.com
omniglot.com
scriptsources.org
britannica.com
onlinelibrary.wiley.com
exactphilosophy.net
psychicscience.org
wikipedia.org
hindidevanagari.com
hindupedia.com
banglapedia.com
tamilheritage.org
indianetzone.com
hinduwebsite.com
exoticindianart.com
ancientindianwisdom.com
bhagavaditavsa.com/sound.htm
ravikhanna.com
collectivepsyche.com/cymatics
inannareturns.com/articles/
    shivasutras/sutra
visablemantra.org
tantra-kundalini.com

yogamag.net
chetanananda.com
beyondweird.com/ck/index.htm
    (chakras)
lantsha-vartu.org
kalachakra.org
soravj.com/showcase/yantra/yantra
aghori.com/yantra
chinesemedicalclasses.wordpress.com
baharna.com/iching
chinaknowledge.de
fengshui4everyone.blogspot.com
chinesefortunecalendar.com
taoistiching.org
iching123.com
yourchineseastrology.com
taoist-sorcery.blogspot.com
chinasage.intro
weebly.com/compass-school
thegreattao.com
goldenelixir.com
astrologyking.com/chinese-astrology
viewofchina.com

YOU TUBE

sanskrit
varna shiksha